Zionism and Judaism

Why should anyone be a Zionist, a supporter of a Jewish state in the land of Israel? Why should there be a Jewish state in the land of Israel? This book seeks to provide a philosophical answer to these questions. Although a Zionist need not be Jewish, nonetheless this book argues that Zionism is a coherent political stance only when it is intelligently rooted in Judaism, especially in the classical Jewish doctrine of God's election of the people of Israel and the commandment to them to settle the land of Israel. The religious Zionism advocated here is contrasted with secular versions of Zionism that take Zionism to be a replacement of Judaism. It is also contrasted with versions of religious Zionism that ascribe messianic significance to the State of Israel, or that see the main task of religious Zionism to be the establishment of an Israeli theocracy.

David Novak holds the J. Richard and Dorothy Shiff Chair in Jewish Studies as Professor of Religion and Philosophy at the University of Toronto. He is a Fellow of the Royal Society of Canada and of the American Academy for Jewish Research. He is President of the Union for Traditional Judaism and Vice-President of the Institute on Religion and Public Life. Dr. Novak also serves as a Consulting Scholar of the James Madison Program in American Ideals and Institutions at Princeton University and as a Project Scholar of the Berkley Center for Religion, Peace, and World Affairs at Georgetown University.

In Memoriam
Mircea Z. Cohn

"Acquire a friend for yourself." Mishnah: Avot

Zionism and Judaism

A New Theory

DAVID NOVAK
University of Toronto

CAMBRIDGE
UNIVERSITY PRESS

CAMBRIDGE
UNIVERSITY PRESS

32 Avenue of the Americas, New York NY 10013-2473, USA

Cambridge University Press is part of the University of Cambridge.

It furthers the University's mission by disseminating knowledge in the pursuit of education, learning and research at the highest international levels of excellence.

www.cambridge.org
Information on this title: www.cambridge.org/9781107492714

© David Novak 2015

This publication is in copyright. Subject to statutory exception
and to the provisions of relevant collective licensing agreements,
no reproduction of any part may take place without the written
permission of Cambridge University Press.

First published 2015
First paperback edition 2016

A catalogue record for this publication is available from the British Library

Library of Congress Cataloguing in Publication data
Novak, David, 1941–
Zionism and Judaism : a new theory / David Novak.
  pages   cm
ISBN 978-1-107-09995-1 (hbk.)
1. Zionism and Judaism. I. Title.
DS149.N8927 2015
320.54095694–dc23   2014045608

ISBN 978-1-107-09995-1 Hardback
ISBN 978-1-107-49271-4 Paperback

Cambridge University Press has no responsibility for the persistence or accuracy of URLs for external or third-party internet websites referred to in this publication, and does not guarantee that any content on such websites is, or will remain, accurate or appropriate.

Contents

Preface		*page* vii
Abbreviations		xi
Introduction		xiii
1	Why Zionism?	1
	Introduction	1
	Political Rhetoric	3
	Psychological Motivation	7
	Jewish Celebration/Jewish Commemoration	9
	Reasons of the Commandments	11
	Four Kinds of Jews – Four Kinds of Non-Jews	18
2	Was Spinoza the First Zionist?	23
	Ben-Gurion and Spinoza	23
	Spinoza's Inversions of Classical Jewish Theology	26
	The Proto-Zionist Statement	35
	Spinoza's Old-New Judaism	44
	Spinoza and the Zionist Dilemma	46
3	Secular Zionism: Political or Cultural?	48
	Secular Zionism	48
	Political Zionism	50
	Cultural Zionism	66
	Hebrew Jurisprudence	83

4	Should Israel Be a Theocracy?	86
	What Is Theocracy?	86
	The Primacy of Theology	91
	God Chooses to Create the Universe as God's Possession	100
	God Chooses to Create the Human Person	112
5	Why the Jews and Why the Land of Israel?	119
	God Chooses Israel	119
	God Chooses the Land of Israel	139
6	Can the State of Israel Be Both Jewish and Democratic?	153
	Jewish Religion and Secular Law	153
	The Problem with Current Israeli Secularism	159
	Principled Agreement	161
	Whose Democracy?	162
	Divinely Sanctioned Secularity	166
	Authentic Jewish Secularity	171
	The Commandment to Acquire and Settle the Land	177
	A Communal Obligation	186
	Human Volition	191
7	What Could Be the Status of Non-Jews in a Jewish State?	197
	Rethinking the Status of Non-Jews	197
	The Resident-Alien	200
	The Equalization of Civil Rights	208
	Potential Jews	213
	Non-Jewish Autonomy	215
	Right and Might	219
8	What Is the Connection Between the Holocaust and the State of Israel?	225
	Historical and Political Sequences	225
	Holocaust Theologies	228
	Messianic Theologies	238
	Theory and Praxis	240
	Another Messianism	244
Index		251

Preface

Almost twenty years ago, a rather unfriendly reviewer of my work accused me of being oblivious to the two most important events in the modern history of the Jewish people (and maybe the entire history of the Jewish people): the Holocaust and the establishment of the State of Israel. I guess he presumed that to be the case, as my work had been primarily in such "universal" areas as Jewish-Christian relations and natural law theory. He even seemed to imply that I might, therefore, be an anti-Zionist and someone who refused to see the Holocaust as a particularly Jewish tragedy. Despite the fact that I didn't respond to these charges (which were made only en passant in a general article), they have stuck in my mind nonetheless. Though I am a Zionist and I do appreciate what the Holocaust means in particular to us Jews, perhaps "my own vineyard I did not watch" (Song of Songs 1:6). In other words, in the dialectic between the universal and the particular, with which any serious thinker has to be concerned, whenever you are absorbed in one of these two poles, you should start looking in the direction of the other pole. So, because of that, from time to time, I did write several articles that deal with the State of Israel. When it comes to the Holocaust, though, I have only mentioned it in writing from time to time, maybe because I did not experience it myself, but have only heard about what it was like to be there from the survivors I have been privileged to have as friends. Only in Chapter 7 of this book have I been able to deal with the Holocaust, in what I hope is an ingenuous way. But, because I have been privileged to personally experience the vibrant life of the State of Israel, there is more I can write about it. Several of these writings are mentioned in the notes of this book. And, because one can only see with one's own eyes, that is, from one's own personal perspective, what I have to say about Israel will have to be a reflection on the theory that justifies its founding and continued existence: Zionism. That is because, being a Jewish theologian or philosopher of Judaism, I cannot reflect on anything otherwise than that way.

During the last ten years or so, I have had the opportunity to lecture and give conference presentations in various places on some of the points developed in this book. I am grateful to the academic audiences who gave me a patient and respectful, yet critical, response to my original presentation of these points to them. Thanks are due to my hosts and listeners at the following locations: Academic Institute of Theology (Lugano), Bar-Ilan University, Cambridge University, Collège des Études Juives de l'Alliance Israélite Universelle (Paris), University of Dallas, Ethikon Institute (San Francisco conference), Foundation for Jewish Culture (Ashkelon conference), Jewish Theological Seminary, Princeton University, Shalom Hartman Institute (Jerusalem), University of Toronto, Van Leer Institute (Jerusalem), University of Wisconsin (Madison), and Yale University.

Over the years, though, I have had the opportunity to discuss and consult with various friends and colleagues about many of the points discussed in this book. The following names come to mind: Salomon Benzimra, James A. Diamond, Anver Emon, Eugene Feiger, Dov Friedberg, Lenn Goodman, Yoram Hazony, Menachem Kellner, Alan Mittleman, (the late) Richard John Neuhaus, Derek Penslar, Kurt Richardson, Abraham Rotstein, Shimon Shitreet, Rabbi Asher Turin (with whom I have discussed almost every rabbinic text dealt with here), and Michael Walzer. I also thank my University of Toronto doctoral student Yaniv Feller for helping me obtain some important Israeli papers needed in research for this book.

Preface

The writing of this book was made more of a dialogue by the invitation of my friend Baruch Frydman-Kohl, Senior Rabbi of the Beth Tzedec Synagogue here in Toronto, to deliver a series of eight lectures in his synagogue in fall of 2012 on the topic "Zionism: Eight Tough Questions." This lecture series was called "The Michael John Herman Memorial Lectures," owing to the generosity of Michael Herman's widow, Mary Ellen, and her children, to whom I am grateful. I was especially honored to deliver these lectures in Michael's memory, because he was a true intellectual who had studied with me briefly, and who was deeply interested in Judaism, Zionism, and philosophy. The lectures gave me the opportunity to present some of my thoughts on Zionism to an intelligent (mostly Jewish) audience in Toronto, whose Jewish community is outstanding in its Zionist commitment. The experience of presenting these thoughts, plus the experience of getting and responding to lively, critical questions, have enabled me (I hope) to make the book personally engaging and a bit less "academic" (in the pejorative sense). Here I have to thank Rabbi Frydman-Kohl for his comments, and for leading the discussion that followed each lecture. Special thanks to my research assistant, Cole Sadler, a doctoral student at the University of Toronto. Cole and I listened to a recording of each lecture shortly after each lecture had been delivered. His intelligent enthusiasm was of great help to me in transposing what had been said into what was now to be written. He also prepared the index. And I thank the University of Toronto, my happy academic home for the past eighteen years, for the use of the research funds of my J. Richard and Dorothy Shiff Chair in Jewish Studies.

I thank my editor at Cambridge University Press, Lewis Bateman, and his colleague Shaun Vigil, for their confidence in my work and their strong support for its publication.

Finally, the dedication. The lectures the book is based upon were first promoted at Beth Tzedec by my friend Mircea Cohn, an active member of the congregation and its Adult Education Committee. Mircea was a Romanian Jew who fled Communist Romania (where he had survived the Holocaust by being fortunate enough to live in Bucharest during World War II) and came to Canada in the 1960s. For many years, he was a distinguished professor of mechanical engineering at the University of Waterloo, before retiring to Toronto to live near the University of Toronto. Mircea was a staunch Zionist, a true European intellectual, and a great connoisseur of music, which my wife Melva and I spent many wonderful times listening to with him and learning its deeper significance from him afterward. Mircea was a regular participant in my seminars (and those of other colleagues in Jewish Studies and Philosophy), where he not only inspired the much younger students by simply being there for the purest reasons, but also elevated the level of discussion with his penetrating questions and insights. The Talmud says: "One should not take leave of his friend except during a discussion of a word of Torah, and thereby remember him" (B. Berakhot 31a). I mention this now, because my last conversation with Mircea was on the night of the last of the Herman Lectures, when he told me he wanted to get together with me to discuss the book on the basis of the notes he had taken during and after them on the ideas presented in them. Alas, Mircea was taken from this world before we could have that conversation. So, I dedicate this book to his memory, with the hope that perhaps we might yet have that conversation somewhere else at some other time.

Abbreviations

B	*Talmud Bavli (Babylonian Talmud)*
M	*Mishnah*
MR	*Midrash Rabbah*
MT	*Mishneh Torah* (Maimonides)
T	*Tosefta*
Tos	*Tosafot* (medieval glosses on *Talmud Bavli*)
Y	*Talmud Yerushalmi (Palestinian Talmud)*

NOTE: All translations, unless otherwise noted, are by the author.

Introduction

Zionism and Judaism: A New Theory is just that: the presentation of a new theory of Zionism with detailed argumentation, citation, and references. To give readers a quick overall view of the development of the book's thesis, summaries of the highlights of each chapter are given here. It is hoped that this will initially attract the attention of potential readers and, perhaps, interest you enough to read the whole book or major parts of it. The summaries will show potential readers both *what* is in the book and *how* the book's trajectory moves through the book's various detailed discussions sequentially. I also refer readers back to the specific listings in the Contents. *Why* the book has been written and presented to the public, though, can be understood only from a fuller reading of the text.

Chapter 1: Why Zionism?

The occasion for writing the book is the fact that the legitimacy of the State of Israel, the object of the Zionist project, is under philosophical-theoretical attack, especially by those who argue that Zionism is antithetical to Judaism. Therefore, Zionists need to be emotionally motivated to respond to these attacks, but even more to respond with reasoned arguments. Zionists must show that Zionism is deeply rooted in the Jewish tradition, and that the celebration of the founding and continuation of the State of Israel (whether secular or religious) is a justified moral obligation. This kind of justification is fully consistent with the Jewish tradition of enquiry into the "reasons of the commandments." Various kinds of Jews and non-Jews are designated as those to whom these arguments will be intelligible and, perhaps, persuasive.

Chapter 2: Was Spinoza the First Zionist?

This chapter begins with what a number of thinkers have taken to be the true historical origin of modern Zionist thought. In this spirit, the first prime minister of the State of Israel, David Ben-Gurion, requested that the ban of excommunication (*herem*), issued against the philosopher Baruch Spinoza in 1656 by the rabbinical court of Amsterdam, be rescinded. The primary reason for this posthumous request was, primarily, because Spinoza, in a few enigmatic sentences in his *Tractatus Theologico-Politicus*, had envisioned the reestablishment of a Jewish state (the Zionist project). Here Spinoza's radical reinterpretations of classical Jewish theology are discussed, with the suggestion they are not as radical a departure from Judaism as many modern secularists presume. Finally, it is argued that Spinoza's thinking, especially about a reestablished Jewish state, still present a challenge to contemporary Zionist thought.

Chapter 3: Secular Zionism: Political or Cultural?

Here the secular Zionism that emerged at the end of the nineteenth century in Europe is discussed in its two chief types: political Zionism, epitomized by Theodor Herzl, and cultural Zionism, epitomized by Ahad Ha`Am. This new secular Zionism is contrasted with the more traditionally religious proto-Zionism of rabbis such as Judah Alkalai and Zvi Hirsch Kalischer. The philosophical inadequacy of the Zionist thought of both Herzl and Ahad Ha`Am (and, by implication, their epigones) is shown by examination of the inconsistencies of their thought, plus their radical departure from classical Jewish religious thought (which need not be rejected as untenable in modern times). It is then argued that the movement to incorporate the "non-religious" aspects of traditional Jewish law (*halakhah*) into the explicitly secular system of Israel law is problematic, as traditional Jewish law in terms of its warrant in divine revelation and its purpose in applying divine kingship to the life of the Jewish people, whether in civil or ritual matters, is inherently religious. Attempts to incorporate its political legislation into a secular system of law is disingenuous, being too religious for secularists and too secular for religious Jews.

Chapter 4: Should Israel Be a Theocracy?

"Theocracy" usually means a polity under the control of dictatorial clerics, a political idea and reality that rightly offends modern adherents of democracy. But the original meaning of "theocracy" (and true to its etymology) is a polity that looks to divine law (for Jews, the Torah) for governance. Here it is argued that a cogent Zionist theory requires an affirmation of this kind of theocracy for the Jewish State of Israel, even if that only means that, at present, the Jewish state looks to the Torah for its general warrant. Only that kind of affirmation could make the State of Israel a truly *Jewish* state. This means that theology, understood as both a philosophical method and the content of the God-saturated Jewish tradition, would best be employed in the development of an adequate Zionist political theory. And this means that Zionist theorists must go deepest into the ontological foundations of Judaism, especially the doctrine of the freely choosing God, whose choices (as understood by Jewish theology) begin with God's choice to create the universe and God's choice to create human persons in His own image. It is advised at the outset of the latter part of this chapter that readers who are not interested in this kind of ontological speculation can skip this discussion if they like, and they can pick up the political discussion in Chapter 5 without losing the train of thought of the overall argument of the book.

Chapter 5: Why the Jews and Why the Land of Israel?

The primacy of divine election discussed in Chapter 4 is picked up in this chapter. Here the discussion begins with the well-known (and often misunderstood by both its adherents and its enemies) doctrine of God's election of the Jewish people for a unique covenantal relationship between God and his people: what it means for the Jews themselves, and what it means for the wider human world in which Jews interact with others, both as individuals and as an historical community. It is then argued why the covenantal election of the Jewish people requires the divine election of a particular land for their communal life to be centered.

Chapter 6: Can the State of Israel Be Both Jewish and Democratic?

Here the statement that "Israel is both a Jewish and a democratic state" is critically examined. There is an attempt to rationally refute the arguments of secularists who assert that Israel should be a democratic state with some vague connection to the Jewish tradition (in its most universal aspects). It is then proposed that as a secular polity Israel looks to American and Canadian models (rather than the more radical French model) that accept the idea of a divine law as the primary warrant for the state's moral legitimacy, yet doesn't look only to any particular historical revelation for its warrant. However, a Jewish state needs a specific Jewish warrant, and that warrant could be the biblical commandment for the Jewish people to "inherit and settle" the land of Israel. The different views of Maimonides and Nahmanides as to the source and meaning of this obligation are examined. It is suggested, in a way different from these two medieval views, that this obligation is a communal one, and that individual Jews have the right to decide whether or not they want to be the individuals who actually perform the mandated Jewish inheritance and settlement of the land of Israel. Finally, it is shown that whereas the mandates prescribe a number of specific obligations, both for individuals and for the community, the Jewish people themselves have the right to choose the kind of government they want to be governed by, as long as it is consistent with the Torah. That choice very much depends on what Jews think is the best way to fulfill their political needs at any particular time in their history.

Chapter 7: What Could Be the Status of Non-Jews in a Jewish State?

The status of non-Jews in a Jewish polity must be rethought, as this is such a new reality for the Jewish people, something as new as having come to be in 1948 with the founding of the State of Israel. The way to do this is to rethink and revive the Talmudic institution of the *ger toshav*: "resident-alien." A *ger toshav* is conceived to be a gentile who wants to live as a citizen (albeit a second-class citizen) in a Jewish polity, but without fully converting to Judaism. And, although according to the traditional sources (where this institution is discussed hypothetically, because it was recognized to be an anachronism) a *ger toshav* has a few civil disabilities, these could be intelligently removed to give him or her full civil equality, whether by more conservative reinterpretation or by more radical fiat. The revival of this institution would also give authentic Jewish status to gentiles who live in the State of Israel and who want to participate fully in its civil society, but who are not ready (or never will be ready) to fully convert to Judaism as an explicitly religious act. Finally, this chapter suggests that the *ger toshav* is not only an individual status, but also a communal one. That is, a non-Jewish polity in the land of Israel could be recognized by the religiously constituted Israeli Jewish community, that is, if they accepted the universal moral (or Noahide) law the Jewish tradition recognizes to be binding of all humankind, and they affirm the God-given right of the Jewish people to inherit and settle the land of Israel with political sovereignty.

Chapter 8: What Is the Connection Between the Holocaust and the State of Israel?

The political connection of the Holocaust and the State of Israel is obvious. Recognition of the right of the Jewish people to a state of their own in their ancestral homeland was very much argued for, by both Jews and non-Jews, to have been made a necessity by the experience of the Holocaust by the stateless Jewish people. But the connection goes much deeper than that so, in fact, this connection soon caught the interest of Jewish theologians. The theologies of Joel Teitelbaum (Satmar rebbe) and Richard Rubenstein are critically examined and rejected: Teitelbaum, who argues that Zionism (and its project, the State of Israel) is the sin of the Jews for which the Holocaust was the appropriate divine punishment; Rubenstein, who argues that because of the Holocaust, Jews must relinquish their traditional belief in a beneficent God and only rely on themselves, especially on themselves as a people who now have a state of their own, one that is capable of defending them from annihilation. Next the messianic theology of a religio-nationalist like Tzvi Yehudah Kook is critically examined, and questioned concerning its messianism that sees the State of Israel as being an actual cause of the final redemption of the Jewish people, and that sees the Holocaust as a necessary step in that divine project. Finally, the suggestion is put forth that all of these Holocaust theologies are, in effect, an insult to the survivors of the Holocaust, and there is the primary responsibility to comfort, not torment (however unintentionally) the survivors, whose mourning for those they lost and what they lost is lifelong. Another less presumptuous messianic theology is suggested in conclusion.

Considering how much of the theory presented in this book still needs to be thought out, I think that anything more than this tentative ending of the book would be presumptuous and premature.

I

Why Zionism?

Introduction

To be a Zionist is to be personally committed or loyal to the existence of the State of Israel as a Jewish polity. There are many Zionists in the world today; most of them are Jews, but there are many non-Jewish Zionists too. Usually, one doesn't have to think of reasons for any such personal commitment, that is, when one's world is going along in its normal course, when it is "business as usual." Only when there are attempts to invalidate this personal commitment does one feel the need to react to the charges made against that personal commitment. When this happens, the first reaction is to protest by expressing personal outrage at the attempt to deny legitimacy to a personal commitment so close to one's heart. But surely, subjective reaction is not enough, especially when the attempt to invalidate such a personal commitment seems to be in the form of rational arguments against what a Zionist is actually committed to, which is to the Jewish State of Israel. When this happens, a Zionist needs to respond rationally by trying to articulate just *why* he or she is committed to the State of Israel, as this personal commitment is now being attacked with arguments (whether good or bad), not just with accusations.

To ask *why* one is committed to Israel is first to pose an ethical question to oneself – one that can be answered only by oneself for oneself. Rational persons need to justify to themselves and then to others why they do what they do.

A Zionist commitment is certainly under such an articulate attack here and now, perhaps as never before. Who could doubt that? That attack is not only military, not only economic, not only diplomatic. It is personal. Even if the attack is not addressed to someone personally, it still goes to the heart of a commitment that is close to a Zionist's identity as a person. It says a lot about *who* he or she is, that is, who is acting so passionately (as do many Zionists). Because this is a challenge for others like oneself, with whom one has something significant in common, the personal question is not only ethical; it also becomes political. The political question is: Why does the State of Israel have a claim on anybody's loyalty? This question, however, can be answered only by making good public arguments for why the Jewish state (*medinah yehudit*) in the land of Israel (*b'erets yisra'el*) should have been founded originally; why it should exist here and now; and why it should continue to exist into the future. Only then can anyone understand why he or she should be personally committed to Israel. So, it is not just that one *wants* the State of Israel to exist because of his or her personal *desire* for it to exist. Rather, a person truly wants the State of Israel to exist because it has the *right* to exist, whether any individual person wants that or not. The matter is public, not private. One's desire that the State of Israel exist (and flourish) is not what legitimizes the state's existence; instead, the state's rightful existence legitimizes a person's desire that it should exist.

To talk of "rights" is to engage in political discourse inasmuch as the concept of *rights* is inherently political. But Israel's right to exist is not just a "diplomatic" case to be made to the external world; it is a *personal* case to be made to oneself first and foremost. Yet this personal case is not something one makes as an individual based on his or her own subjective motives. Rather, this personal case is communal: it is the claim of a community of persons (plural). This *personal/communal* claim must be made prior to the external diplomatic case that is made to those outside one's own community. In fact, the external diplomatic case rings hollow unless the internal communal claim has been made intelligently and accepted beforehand. To the outside world, one makes the case that argues anonymously or universally: Israel's right to exist is the right of *any* nation to *a* state of *its* own in *a* land of its own. But, personally one must say: Israel's right to exist is the claim of the Jewish people to exist in *their* own state in their own land. How can one argue effectively for the right to live in a house if one doesn't have personal reasons for wanting to live in *this* house? That is, what is it about this house that makes one want to live in it with one's own family? Why was this house built at all? These reasons are existential insofar as they are about what lies at the core of one's personal/communal existence. Surely, one needs to feel claimed by his or her community that is exercising its right over its members before one can make any communal claim on others. Minimally, that claim on others is the right not to be impeded by others in one's own existence or survival. Maximally, that right is the claim on others for assistance in one's own struggle for survival.

Political Rhetoric

Zionists who are politically astute know and have taught others how to deal with the anti-Zionist war against Israel's right to exist, or even Israel's right to have ever existed in the first place. To be sure, Zionist orators often invoke the emotional factors that motivate passion for Israel, though that seems to be more for rhetorical affect than to actually express any psychological insight. Nevertheless, Zionists are becoming more and more adept at getting beyond mere rhetoric by pointing to various international political agreements that make Israel's existence as a polity or nation-state among the nations (that is what "inter-national" means) an indisputable political fact, and that the burden of proof is on those who would deny that fact. Along these lines, the following political facts are cited: the Balfour Declaration of 1917, when the British Government recognized the right of the Jews to a "homeland" in Palestine; the San Remo Resolution of 1920 (ratified by the League of Nations in 1922) that internationally recognizes the right of the Jews to that homeland; the United Nations' partition of Palestine into Jewish and Arab political spheres in 1947; the recognition of Israel by both the United States and the Soviet Union in 1948; the acceptance of the State of Israel into the United Nations as a member state in 1949; and the peace treaties between Israel and Egypt in 1979, and between Israel and Jordan in 1994.

All of these political facts are testimony that the right of the State of Israel to exist as a nation-state in the world has been recognized in one way or another by the world, that is, by others.[1] Yet, when it comes to the question of why Jews (and their friends) not only should recognize Israel's right to exist, but also should be personally or dutifully committed to Israel's existence, that is too often left to rhetoric rather than to reason. When Jews are at home among themselves, the emotional card is usually played. Pride in the courage and success of Israeli sisters and brothers in not only persevering, but also flourishing, is conjured up. Or, Jews conjure up their fear of what might happen to them if (God forbid!) they didn't have the military power of the State of Israel to protect them from their enemies, which is a fear that becomes intensified by memories of the time of the Holocaust when large numbers of Jews became "stateless," powerless, displaced persons, deprived of their political rights, even their right to life, and thus totally vulnerable to whoever would destroy them – and who almost did. Non-Jewish friends of the Jewish people – who are much more than diplomatic, economic, or political allies – very much resonate to these concerns.

Certainly, all of these emotional factors, which political rhetoric makes such good use of, are important. Who could deny that? Never underestimate the importance of psychological motivation. Without it, no person would desire to do anything

---

[1] Israel's *Declaration of Independence* (in Hebrew *megillat ha'atsma'ut*) says: "This recognition by the United Nations of the right of the Jewish people to establish their state is irrevocable … Thus the members and representatives of the Jews of Palestine and of the Zionist movement … hereby declare the establishment of a Jewish state in the land of Israel to be known as the State of Israel." (en.wikipedia.org/wiki/Israeli_Declaration_of_Independence#the_scroll)

of personal significance. More than that, though, one certainly needs to know how to argue in terms of realpolitik against those who charge that Israel is a pariah state having no right to exist, now or ever. Politics in the usual sense employs the tactics of realpolitik, in which the best defense is often a good offense. Nevertheless, however necessary realpolitik and psychologically effective rhetoric are, neither of them or even both of them together is sufficient to inspire active Zionist commitment and sustain it intelligently. For that philosophy is needed – not philosophy as a detached view of the world from nowhere in particular, but rather philosophy as the search for the reasons or purposes that make what one does in the world something worthy of free, intelligent human persons. That is, one needs to ascertain the purposes that make his or her life, especially the communal life a person lives together with his or her own people, worthwhile. (Philosophers call that "teleology," i.e., "speaking of ends or purposes.")

As for political strategy, the nineteenth century Russian Jewish thinker Judah Leib Gordon was wrong when he famously counseled: "Be a Jew in your tent, but a human being [*ben adam*] when you depart from it."[2] No! "Jewishness" should not be seen as a private particularity that Jews must leave back home when exercising their universal human rights publicly (in this case, the claim of *any* people on the world for a state of *their* own). Yet too many modern Jews did take Gordon's advice to heart, becoming so enamored of the wider world that they couldn't wait to depart from their "tent," never wanting to come back to what they saw as the narrowness of the tent they wanted so desperately to escape from. However, contrary to Gordon and those who still think like him, Jews should see (and be seen by their friends) that their presence in the wider world is an integral

---

[2] This is from Gordon's 1863 poem, "Awake My People!" The Hebrew original is found in *The Writings of Judah Leib Gordon: Poetry* [Heb.] (Tel Aviv: Dvir, 1956), 17–18. A full English translation of the entire poem is found in Michael Stanislawski, *For Whom Do I Toil? Judah Leib Gordon and the Crisis of Russian Jewry* (New York: Oxford University Press, 1988), 50. For an astute historical analysis of the poem, see ibid., 50–67.

aspect of their Jewishness, not a replacement for it altogether. Making one's political case *to* the world no doubt means there are times when one needs to be a proactive participant *in* the world, because no people can survive politically isolated *from* the world, especially in an age of globalization, whether militarily, economically, diplomatically, or intellectually. Nevertheless, Jews are still very much part of a higher – not lower – realm called "the house of Israel" (*bet yisrael*); and it is the realm to which Jews can and should regularly return because it is their true place in the world. Without it, Jews come from *nowhere* and more and more become anonymous *nobodies*, what used to be called "rootless cosmopolitans."[3]

At this level, then, asking the question, "why be a Zionist?" is to ask the larger question "why be Jewish?" That question is more than a rhetorical one, for it assumes that not being a Zionist, or not being Jewish, is a real option in the world today, which it is. The notion that Jews simply *have to be* Zionists because the world will not let them be anything else, or Jews simply *have to be* Jews because the world will never let Jews forget the accident of their birth to Jewish parents, is simply not true. We certainly know that it is not true today, when even the worst enemies of the Jews are not checking individuals' ancestries like the Nazis did. The enemies of the Jews might be evil, but their evil is not the evil of genocidal racism – which, however, doesn't make the new threat of genocide from twenty-first- century enemies any less lethal though.

Political strategy, necessary as it no doubt is, does not give one *reasons* for being committed to the existence of Israel. Political strategy doesn't answer the question of why Israel itself ought to exist. It only enables one to counter the claims of enemies of the Jews that Israel should not be recognized as a nation-state in the international arena. In making this case, though, one doesn't have to look for reasons as to why he or she should be actively committed to Israel's existence, survival, and flourishing. One only needs to counter the charges of legal and political illegitimacy by

---

[3] See en.wikepedia.org/wiki/Rootless_cosmopolitan

pointing to undeniable legal and political facts. This is like showing your notarized lease to somebody who denies you are the rightful tenant in your own house and claims you are a poacher there. But this evidence in no way explains why you are living in this house, and why you and your family should continue living in this house, and why your true friends can well understand and empathize with that. And it doesn't tell you or your children why you or they shouldn't move out of the house whenever it is no more to your or to their liking.

Psychological Motivation

As for psychological motivation, one is most at home when one feels at home. And one feels most at home when one is doing deeds that identify this home as one's own. Strong feelings for Israel are very much part of Jews being at home in the world. To ignore these emotions or attempt to leave them behind would turn a person into a random individual in the world. To be emotionally motivated even without good reasons why is still better than not being motivated at all. To slightly paraphrase an opinion in the Talmud: one should learn Torah and keep the commandments even for an extraneous reason (*she-lo li-shmah*), because from out of the extraneous reason one might well come to do this for the inherent or true reason.[4]

Assuming, nevertheless, that Jews should remain at this psychological level is inadequate to the task of being Jewish, and of being a Zionist which I think is a major, indispensable component of being Jewish today. Emotion is where one begins, and emotion always accompanies everything significant one is able to do, but the emotional level is not where a fully intelligent human life stops or should become fixated. Emotion is not fully adequate to our existence as persons, because it doesn't tell us *why* we should perform certain acts other than that they make us feel good about ourselves (a current refrain in today's pop psychology). In other words, psychological motivation does not

[4] B. Nazir 23a.

supply or discover reasons that guide our actions to goals that beckon us to act *because* of them, which means acting for the sake of these goals or purposes (or what philosophers like to call "ends"). Feelings without reasons do not point us in a definite direction, one whose end is knowable; instead, feelings alone throw our actions around every which way. Emotional intensity should always accompany important rational action, but it cannot justify it.[5] Without reasons to enable us to privilege one emotion over another, when one emotion is pushing us to act one way and another is pulling us to act the opposite way, we are frequently paralyzed in our emotional ambivalence. Or, without reason to judge which feeling takes precedence when there are two or more in conflict, one could feel one way today and quite otherwise tomorrow, and in each case act accordingly. Or, without reason to judge which feelings are justified and which are not, we are easily led by those who are clever enough to know how to manipulate people by playing to their psychological blind spots. At this level of arrested human existence, we cannot actually *decide* to act one way rather than the opposite way. At this level of human existence, there is no criterion for deciding or judging what to do as our own intelligent choice. At this level we can only react to forces that seem to have no respect for us as free, rational persons.

Immanuel Kant said: "Thoughts without content are empty; intuitions without concepts are blind."[6] By analogy I would say: Feelings without reasons directing us to act are dumb; reasons without feelings motivating us to act are personally detached. But we must begin with emotionally charged action. Celebration of a founding event, what the Jewish philosopher Emil Fackenheim (d. 2003) called a "root experience," is a key example of such emotionally charged action; and it is emotionally charged action that is public, not private, and structured, not spontaneous.[7]

---

[5] See Plato, *Philebus*, 20E–22E; Aristotle, *Nicomachean Ethics*, 10.2/1172^{b}26–35.
[6] *Critique of Pure Reason*, B75.
[7] *God's Presence in History* (New York: Harper Torchbooks, 1970), 8–14.

Jewish Celebration/Jewish Commemoration

Let us now look at *how* Jews celebrate *Yom ha`Atsma'ut*: Israel Independence Day, which commemorates the founding event of the State of Israel as well. This is certainly an emotionally charged activity for most Jews, and for many friends of the Jews. Now, it is still too early to tell just what uniform communal form or "ritual" the celebration of *Yom ha`Atsma'ut* will take hold among the great majority of the Jewish people.[8] Yet the celebration of this great event (and perhaps some other similar events as well) will have to take some definite ritual form if it is to continue to be celebrated by the Jewish people in any coherent way. Without this kind of ritual formalization, this celebration will not be a commemoration by which Jews renew their own personal identification with an event more and more of them did not actually experience themselves. Instead, this celebration will become a nostalgic occasion for those who did experience this event to remind those who didn't actually experience it of how it belongs to them alone. But then, this kind of nostalgia will most likely fade away once those who actually experienced it are no longer here in this world. Only with this kind of ritual formalization or codification will Israel Independence Day become like the other great events that Jews celebrated with definite, legally structured, rituals like the Passover *seder* or the Hanukkah lights. Celebratory rituals have staying power only when they are taken to be positive commandments (*mitsvot aseh* in Hebrew) structured by law (*halakhah* in Hebrew). Thus emotionally charged action, like the celebration of *Yom ha`Atsma'ut*, needs to take on public form that can be handed down from one generation to another (that is what "tradition," *masoret* in Hebrew, means) with historical continuity.[9]

Furthermore, we need to consider whether such public ritual forms need to be "religious," that is, whether they have to have a connection to God, or whether they can simply be the "cultural"

---

[8] See B. Avodah Zarah 36a. See MT: Rebels, 2.7.
[9] M. Avot 1.1.

celebration of national or civic "holidays" rather than the cultic celebration of "holy days" (*haggim* or *yamim tovim* in Hebrew) in the literal sense. Whether religious or secular, though, commemorative rituals like these make sense only when they are accepted as moral imperatives. So, if there is a moral imperative to celebrate the founding of the State of Israel in whatever way, then that imperative must be seen as part of the larger imperative to support the continuing existence of the State of Israel. But, if the celebration of the founding event is severed from the larger present imperative to support (in whatever way) the State of Israel as a personal obligation, this celebration will degenerate into sentimentality. This kind of sentimentality is dangerous, because it diverts attention from present tasks by indulging the desire to flee from the present into a frequently romanticized past. Such sentimentality makes one ignore how present tasks point one into the future *before* one can retrieve his or her past for its useful precedents to inform present activity. Unlike this kind of sentimentality, one should not be interested in the past for its own sake; instead, the value of the past is when it shows one how to celebrate its great events in the present, thereby renewing these great events here and now. In fact, too much "historicism," which can be taken to be sentimentality intellectualized, still disconnects the past from the present in a way that provides "decent burial" for the past rather than retrieving one's own past for one's own active present, in which the State of Israel's life and its founding event are so indispensable.

Now the moral imperative to celebrate great events is not something that a group of rabbis simply decided is good for the Jewish people to do. It is not something that comes from the top down, so to speak. Instead, it comes from the bottom up. That is, popular celebrations of great events crop up by themselves as it were. Only thereafter do those responsible for structuring custom into law fulfill that responsibility accordingly. The structured celebration of Hanukkah is the best example of this process. It celebrates the defeat of the Hellenistic Syrian regime and their assimilationist Jewish collaborators by the Maccabees in 164 B.C.E., who then set up an independent Jewish state in the land of Israel. A significant part of that national victory was the cleansing of the Temple in Jerusalem of the pagan cult that had been introduced there by the assimilationists. This event, epitomized by the rekindling of the Menorah in the Temple, gradually became a popular celebration of a festival (*hag*), even though there was no specific scriptural basis for this new holyday. Eventually, the rabbis formalized that popular celebration with a prescribed ritual format (kindling lights for eight consecutive evenings), even proclaiming that the specific ritual is to be celebrated as something commanded by God.[10] This seems to be a Jewish version of the Latin saying, "The voice of the people is the voice of God (*vox populi vox dei*)." It is hoped that the celebration of *Yom Ha`Atsma'ut* will follow a similar historical trajectory. It is hoped that just as the ancient rabbis persuaded enabled the Jewish people to celebrate Hanukkah because the Maccabean victory enabled the Jewish people to return to authentic Jewish life (epitomized by the lighted Temple), so will current or future Jewish teachers persuade the Jewish people to return to authentic Jewish life (which will be epitomized by the messianic rebuilding of the Temple in one way or another).

Reasons of the Commandments

I mention all of this now, because those who are unable, let alone unwilling, to celebrate the existence of the State of Israel with others as a moral imperative, one that is part of a larger moral imperative, are in a very poor position to understand themselves, let alone explain to others, not just *how* the State of Israel came to exist, but *why* it ought to exist. (The "how" question is for historians to answer; the "why" question is for philosophers to answer, hence this book.) Now in the Jewish tradition, what ought to exist is something that we have been commanded to bring into and maintain in existence. (Think of the commandment to procreate, i.e., to conceive and birth children, plus raise them to maturity.[11]) For most Jews today, to support the

---

[10] B. Shabbat 23a re Deut. 17:11.
[11] Gen. 9:7; M. Yevamot 6.6; B. Kiddushin 29a.

existence of the State of Israel is a commandment (a *mitsvah*), whether they are aware of the imperative force of what they are doing or not. (The nature of this particular commandment is explored in Chapter 6.)

Although there have been those in the Jewish tradition who have asserted that commandments are best obeyed when no questions about their meaning are asked, the preponderance of the tradition has encouraged the search for "the reasons of the commandments" (called *ta`amei ha-mitsvot* in Hebrew). That is because understanding these reasons helps those who believe there is a moral imperative for them to act a certain way to act that way more intelligently.[12] Understanding the reasons helps one see that these commanded deeds are meaningful or intentional acts worthy of intelligent persons, that these deeds are not just blind behavior that is unworthy of intelligent persons. In other words, understanding *why* you are doing something definitely improves *how* you actually do it.

Nevertheless, in the old "religious" (in Yiddish, *frum*) approach, what my late revered teacher Abraham Joshua Heschel called "religious behaviorism," Jews were often told: "Just do *mitsvot*; don't ask why!" (In Yiddish: *fregt nisht kashes!*).[13] In modern times, this was a kind of panic reaction to the arguments (and they were arguments) of non-Orthodox or anti-Orthodox Jews to give reasons, not for why Jews *should* keep the commandments, but rather *why Jews shouldn't* keep them.[14] So, for example, it has been argued, the Jewish dietary prohibitions (*kashrut*) are no longer binding because they were originally given to keep Jews separate from the gentiles in their cultural practices such as the way Jews eat together; but now, having won political equality with the gentiles, Jews should not maintain practices like *kashrut* that keep them as separate from the gentiles as Jews were when we were their political inferiors, being confined in the

---

[12] See Maimonides, *Guide of the Perplexed*, 3.26.
[13] *God in Search of Man* (New York: Farrar, Straus and Cudahy, 1955), 320–35.
[14] Talmudic precedence for this "fideistic" view is on B. Sanhedrin 21b re Deut. 17:16–17.

Reasons of the Commandments

ghetto of the gentiles' making. In other words, for these opponents of tradition the original reason no longer applies; hence the practice it once explained well should be dropped as an anachronism. The reason seems to be no longer valid. Indeed, since childhood I have heard the same arguments from anti-Zionists, that is, Zionism and the practices it entails make us "foreign" when we should be more like the people we live among, especially when the majority of the gentiles do not seem to want us to be "foreigners."

Instead of trying to present better reasons for keeping the commandments, including the commandment to support Israel, too often the kneejerk response has been directed against the *persons* themselves (i.e., an *ad hominem* putdown) rather than actually dealing with the arguments themselves (i.e., *ad rem*). The reaction too often has been condemnation, that is, castigating those making the arguments by accusing them of being ashamed of being different, and wanting the Jews collectively to disappear. In other words, they are often accused of being "self-hating" Jews. This kind of condemnation was what someone as brilliant as the Israeli historian-philosopher Gershom Scholem (d. 1982) in the 1960s directed against his old friend, the by then anti-Zionist political philosopher Hannah Arendt (d. 1975). Scholem accused Arendt of having no *ahavat yisrael* or "love of the Jewish people," her own people.[15] Arendt's response was that she didn't see why she should love any people (other than her friends). But this was something far beneath the type of rational argument both she and Scholem, being the philosophers they both were on their better days, were quite capable of making. In both cases, what we see is intellectuals essentially engaged in emotionally motivated name-calling.[16]

---

[15] Scholem's letter of June 23, 1963 to Arendt, which was his response to her *Eichmann in Jerusalem* (New York: Viking Press, 1963), and Arendt's quick reply of July 24, 1963, are printed in Hannah Arendt, *The Jew as Pariah*, ed. R. H. Feldman (New York: Grove Press, 2001), 241–51.

[16] See S. E. Aschheim, *In Times of Crisis* (Madison: University of Wisconsin Press, 2001), 73–85.

The anti-Zionist arguments are still arguments, however grating they might be emotionally to Zionists. As such, they must be countered with better arguments, not condemnations that make Zionists look dumber than they really are, and that make their adversaries look smarter than they really are. Condemnatory public rhetoric lowers the level of public discourse. No matter how bad the arguments of the Jewish anti-Zionists might be, they are still arguments nonetheless. As such, they must be countered with good arguments. (And, if they are good arguments, then they must be countered with better arguments.) However, though these challenges to one's beliefs and practices (about which a person is so passionate) are only the occasion for one's having to look for reasons of these beliefs and practices, that person still needs them as a way of motivating him- or herself. Yet looking for these reasons is valuable in and of itself. Action (which is what this looking for reasons is) is more important than reaction. Reactionary responses alone usually counter anti-Zionist arguments with condemnations that employ the slogans of propaganda rather the rational insights of the Jewish tradition. That is not good for Zionism and the Jewish tradition of which it is the greatest contemporary manifestation. It turns Zionists into an essentially special interest group; and it turns Zionism and the whole Jewish tradition in which it is truly rooted into an ideology rather than the profoundly intelligent way of life Judaism so magnificently is. These anti-Zionist arguments should be regarded as a challenge to Zionist thought, stimulating thoughtful Zionists (and their sympathizers) to discover new and better reasons for their Zionist commitment than they had before they were so challenged. But what are these *Jewish* anti-Zionist arguments?

The most cogent Jewish anti-Zionist argument (to my mind anyway) is the one that argues that the main purpose of the Jews and Judaism in the world today is to be a "light to the nations."[17] That almost always means being a force for social justice internationally. (That is an argument made by some liberal religious

---

[17] This is dealt with more fully in Chapter 5, p. 132.

non-Jewish anti-Zionists, who are not intentionally antisemitic.) But how can Jews do that (they say) when so much of their time and energy is taken up with defending Israel from enemies they wouldn't have if Jews hadn't become a nation-state? And, when one counters that argument by saying that secure Jewish existence today requires a Jewish state, they counter-argue that the lives of Jews are made more precarious because of Israel's precarious position in the world today. That is their realpolitik argument, which becomes their philosophical argument when they argue that the State of Israel, by making the Jewish nation-state be at the center of Jewish existence, hinders rather than helps the true purpose of the existence of the Jewish people in the world.

These "internationalists" or "universalists" seem to think that the Jewish people should exist primarily for the sake of the world. In fact, though, the Jews exist for the sake of their covenantal relationship (*brit*) with God. Now the nations of the world can, and sometimes do, take notice of that fact. But that notice is a possible effect of that fact being made known; it is not the essential reason for that fact's coming to be.[18] The Jews are a people because of the Torah, the content of God's covenant with them, which was most famously expressed by the ninth-century Jewish thinker Saadiah Gaon.[19] Jews should be happy when the nations of the world notice the vitality of their covenantal life, but the covenantal life is not lived primarily to impress gentiles or influence them.

Furthermore, these new Jewish anti-Zionists do not seem to be making the old anti-Zionist argument that the Jews are not a people, but only a voluntary association of like-minded individuals (something like a Protestant denomination or a political party).[20] Hence, the political loyalty of these Jewish individuals should only be to the country of the people these individuals

---

[18] Philosophers would say it is a *ratio cognoscendi* (reason for knowing), not the *ratio essendi* (reason for being). See Kant, Critique of Practical Reason, A5:4, note, trans. W. S. Pluhar (Indianapolis: Hackett, 2002), p. 5, n. 25.

[19] *Book of Beliefs and Opinions*, 3.7.

[20] See Leora Batnitzky, *How Judaism became a Religion* (Princeton, NJ: Princeton University Press, 2011).

have themselves chosen to become part of as equal citizens. Until 1933, there were still many German Jews who called themselves "German citizens (*Deutsche Staatsbürger*) of the Mosaic faith (*Glaube*)." In the United States, for example, Zionists were charged with having "dual loyalty," hence having questionable or ambivalent loyalty to the United States, by such groups as the militantly anti-Zionist "American Council for Judaism." Nevertheless, these new Jewish anti-Zionists are not patriots of countries other than Israel. Instead, they are most often Jewish "internationalists" who are generally opposed to all nationalism in general, and Jewish nationalism as Zionism in particular. Thus they see Zionism making *Jewishly* unwarranted claims on them, and on all other Jews as well. And, in fact, there are even some Israeli Jews who espouse similar Jewish anti-nationalism/anti-Zionism. So, their anti-Zionism is not their rejection of Judaism; instead it is their mistaken notion that Zionism and Judaism are incompatible, even at odds with each other.

Zionists, therefore, need to show why a people needs a purpose for its existence, and why the Jews need such a purpose especially. Zionists need to show why their Zionist commitment to the State of Israel is rooted in the Jewish tradition, and then how Zionism furthers rather than hinders the great purpose for which Jews and Judaism exist and ought to continue to exist. Accordingly, one has to show by means of rational arguments why Zionism is integral to Judaism, and why anti-Zionism is an aberration from Judaism.

Finally, though, there those who protest any attempt to discover and then argue for a raison d'être of the State of Israel, or of the Jewish people. They assume that only enemies of Israel and of the Jewish people ask of them what is not asked of any other people or state in the world. Why does Israel have to justify its existence when no other nation has to justify its existence? Well, it is true that many nations in the world do not have to justify their presence in the world to others, yet their thoughtful citizens do have to justify the founding of that nation and its continued existence in the world to themselves and to their fellow citizens. After all, why should anybody struggle, fight, or even risk his or her life to preserve their nation when there are easier options: national extinction, assimilation into or subjugation to some other nation that does affirm its raison d'être over all others. Think of how the former Soviet Union lost its raison d'être (however bad it may have been) and quickly ceased to exist as a nation therefore. Think of how the Cornish people simply assimilated into the English people. Think of how the French nation subjugated or surrendered itself (at least officially) to the German nation in 1940, because of what seems to have been the basic loss by the French people of their raison d'être, that is, their will to survive as a distinct nation for a reason more than mere survival per se.[21]

Even individual persons need such a purpose to keep on living and working in the world; think of how many individual persons disintegrate mentally and even physically when they lose their reason for living and working. Indeed, there are survivors of the Holocaust who have told me how, even in the hell of a place like Auschwitz, they still wanted to survive and made superhuman efforts to survive, who never lost hope for their future liberation from this hellish world, because they had hope for their possible return to the life of Torah and its commandments of which they had been presently robbed by their evil Nazi oppressors. And, they actually wanted not just to regain what had been taken from them, but to live that way of life again even more fully than before.[22] This purpose, of course, which is always the communal purpose of the Jewish people, is much more than what some call the "life plan" of individuals.[23]

---

[21] For a profound insight into what happens when a people loses its positive raison d'être, no accident written by a great French philosopher in exile from France during World War II, see Jacques Maritain, *Natural Law and the Rights of Man*, trans. D. C. Anson (San Francisco: Ignatius Press, 1986), 122–25.

[22] See David Weiss Halivni, *The Book and the Sword* (New York: Farrar, Straus & Giroux, 1996).

[23] Cf. John Rawls, *A Theory of Justice* (Cambridge, MA: Harvard University Press, 1971), 409.

Four Kinds of Jews – Four Kinds of Non-Jews

There are, it seems, four kinds of Jews, plus four kinds of non-Jews in relation to Zionism, and their different reasons for being Zionists or Zionist sympathizers must be addressed separately. And, in the course of this book, I try to keep my different readers in mind.

First, there are Jews with no commitment to either Judaism or Zionism. They are especially difficult to address when they are Jews who once did have a commitment to Judaism (with or without a commitment to Zionism), which they have subsequently repudiated in one way or another. Usually, though, this kind of Jew makes arguments that are not essentially Jewish. In fact, they are almost always the same type of anti-Israel arguments made by non-Jewish opponents of the State of Israel, that is, that the State of Israel lacks international legitimacy. That being the case, their arguments should be countered no differently than one would counter the same arguments when made by a non-Jew. Nevertheless, this kind of anti-Zionist Jew is more often not someone who once did have an experiential connection to Judaism (with a Zionist component or not) and then lost it, but rather someone who has "never been there" so to speak (what the Jewish tradition has called *tinoq she-nishbah* or the "child kidnapped by gentiles").[24] The task for Zionists is to try to immerse them in authentic Jewish experience in which active Zionism is now an essential component. Only then can this kind of "reborn" Jew begin to intelligently search for the reasons of why he or she is doing what he or she is now doing. As Aristotle pointed out, you can discuss ethical purposes only with someone who has had some experience in living a distinctly ethical life.[25] So, too, you can discuss the reasons of the commandments (like the commandment to support

---

[24] B. Shabbat 68a. See David Novak, *The Election of Israel* (Cambridge: Cambridge University Press, 1995), 259–61.
[25] *Nicomachean Ethics*, 1.3/1095a2–10.

Israel) only with someone who has been living a Jewish way of life, however partially.

Second, there are Jews who have a commitment to Judaism, but who have no commitment to Zionism. When they are explicitly anti-Zionist, they must be shown that they have distorted the Jewish tradition by making Zionism antithetical to it. Much the same counter-arguments apply to both ultra-traditionalist anti-Zionists and ultra-liberal anti-Zionists. To the ultra-traditionalists for whom Zionism is too worldly, to them let it be said: Jews are participants in the external world whether they like it or not. Zionism enables Jews to function in that world most intelligently and in the most politically effective way, that is, navigating *in* the world without being swallowed up *by* the world; and this is warranted by the Jewish tradition. And to the ultra-liberals for whom Zionism is the kind of Judaism that is not worldly enough, let it be said: Any worldliness that makes the chief purpose of Judaism to be its function for enlightening the non-Jewish "other," that is a recipe for the demise of the Jews, for the Jews then become somebody else's servants rather than residents in their own home. Only in their own home are Jews meant to be neither their own masters nor somebody else's servants, but intimate guests of God's. Zionism enables Jews to best live as God's guests in the land of Israel, the land God had chosen for them to dwell in as a people.

Third, there are Jews for whom Zionism has become a substitute for Judaism. They usually argue that Judaism was needed to keep the Jews intact as a people without a land of their own, and without a state of their own there. However (in this view anyway), once Jews do have a land of their own with its own state, Judaism has outlived its national usefulness. In fact, some of them argue that Judaism hinders the Zionist project by providing a way of life that Jews outside of Israel can live and call adequately (if not sufficiently) Jewish. For them, superseding Judaism is superseding Diaspora existence (called *shelilat ha-golah,* literally the "negation of the exile"), which they think has no right to continue to exist. (Somehow, after the Holocaust,

I cringe at any suggestion that any group of Jews has no right to exist, even if that suggestion does not extend to denying the right to exist to their Jewish bodies.) To them let it be said: Judaism is the trunk of which Zionism is the branch. Though a trunk needs to branch out or it *will* die, a branch detached from its trunk is *already* dead. Thus Judaism can exist without Zionism, though inadequately today as has just been noted, but Zionism loses both its origin and its end when severed from Judaism. In the same way, Israel loses its purpose for existing, its raison d'être, when it cuts itself off from the Jewish people's past history, present existence, and future hope.

Fourth, there are Jews for whom their Zionism is a unique manifestation of their Judaism in and for the modern world. They need to see *how* the integral connection of Zionism to Judaism has functioned, which is the job of historians; and *how* it actually does function and ought to function, which is the job of Jewish ethicists, or who we now call "halakhists" of one brand or another. They need to see *why* Zionism is a necessary manifestation of Judaism, and *why* Judaism or the Torah exists and ought to continue to exist, borne by the living Jewish people in the world. That is the job of Jewish philosophers.

Finally, it seems to me from my own experience in regularly talking with non-Jews that there are four kinds of non-Jews who might well be interested in this book, who might well understand its arguments in one way or another, and who might empathize or even sympathize with them.

First, there are Christians who see themselves to be part of God's covenant with Israel/the Jewish people, who do not think the Church has supplanted the Jewish people as Israel. They are convinced that God is keeping His biblical promise to the Jewish people by letting the Jewish people return to the land of Israel and settle it. They are, therefore, committed to the existence of the State of Israel as a contemporary manifestation of the covenantal reality, which they sympathize or identify with.[26] (They

---

[26] See Shalom Goldman, *Zeal for Zion: Christians, Jews, and the Idea of the Promised Land* (Chapel Hill, NC: University of North Carolina Press, 2009),

should be differentiated from Christian "millenarians," who hope that Israel's struggles with her enemies will bring about Armageddon, i.e., the end of the world as we know it in some sort of apocalypse, after which the Kingdom of God will descend into the world.) In fact, it is sometimes embarrassing for Jewish Zionists to learn that there are Christian Zionists who have better biblically based theological arguments for their Zionism than many Jews have for their own Zionism.

Second, there are Muslims who can appreciate why Jews need a state of their own, which is theologically legitimated by its being founded in its acceptance of a divine command to establish such a theopolitical entity.

Third, there are secular non-Jews, who see analogues in Zionism to their own nationalism, and who appreciate how many Zionists have tried to make the Jewish nation-state eschew the type of nationalism that degenerates into racism, chauvinism, and militarism.

Fourth, there are non-Jews who admire the determination of Israel to survive against great odds, and who want their own people to learn how the Jews have done that best when they have been faithful to the cultural resources of the Jewish tradition.

With this Zionist project of ours these four kinds of non-Jews might empathize or even sympathize with each in their own way. Hence this book, though written primarily for Jews, tries to speak to non-Jews as well, not apologetically, but by showing them how they can include themselves in this reflection on Zionism, even in the Zionist project, in a way that is consistent with their own traditions and ideologies. They too need to see how integral Zionism is to the Jewish tradition: past, present, and future. Furthermore, non-Jewish readers will be especially interested in the arguments presented in Chapter 6 that show how the civil rights of non-Jews, both individual and collective, are recognized and endorsed in the Jewish normative tradition.

270–308. For the importance of the land of Israel in the Christian tradition, see Robert Louis Wilken, *The Land Called Holy* (New Haven, CT: Yale University Press, 1992).

Let us now look as the beginnings of modern Zionism, which by the late nineteenth century had taken a decidedly secular turn. A strong case can be made for designating Baruch Spinoza (1632–1677) the first modern Zionist. Many of the early Zionists thought so. The question is, though, whether Spinoza himself was really as secular (in the contemporary sense of the term) as many have long thought and still do think, or not.

2

Was Spinoza the First Zionist?

Ben-Gurion and Spinoza

In 1954, no doubt beset by great national and international challenges, the first Prime Minister of the quite recently reestablished State of Israel, David Ben-Gurion, nevertheless still took the time and effort to write a rather odd letter, or at least, a rather odd letter for a politician to write. The letter was addressed to the *Hakham* or Chief Rabbi of the Sephardic community of Amsterdam, Salamon Rodrigues Pereira, whose community still carries the official name *Portugees-Israëlitische Gemeente*. In this letter, Ben-Gurion requested from Rabbi Pereira that his rabbinical court (his *bet din*) repeal the ban of excommunication (the *herem*) placed upon a former member of his community almost 300 years earlier in 1656.[1] That former member of the community was Baruch Spinoza, a man already controversial in his own day, and who has remained the subject of much controversy ever since.

Ben-Gurion's reason for making this odd request was because he regarded Spinoza's excommunication from his native Jewish community to be an embarrassment to the Jewish people. For Spinoza was the man whom Ben-Gurion thought was the

---

[1] http://archive.jta.org/article/1954/07/26/3040463/amsterdam-jewish-community

greatest Jewish thinker since the biblical prophets, as well as now considered a world renowned philosopher, assumed by many to be in the same league with Plato, Aristotle, Kant, and Hegel.[2] Yet this great Jewish philosopher was rejected by his own Jewish community, acting in the name of the entire Jewish people! Although Spinoza left the Jewish community voluntarily, the ban but confirmed the community's agreement with his own choice, and Spinoza did not at all regret his choice, none of these facts would have dissuaded Ben-Gurion from requesting what could only be Spinoza's posthumous, symbolic reinstatement into the Jewish people.[3] Furthermore, even though Ben-Gurion surely knew that Rabbi Pereira's answer would be "no," nonetheless that too would not have dissuaded him from making this radical request of this very traditional rabbi. Ben-Gurion was making more of a public statement than a private request.

There were two reasons for Pereira's predictably negative reply. One, Pereira invoked the Talmudic principle that a later rabbinical court may not repeal the decision of an earlier rabbinical court unless the members considered themselves "greater in wisdom and in number of disciples."[4] Unlike Baruch Spinoza, Salamon Rodrigues Pereira had no problem accepting the authority of his predecessors as he had received it through the normative Jewish tradition. (As an aside, I remember seeing Rabbi Pereira in the Spanish-Portuguese Synagogue in New York when I was fourteen years old. He certainly looked and acted as if he had just stepped out of one of Rembrandt's portraits of seventeenth century Amsterdam rabbis.) Two, it seems Pereira himself agreed with his predecessors: Spinoza was indeed a denier (*apiqoros*) of

---

[2] In his essay, "Cultural Independence," Ben-Gurion called Spinoza "the greatest philosopher coming out of the Jewish people in the 17th century, and one of humankind's most profound thinkers." *Vision and Way* 4 [Heb.], 2nd ed. (Tel Aviv: Mapai, 1956), 54. Note, also, his essay, "Eternal Israel," in which he places Spinoza (and Einstein, himself a Spinozist of sorts) among the best Prophets and Sages of the Jewish people (ibid., 309). See David Novak, *The Election of Israel* (Cambridge: Cambridge University Press, 1995), 25, n. 6.

[3] For the historical context of this *herem*, see Steven Nadler, *Spinoza: A Life* (Cambridge: Cambridge University Press, 1999), 116–54.

[4] M. Eduyot 1.4. See, also, B. Shabbat 112b.

everything Judaism is based upon. In other words, had he been there in 1656, Pereira would have agreed with the decision of the court of his predecessor, Saul Levi Morteira, a formidable talmudist and theologian, who had been a teacher of Spinoza in the Amsterdam *yeshivah*, the school where Spinoza seems to have been the most promising student. (Also as an aside, I remember meeting Rabbi Pereira's son in New York in the mid-1980s, and when I asked about his father's exchange with Ben-Gurion, Pereira-fils was convinced that Pereira-père meant every word he wrote back to David Ben-Gurion in 1954.)

The primary reason Ben-Gurion would not have been dissuaded by Pereira's predictable rejection of his request is that Spinoza was, for him, the first Zionist – and Zionism is, for Ben-Gurion, a clear break with the rabbinically dominated Jewish past against which Spinoza gave the best theoretical justification for its being overcome in general, and having been overcome by Baruch Spinoza himself in particular.[5] Considering Ben-Gurion's low opinion of both rabbis and traditional – that is, rabbinic – Judaism, it is clear why he wanted Spinoza back in the Jewish fold. Spinoza was taken to be a precedent for his kind of Zionism, and it was a precedent from a philosopher whom Jewish intellectuals, non-Jewish as well as Jewish, greatly respected. If these intellectuals respected Spinoza's philosophical and political break with the past in general, then perhaps they could be made to respect Spinoza's break with the rabbinically dominated Jewish past in particular, especially that Jewish past in which Ben-Gurion's kind of Zionism would have gotten no respect. For Ben-Gurion and others like him, Spinoza was the prototype of the new kind of Jew they thought themselves to be, and the new kind of Jew they wanted Israeli Jews, especially, to become. The question is whether or not Spinoza is really the kind

---

[5] See Ben-Gurion's "State as Exemplary End and Means," *Vision and Way* 5, p. 78. For a thorough study of Spinoza's reception by subsequent Jewish thinkers, especially by Zionists, see Daniel B. Schwartz, *The First Modern Jew: Spinoza and the History of an Image* (Princeton, NJ: Princeton University Press, 2012), 113–53. Also, see *Spinoza: Dreihundert Jahre Ewigkeit*, 2nd ed., edited by S. Hessing (The Hague: Martinus Nijhoff, 1962).

of precedent a secular Zionist like Ben-Gurion was hopefully looking for. Indeed, as we shall see, Spinoza is as much of a challenge to contemporary secular Zionism as he always has been to religious Zionism from his time on.

Spinoza's Inversions of Classical Jewish Theology

Before we look at the one long sentence in Spinoza's *Tractatus Theologico-Politicus* that so impressed Ben-Gurion and other secular Zionists, we need to raise four questions. One, how radical was Spinoza's break from Judaism? Two, is what might be called Spinoza's "proto-Zionism" as radical a break from Judaism as Ben-Gurion seems to have thought it to be? In other words, how truly "secular" was Spinoza's "Zionism"? Three, does Spinoza have anything to offer the current dilemma of Zionists, namely, what would make Israel as a state of Jews (*medinat yehudim*) an authentically *Jewish* state (*medinah yehudit*), that is, a state that could be justified by appealing to at least some kind of Judaism? Could Spinoza be used to justify the existence of a Jewish state in the land of Israel *theologically*? (Like it or not, as we shall seen, Judaism is inextricably theological because the "God-question" is ubiquitous therein.) Four, does Spinoza's break from conventional Jewish theology make any "theological" reading of him self-contradictory, or does Spinoza have his own theology, which has at least some correspondence with Jewish tradition? I submit that dealing with these four questions will enable us to see what for many might well be a *new* Spinoza, especially Spinoza as a *new* kind of Zionist.

How radical Spinoza's break with the Jewish past was is arguable, as we shall see. Yet he certainly broke with what seems to have been unanimous Jewish religious opinion in his own time. And, even though he could have hardly predicted the subsequent effects of his break in later Jewish history, those effects have been profound, so profound that they are now still operative in the life of the Jewish people – and perhaps in the whole Western world – now more than 350 years later.[6]

---

[6] See Schwartz, *The First Modern Jew*, 1–32.

Spinoza's break can be seen in what I would like to call his three "inversions" of the conventional theology of most of his contemporaries, both Jewish and Christian. What seems to be Spinoza's Zionism or "proto-Zionism" is best understood in the context of all three of his inversions of the conventional Jewish theology of his time.

Spinoza's first inversion: Whereas Jewish tradition had taught that God elected Israel in the covenant (the *brit*), Spinoza inverted that relation to assert that Israel elected God through a "social contract" (a *pactum*).[7] In Spinoza's view, just as an individual person has the right to be a party to the social contract of the particular society he or she chooses to live in, so does that person have the right to choose his or her religion. As such, one has the right (although not always the opportunity) to disaffiliate with any religious community he so chooses, even if one happened to have been born into that community.

Conversely, according to traditional Jewish law (*halakhah*), no Jew can ever leave the Jewish people, at least de jure, as one's Jewish being is not the result of one's own choice to be Jewish. Being Jewish is something one is born into; thus it is as involuntary as is one's birth.[8] That is why Spinoza's forbearers who had converted to Christianity in Spain and Portugal (called "marranos," when their conversion was under duress and the Christian commitment had only been feigned by the *conversos*) were not

---

[7] *Tractatus Theologico-Politicus* [TTP], chapter 16, trans. M. Silverthorne and J. Israel (Cambridge: Cambridge University Press, 2007), p. 205. See David Novak, *The Election of Israel*, Cambridge: Cambridge University Press, 1995, 31–44.

[8] B. Kiddushin 68a re Deut. 7:4; M. Avot 4.29. In fact, even converts (*gerim*) are considered to have been "born again" into the Jewish people rather than being considered to be voluntary parties to a social contract (B. Yevamot 22a), which like all contracts can be terminated. See David Novak, *The Jewish Social Contract* (Princeton, NJ: Princeton University Press, 2005), 30–34. That is also why a properly conducted conversion (*giyyur*) can never be nullified (B. Yevamot 47b; MT: Forbidden Intercourse, 13.14–16), because being a covenant (*brit*) it is not based on a contract (B. Keritot 9a). And that is why a gentile who converted him- or herself, that is, without being officially accepted by a rabbinical tribunal (*bet din*), is not considered to be a true convert (*ger tsedeq*), and thus requires a proper conversion and its officially supervised rites (B. Yevamot 47a re Deut. 1:16).

considered to have ever become gentiles de jure.⁹ Moreover, even for coverts to Judaism, their choice to become Jewish is only a necessary condition, but not a sufficient cause, of their actually being accepted into the Jewish people.¹⁰ Thus a forced conversion (like a forced marriage or divorce) can be annulled, nor can any gentile force a rabbinical court to convert him or her.¹¹ (A rabbinical court might have reasons, either intrinsic to the case before it or because of public policy concerns extrinsic to the case before it, to reject an application for conversion.¹²) Yet, these *conversos*, not having any experience with living a normative Jewish life in a traditional Jewish community, are in fact almost like candidates for conversion to Judaism in the sense they require a process of integration into normative Jewish praxis and education or indoctrination in the theology underlying normative Jewish praxis, both of which neither converts nor "returnees" (*ba`alei teshuvah*) to Judaism have any experience with.¹³ In other words, like the covenant itself, their de jure

---

⁹ B. Sanhedrin 44a. In this text the words of Scripture, "Israel has sinned" (Josh. 7:11) in interpreted to mean "even when they have sinned, they are all still Israel." This refers to the people Israel collectively as is clear from the context of the scriptural words and the Talmud's interpretation of them. In fact, this interpretation of the indelibility of the covenantal election of Israel might very well be a Jewish polemic directed against Christian supresessionist claim that God had replaced the Jewish people with the Church because of the sins of the Jews. However, in medieval sources, where there was concern about the apostasy of individual Jews, the words of Josh. 7:11 and their interpretation in the Talmud text were taken to refer to individual Jews who had apostasized by converting to Christianity (whatever their motive). In other words, the message was: "You can always come back home to the Jewish people, since you never really left home in the first place." See Novak, *The Election of Israel*, 138–43, 189–99. This text, no doubt, played an important role in the reintegration into Judaism of Spinoza's *marrano* forbearers by the newly formed Sephardic-Dutch Jewish community.

¹⁰ B. Ketubot 11a.

¹¹ B. Baba Batra 48b; M. Gittin 9.8; B. Gittin 88b.

¹² B. Yevamot 23b. Also, Jewish courts couldn't accept gentile converts when Christian or Muslim polities, in which they were at best resident-aliens, prohibited and severely punished even Jewish acceptance of converts who came to Judaism on their own initiative and not because of any overt proselytizing on the part of Jews.

¹³ B. Shabbat 68a; see Novak, *The Election of Israel*, 259–61.

status is involuntary, but the lived reality of their status de facto requires their active, voluntary acceptance of it as a necessary condition.[14]

The historical effect of Spinoza's first inversion, that is, voluntary religion, came about when Jews had to reinvent their political status in the newly emerging nation-states in the eighteenth century (beginning with Prussia). In these nation-states one's religion was considered to be an individual *choice*. That is, instead of being born, involuntarily, into the traditional community or people of one's birth (or infant baptism) and thus having the duty to accept its authority, one now had the right to *confess* his or her adherence to that community or to any other community – or to no community (being a citizen whom German law would later call *konfessionlos*, i.e., "without any particular religion").

As for this last option, Spinoza not only provided theoretical justification, but he also became an archetype for it. He was probably the first Jew who left the religious Jewish community (the only kind of Jewish community available at the time), yet who affiliated with no other religious community. As such, he was unlike his *converso* ancestors in Spain and Portugal, who under duress renounced Judaism by becoming Christians publicly (and thus known as *marranos*). And because their conversions to Christianity were as involuntary as was their Jewish birth, Spinoza's voluntary departure from the Jewish religious community was essentially different from theirs. Indeed, his inversion of the classical doctrine of election justified his own voluntary decision to leave the Jewish religious community per se (and not just the Jewish community of Amsterdam).

In his *Tractatus Politicus*, Spinoza wanted religious affiliation to be, in what he wanted to be a new kind of democratic polity, "the business of the private man" (*officium viri privati*).[15] Morality, conversely, is public; it is for the sake of political order

---

[14] B. Shabbat 88a-b re Exod. 19:17, Est. 9:27, and Prov. 11:3.
[15] *Tractatus Politicus*, 3.10, trans. S. Shirley (Indianapolis: Hackett, 2000), p. 53; also, ibid., 6.40, p. 75.

and public safety.[16] And in this kind of polity, an individual citizen's acceptance of its political authority and his or her obedience of its moral precepts is not to be a voluntary matter. The state has the right to coerce acceptance of its authority in the face of rebellion or sedition; and the state has the right to enforce its morality when faced with resistance or indifference.

We now come to Spinoza's second inversion: Whereas Jewish tradition had taught that morality needs a religious justification, Spinoza inverted that relation to propose that religion needs a moral justification, that is, a justification that appeals to a revealed text or Scripture.[17]

The traditional religious justification for morality is that it is part of the overall revelation of God to a particular people at a particular time in a particular place. This revelation is neither the invention of human will nor is it is the discovery of human intellect. Instead, it is God's uniquely supernatural intrusion into the affairs of this particular people. It is what has been revealed *to* the people; it is neither what has been invented nor what has been discovered *by* them. The purpose of the revelation is to establish an ongoing relationship between God and *His* people. That relationship is what is now called a "covenant" (*brit* in Hebrew). The structure of that covenantal relationship is the *Torah*; the content of that relationship is the commandments (the *mitsvot*) to be performed by the people.[18]

Because God is primarily related to a people, a communal entity, some of the commandments pertain to the direct relations among the people (the interhuman realm rabbinic tradition calls *bein adam le-havero*). That is what we would now call "morality." But, by means of revelation, the people are directly related to God, so some of the commandments directly pertain to that relationship (the divine–human realm rabbinic tradition calls *bein adam le-maqom*).[19] This is what we now call "religion." Both realms, the

---

[16] Ibid., 5.2, p. 61.
[17] Hence even commandments generally considered to be rationally evident are still referred back to scriptural texts, either generally or specifically (B. Yoma 67b re Lev. 18:4; B. Sanhedrin 56b re Gen. 2:16 and 58a re Gen. 2:24).
[18] B. Berakhot 5a re Exod. 34:12; B. Hagigah 3b re Eccl. 12:12.
[19] M. Yoma 8.9.

interhuman and the divine–human, are necessary components of the covenantal reality. But which realm is more important? Which realm justifies the other in a hierarchy that cannot be cogently reversed?

Surely, what pertains to God-and-humans takes precedence over what pertains to humans-among-ourselves, because God the Creator is greater than even humans, the creatures with whom God has the most in common (because humans are created in the image of God). Therefore, the human relationship with God takes precedence over the relationship we humans conduct among ourselves.[20] Yet, because this divine–human relationship operates in this world of human plurality, the precedence of the divine–human relationship must *ground* the interhuman relationship. Without that theistic grounding, the interhuman relationship inevitably claims to be self-sufficient or "autonomous." Nevertheless, if it isn't correlated with the interhuman realm, the divine–human relation will inevitably become ascetic or world denying. So, for example, in the ancient Israeli polity (the polity that so impressed Spinoza), the Sanhedrin, the national Supreme Court and Legislature that ruled on moral as well as religious matters, met in an outer precinct of the Temple, the locus of the nation's cult or *religio*.[21] The Temple cult, though, was not conducted in any precinct of the Sanhedrin.[22]

This subordination of morality to religion is cogent only within a life-system that provides its members with the means for a *direct* relationship with God. In Judaism, those commandments (*mitsvot*) that we would now call "rituals" or "ceremonies" are the means whereby Jews are directly related to God. And all of these rituals, in one way or another, commemorate

---

[20] B. Berakhot 19b-20a re Prov. 21:30; B. Yevamot 6a re Lev. 19:3; B. Sanhedrin 74a. Nevertheless, on certain less important issues, the interhuman relationship takes precedence over the divine–human relationship. See B. Berakhot 20a and Rashi, s.v. "shev v'al ta'aseh" re B. Yevamot 90b; B. Shabbat 127a re Gen. 18:3.
[21] *Sifrei*: Deuteronomy, no. 152; M. Sanhedrin 11.2; B. Sanhedrin 41a and Rashi, s.v. "ela dinei nefashot"; Y. Horayot 1.1/45d re Deut. 17:8.
[22] M. Middot 5.4; B. Yoma 25a.

and celebrate the historical events through which God directly presented Himself to His people, and whose commemoration and celebration enable His people to enjoy intimate covenantal community with God.[23] These rituals regularly *re-present* these events when symbolically reenacted by the people. That assumes God operates through *temporal* events, events that God has *freely chosen* to effect, yet which God could have just as freely chosen not to effect.[24]

However, what if that is *not* how God acts? What if God's relation to any particular event in the world is remote and indirect? What if God is first or prime cause, but never the immediate or proximate cause of any event in the world? What if God, to use a more British metaphor, never "jumps the [cosmic] queue"? Or, to use a more American metaphor, what if God never "does an end-run" around the great chain of being? If that is true – and Spinoza certainly thought so – a direct relationship with God is impossible within the ordinary interhuman world, the world where politics and law are essential for its duration.[25] The direct relationship with God is possible only for philosophers in their beatific vision of Nature as one totally integrated whole (what Spinoza called *natura naturans*).[26] But, because ordinary people cannot enjoy this kind of philosophical experience, they are only parties to the direct interhuman relationship, the relationship where politics and law reign. Accordingly, for ordinary people, citizens of the state, religious ceremonies should only be for the sake of political harmony, and are to be judged as to how well or how badly they function politically.[27] God is the ultimate, but not the proximate, cause of that political harmony.

---

[23] MT: Benedictions, 11.2.
[24] Nahmanides, *Commentary on the Torah*: Exod. 13:16; also, David Novak, *The Theology of Nahmanides Systematically Presented* (Atlanta, GA: Scholars Press, 1992), 99–124.
[25] TTP, chapter 13, pp. 213–14. See also David Novak, "Spinoza's Conception of Ethics" in *The Oxford Handbook of Ethics and Morality*, eds. E. N. Dorff and J. K. Crane (New York: Oxford University Press, 2013), 102–17.
[26] *Ethics* 5, P36.
[27] TTP, chapter 5, pp. 74–75. Cf. Maimonides, *Guide of the Perplexed*, 3.38–39.

Spinoza's Inversions of Classical Jewish Theology   33

This second inversion of Spinoza's, his subordination of ordinary religion to political morality, paved the way for Reform Judaism, which became the new form of Judaism most suitable (at least in the eyes of its proponents) for a modern secular nation-state claiming political/moral hegemony. Reform Jewish thinkers asserted that their religion is to serve and promote public secular morality; it is not supposed to advocate a "higher" morality stemming from revelation and tradition.[28] Moreover, whereas in premodern times full political acceptance of Jews by Christian polities meant that Jews had to totally renounce their Judaism and become Christians, the new more secular polities only required that Jews, especially, keep their Judaism private and publicly subservient. A Jew was to be "a Jew at home and a human being in public," as the nineteenth century Russian Jewish thinker Judah Leib Gordon famously put it, as we have seen.[29] Here again we see Spinoza's point about religion being "the business of the private man."

Now, by "secular" I do not mean "atheistic," though that is its current connotation. That was surely not the case with any nation-state until the twentieth century. Instead, by "secular" I mean that the newly emerging European nation-states were not appealing to any historical revelation, to any particular religious community, to any traditional hierarchy as a warrant for their legitimacy. Like Thomas Jefferson in the newly independent United States of America, there was an explicit appeal to "Nature's God" – who sounds very much like Spinoza's "natural God" or "divine Nature" (*deus sive natura*).[30] Neither Spinoza nor Jefferson (even though he probably never read Spinoza) was not advocating that politics replace religion; they were only advocating that *revelation-based* religion be subordinate to a public morality that claimed to be ultimately rooted in "Nature's God." There is a big difference between early modern notions of the "secular" and "secularity" and contemporary "secularism."

---

[28] See Schwartz, *The First Modern Jew*, 58–65.
[29] See Chapter 1, p. 5, for the exact wording.
[30] *Ethics*, 4, P4.

In my opinion, those who see Spinoza as a proto-secularist, that is, usually seeing him as a distinguished predecessor of their own modern secularism, are wrong. They are as wrong as those who saw and still see Spinzoa to be an atheist, in the current, anti-metaphysical sense of that designation.[31]

It is notable that until the mid-twentieth century most Reform Jews, who were taken with Spinoza's making religion a morally grounded choice, were anti-Zionists. That is because Zionism seemed to compromise their rather recently gained citizenship in the modern nation-states, something they regarded as a moral and not just a pragmatic necessity. They believed that any revival of the national dimension of the Jewish religious tradition, however dressed up in secular garb, would impede their full political acceptance by these secular, non-Jewish polities. The Jewish religion, however diluted, would become again the same impediment it had been to the full political full acceptance of Jews by the religiously warranted polities of the *ancien régime*. On a more philosophical level, the German-Jewish philosopher Hermann Cohen (d. 1918) saw Zionism fundamentally contradicting the universalism he took to be essential to Judaism.[32]

As we now approach the question of Spinoza's proto-Zionism on the heels of looking at his first two inversions of the Jewish tradition, we need to ask whether Spinoza could be considered to be a proto-Reform Jew in the way the philosopher Moses Mendelssohn (d. 1786) could be considered a proto-Reform Jew (even though he was personally quite traditional, at least in practice)? Or, was Spinoza advocating something else by his proto-Zionism, either something more radical than Reform Judaism, that is, no Judaism at all or a Judaism more conservative than a reformed Judaism, that is, a return to the primacy of

---

[31] See, for example, Yirmiyahu Yovel, *Spinoza and Other Heretics* 1 (Princeton, NJ: Princeton University Press, 1989), 172–77. Cf. Richard Mason, *The God of Spinoza* (Cambridge: Cambridge University Press, 1997), 170.

[32] *Reason and Hope: Selections from the Jewish Writings of Hermann Cohen*, trans. E. Jospe (New York: W. W. Norton, 1971), 163–71; also, idem., *Religion of Reason Out of the Sources of Judaism*, trans. S. Kaplan (New York: Frederick Ungar, 1972), 360–63.

Jewish religion for a Jewish state? This latter alternative, *Jewish religion for a Jewish state*, means much more than Judaism becoming a religious denomination in a non-Jewish state, which was the predominant Reform view until the mid-twentieth century.

The Proto-Zionist Statement

We now come to Spinoza's third inversion: Whereas the preponderance of the Jewish tradition had taught that the Jews must wait for the Messiah to apocalyptically restore them to national independence, Spinoza inverted that relation to assert that the Jews will have to restore themselves to national independence. So let us now turn to that one long sentence from Spinoza's *Theological-Political Treatise* that so convinced David Ben-Gurion and other early Zionists that Spinoza had anticipated in theory what they were working to effect as praxis.

At the end of chapter three of this treatise, in the chapter dealing with "the Vocation of the Hebrews," Spinoza writes about the possible change in the political situation of the Jewish people, and because of it that they might once again become a nation uniquely related to God, as follows:

> Were it not that the principles of their religion weaken their courage [*animos effœminarent*], I would believe unreservedly, given an opportunity, since all things are at some time changeable, they might reestablish [*iterum erecturos*] their state [*imperium*], and God will choose them again [*de novo electurum*].[33]

Ben-Gurion and other Zionists seem to have thought that the key point in this sentence is that their religion "feminizes" them in the sense of making the Jews politically (and militarily) passive. Now the literal term, *effœminare*, is not being used in a literal sexual sense. Were that the case, Spinoza would have said that the Jewish religion makes their bodies passive, which is a typically male view of female sexuality as being essentially passive.[34]

---

[33] TTP, chapter 3, p. 55.
[34] Interestingly enough, whereas Spinoza sees circumcision to have "such great importance as almost to persuade one that this thing alone will preserve their

Instead, Spinoza is speaking of political passivity, that religiously instilled national characteristic that has politically emasculated the Jews. It has thus psychologically robbed the Jews of the ability to actively control their political fortunes by conditioning the Jews to wait for supernatural divine intervention to restore their ancient political liberty to them. Political liberty (what in modern Hebrew came to be called *atsma'ut*) means not being dependent on anyone else – and, apparently, that independence includes being no longer dependent, at least no longer dependent on the miracle-working God of the Bible.

However, Spinoza did not mean that the miracle-working, anthropomorphic God of the Bible is the only one worthy of the name "God." Spinoza was convinced that his ontology is a new and more accurate *natural theology*.[35] Moreover, it is from biblical *political theology* with its assertion of divine kingship, rather than from biblical *dogmatic theology* with its assertion of a supernatural Creator-God, that a theory of God emerges that is not in conflict with the God envisioned by Spinoza's natural theology. And just as Spinoza's natural theology is the meaning of the contemplative religion of philosophers, so is Spinoza's political theology the meaning of the practical religion of the secular polity he hoped for. But, if Spinoza also hoped for such a new *Jewish* secular polity to emerge, and even if that polity is not to be atheistic, would the political theology of that polity have any connection to any kind of *Jewish* religion that has ever been practiced?

For many secularist Zionists, though, even those who like Ben-Gurion are not atheists, to become a modern nation, the Jews had to regain their sovereignty at the expense of any kind of Jewish religion.[36] For the Jewish religion, as it had come down to them, had taught the Jews to wait for the coming of the Messiah as an apocalyptic event, something that would end

---

nation for ever and ever" (ibid.), Maimonides in *Guide of the Perplexed*, 3.49 sees the purpose of circumcision to be the weakening of male libido, that is, what could be seen as "feminizing."

[35] TTP, pref., p. 12.
[36] This will be dealt with in Chapter 3.

human political history rather than return the Jewish people to human political history. So, the Israeli philosopher Yirmiyahu Yovel thinks that this remark of Spinoza (and he takes it to be only a *remark*) is but a warning to the Jews to beware of the messianic pretender Shabbetai Zevi, who was becoming more and more attractive to Spinoza's Dutch Jewish contemporaries and, in fact, to many Christians as well.[37] In this view, Spinoza's remark is only hypothetical. It seems to be saying: "If there were to be any Jewish national restoration, it won't happen because of supernatural divine intervention; instead, it will only come about when Jews seize the opportunity to actively reassert themselves according to their natural right to exercise their own power." Nevertheless, in this view anyway, Spinoza is not seriously suggesting here that the Jews can actually do so; hence Jews should not derive from his words any moral message that this is what they ought to do. One cannot in good faith command what is out of the present range of practical possibility. In this view, Spinoza is only telling the Jews not to let the Jewish religion lead them in a futile path by imparting to them false hopes as it has done in the past. But, if that is what Spinoza really meant, then he is hardly the proto-Zionist Ben-Gurion and others like him made him out to be.

Furthermore, if that is the correct interpretation of this proto-Zionist (and maybe only this "proto-nationalist" statement, as Spinoza doesn't mention the land of Israel as being the necessary site of this independent Jewish state), if this is the correct interpretation, then Spinoza's point "that God will again choose them" is quite problematic. Wouldn't independence from the Jewish religion entail being independent of the God whom the Jewish religion teaches chose the Jews? So, isn't Spinoza contradicting himself in the very same sentence? To save him from such blatant self-contradiction, we shouldn't take the beginning literally, as it is quite consistent with much of what Spinoza says elsewhere, but drop the ending, making it what we now call a "throwaway line"? That is indeed tempting, but I think we have

---

[37] Yovel, *Spinoza and Other Heretics* 1, 190–93.

to assume that Spinoza really meant both the beginning and the end of the sentence, and that he saw them to be consistent with each other – and with his overall political theology or theological politics.

In the proto-Zionist passage, Spinoza makes three points, and these points seem to be admonitions to Jewish action. One, in spite of their religion, the Jews *should not* allow themselves to become passive bystanders when opportunities (*data occasione*) for politically effective action do occur. Two, when the opportunity arises, the Jews *should* reestablish their own state. Three, the Jews *should* assume that the successful reestablishment and endurance of their state is the will of God. This accordingly leads us to ask three questions. First, what kind of religion are the Jews to act in spite of, and is there any other kind of religion that could justify Jewish political activism? Second, what kind of state should the Jews rebuild? Third, why is God's choice of the Jews important for their reentrance into the world of politics?

Most secularist readers of Spinoza have assumed that he was rejecting all traditional religions, such as Judaism and Christianity, and advocating that politics take their place, and that the only place for any religious activity was the very private exercise of the intellect by philosophers, epitomized by their "intellectual love of God" (*amor dei intellectualis*).[38] However, Spinoza was not opposed to all public religion, for he suggested that a new democratic state should devise its own new public religion (something like what Rousseau would later call "civil religion").[39] Moreover, Spinoza was not opposed to all forms of traditional religion. In fact, he also thought that the ancient Israelite state represented in the Bible, if not actually replicable, could still be "quite profitable to imitate."[40] And in that ancient Israelite or "Hebrew state" (*republica Hebræorum*), religion and politics were thoroughly integrated with one another.[41] That

---

[38] TTP, chapter 4, p. 60; *Ethics* 5, P32, corollary.
[39] *Tractatus Politicus*, 8.45, p. 118. See Jean-Jacques Rousseau, *The Social Contract*, 4.8.
[40] TTP, chapter 18, p. 230.
[41] TTP, chapter 17, p. 221; chapter 19, p. 248.

being both what is true and what is desirable about this ancient state, we can now see that Spinoza very much approved of what we now call "Biblical Judaism," especially the religion publicly practiced in the days of the First Temple when the Jewish people enjoyed full political independence.

What Spinoza did not approve of is the Judaism of the late Second Temple period, when the dominant form of Judaism was the religion of the Pharisees, what came to be called "Rabbinic Judaism."[42] And this was the religion that grew up among the Jewish people after they had lost their political independence, when the Jews fell under Rome's heel. As such, it is no surprise to learn that this kind of religion encouraged passivity in its adherents, something the earlier "Biblical Judaism" certainly discouraged.

If or when the Jews get the opportunity to reestablish their own state, then it follows from Spinoza's admiration for the ancient Israelite state that their new state should be a *theocracy*, because the old state to be imitated was a theocracy.[43] Now, unlike its current connotation, "theocracy" does not means what is basically a dictatorship of clerics. Instead, the original meaning of the Greek term, first coined by the first-century Jewish historian Josephus, is "the rule of God" (*kratos tou theou*).[44] And, this is precisely what Spinoza thought made the ancient Israelite state so admirable, for two reasons. One, the warrant for this state, its raison d'être, was continually referred back to God as the First Universal Cause (*causa sui*), thus putting itself within the eternally enduring natural order. Accordingly, you could argue that this political order was rational, being very different from all other states that largely rely on historical chance, blind fate, or the private self-interest of those having power within and over the state. Two, this Israelite state was truly democratic insofar as all its citizens enjoyed the highest degree of equality possible. Why? *Because they were all unequal before God*

---

[42] TTP, chapter 7, pp. 115–17.
[43] TTP, chapter 17, p. 214.
[44] This will be discussed more fully in Chapter 4.

equally. Therefore, no one had more access to God the Sovereign than anybody else. All had equal access to the law regarded as divine, and all were to be equally under divine authority alone. As Spinoza put it:

> The Hebrews did not transfer their right [*suum ius*] to another person but rather all gave their right equally [*æque*] as in a democracy ... It follows they all remained perfectly equal [*æqualis*] as a result of this agreement [*ab hoc pacto*]. The right to consult God, receive laws, and interpret them equally, and all equally without exception retained the whole administration of the state.[45]

Clearly, such equality before the Sovereign would be impossible in any state where anyone else but God is sovereign. In any other kind of state, sovereignty is itself a problem. Why should the citizens recognize anybody human like themselves to have God-like authority over them? Indeed, that would be Spinoza's argument against the state being founded in a Hobbesian social contract, in which the contract designates the sovereign to be "this mortal god" – an oxymoron if there ever was one, as a god is not mortal and a mortal is not god, let alone *the one and only God*.[46] And that would also be Spinoza's argument against Rousseau's "general will," because a collective will is nothing but one individual will subordinating everybody else's will to itself.[47] There is no such thing as "collective will" anymore, what some now like to call "group-think." As with Hobbes' "this mortal god," we have only a difference of degree, but not a difference of kind. But, surely, the sovereign's authority depends on his being taken to be different in kind from those living under his authority. That is why Spinoza's theology makes him a more persuasive political theorist than either Hobbes or Rousseau (or others) – at least in my opinion.

The question of what kind of state the Jews should reestablish, and the question of what it means for the Jews to be re-chosen by God, are two sides of the same coin. For Spinoza argues that

---

[45] TTP, chapter 17, p. 214.
[46] *Leviathan*, chapter 17.
[47] *The Social Contract*, 4.1.

The Proto-Zionist Statement

the success of the ancient Hebrew republic was because of its law, and that this led the Jews to believe that their law's political success must be *because* it is divine, that is, grounded in the divine/natural order of the universe. And the fact that their law is superior, that is, more effective politically than any other state's law, means that the Jews have inferred from that fact their being a special or "chosen" people.[48] But how can this be true, because Spinoza's God is eternal and unchanging? Isn't choosing something one does at a certain point in time, picking one option over another, the options being temporal possibilities? And doesn't making a choice change the chooser from one course of action to another? In other words, what seems to have been chosen in time, in truth is what God wills eternally, and accordingly, it couldn't have been otherwise.[49] Indeed, Spinoza says that like the ancient Hebrews, "we have recourse to this same power of God [as *causa sui*] when we are ignorant of the natural cause of some thing."[50] Now, for Spinoza, will (*voluntas*) is involuntary: it couldn't be otherwise, whereas choice (*electio*) is voluntary: it could be otherwise.[51] Thus God's will couldn't have been otherwise; but God's choices (which Spinoza denies) could have indeed been otherwise. Miracles (whose reality Spinoza also denies) are *when* God chooses to interrupt the customary order of nature.[52] But, for Spinoza, that is impossible, because the eternal, causally determined order of nature admits of no interruptions. To assert that God can intrude into the natural order (when the natural order and God are one and the same) is "a great obstacle to science."[53]

---

[48] TTP, chapter 3, pp. 45–46.
[49] *Ethics* 1, P32. God has freedom of will in the sense of being the first cause who is free *from* any prior external cause, because there is none, because God is infinite and eternal. But God does not have freedom of choice (*liberum arbitrium*), that is, the freedom *to* choose *from* among temporal possibilities, because that would involve divine mutability or change. See Chapter 4.
[50] TTP, chapter 3, p. 25; see chapter 6, p. 89.
[51] See Aristotle, *Nicomachean Ethics*, 3.2-3/1111b5-1112a20.
[52] TTP, chapter 6, pp. 81–83.
[53] *Ethics* 1, P33, scholium 2, trans. E. Curley, *A Spinoza Reader* (Princeton, NJ: Princeton University Press, 1994), p. 107.

Spinoza's idea of will as involuntary and nonselective should be contrasted with the way choice is viewed in biblical-rabbinic theology as voluntary and selective. We see this in the way biblical-rabbinic theology looks at God's choice to love Israel and Israel's choice to love God. These two interrelated loving choices or voluntary love are both proactive and reactive. On God's side of the covenantal relationship, we see this in the benediction recited in the daily morning service (*shaharit*) just before the evocation of the *shema* ("Hear O' Israel: the Lord is our God, the Lord alone" – Deuteronomy 6:4), when God is thanked for being "He who chooses [*ha-boher*] His people Israel in love [*b'ahavah*]."[54] This love is initiatory and selective, for love always intends a singular object: the beloved, and thereby elicits a response from the beloved object now responding as a loving subject.[55] Thus the Torah's command (presupposing the free choice of its addressee): "You shall love the Lord your God with all your heart, with your whole life, and all your might" (Deuteronomy 6:5), which is selective in the sense of being directed to the unique, singular, divine object.

God too is responsive to human desire for His attention, what the kabbalistic tradition calls the "awakening from below" (*it`aruta de-le-tatta*).[56] That this interactive love is enacted in temporal events, either in God's revelations or in the people's deeds, means that this love is truly erotic, which is evident in the Song of Songs and rabbinic exegesis of it. In truly erotic love, the lovers both affect and are affected by each other.[57] Moreover, even though as an emotion is often involuntary (at least in human experience), the Torah seems to teach that the way love is activated is voluntary (and the emotion is engendered by the act rather than engendering it). A person can be commanded to love as a person can be commanded to choose, because in

---

[54] M. Berakhot 1.4; B. Berakhot 11b re Jer. 31:2; Jacob ben Asher, *Tur: Orah Hayyim*, 60.
[55] MR: Song of Songs 8.6 re Mal. 1:2.
[56] *Zohar*: Va-yets'e, 1:164a re Num. 28:2. See B. Yevamot 64a re Gen. 25:21; B. Hullin 60b re Gen. 2:5; MR: Song of Songs 2.32 re Song of Songs 2:14.
[57] MR: Song of Songs 1.11 re Exod. 15:2, Deut. 32:13, and Song of Songs 1:15.

each of these commandments a person is being commanded to actually do something on behalf of the One who is doing the commanding.[58] God can choose whether to lovingly elect Israel or not, and whether to respond to Israel's appeals or not. And Israel can choose whether to respond to God's love or not. So, as we shall see in a later chapter, choice is an essential component of every relationship between God and the universe, and with everything and everybody therein.[59]

Conversely, Spinoza denies that God engages in external relations (everything is within God), and denies that there are temporal possibilities even for God, because all God's relations are internal and universal (hence nonselective). As such, we can see why his treatment of God–human love is a rejection of the biblical-rabbinic theology just noted. For Spinoza, God does not, could not, and would not choose to love anybody else in particular, because for God there is no "other" to love. God does not, could not, and would not choose to elicit anybody else's love in return, because there is nobody "else" to respond to God. And, God does not, could not, and would not respond to anybody's appeal (as in petitionary prayer) to act through temporal events, because everything is already the result of an eternal decree. Regarding selective love, Spinoza says: "Insofar as God loves himself, he loves men, and consequently that God's love of men and the mind's intellectual love of God are one and the same."[60] And regarding responsive love, Spinoza says: "He who loves God cannot strive that God love him in return."[61] In both of these passages, you can speak of will as the immanent first cause, but you can't speak of choice as a temporal event.

Directly attributing everything to God's will (as we now better understand what Spinoza means by it) is not conducive to developing the attention to data immediately present to us that characterizes modern natural science. Nevertheless, that direct divine

---

[58] Deut. 30:19.
[59] See Chapter 4.
[60] *Ethics* 5, P36, p. 260.
[61] Ibid. 5, P19, p. 253.

attribution is quite beneficial for constituting a truly just political order. It is also quite beneficial for developing an appreciation of eternity that characterizes the ontological concern of philosophers who are supposed to thrive (albeit discreetly) in this truly just political order. Both politics and philosophy, then, are to be concerned with eternity.[62] Here again we see that Spinoza was neither a "secularist" in his politics nor an atheist in his ontology or philosophy per se.

It would seem that "chosenness" is what the Jews inferred from their experience of the political success of their own state and its law, that is, from their subjective, temporally located, point of view. But when the philosophers among the Jews think this political reality from "the perspective of eternity" (*sub specie aeternitatis*), which is thinking from God's perspective, they understand that in essence the order and duration of the Jewish state reflect the eternal order of the universe. Hence, when Spinoza talks about God choosing the Jews "again" (de novo), that means the Jews will experience once more *anew* what, in truth, has *always* been the reality.

Spinoza's Old-New Judaism

The last thing to ask here is: What makes the biblical-like state Spinoza seems to hope the Jews might, *mutatis mutandis*, reestablish different from their current political situation in the Diaspora? This question can be best answered when we look at why Spinoza admired the Hebrew polity in the days of the First Temple, but despised the Jewish polity in the days of the Second Temple. First, as we have seen, the Jewish polity in the days of the Second Temple was dependent on another human polity: Rome; and unlike the days of the First Temple, God was not the real Sovereign there. But, second, Spinoza attributes the downfall of the First Temple polity to the growing power and independence of the priesthood, which turned the Hebrew polity into a *theocracy* in the current pejorative sense of that loaded

---

[62] TTP, chapter 17, pp. 214–18; also, ibid., chapter 18, pp. 230–32.

term.⁶³ Theocracy is a state ruled by clerics as a political party, primarily serving their own class interests rather than the needs of the state as a whole, plus claiming greater access to God the Sovereign than that of the other citizens. In other words, Spinoza was consistently and vociferously anticlerical.

There is little doubt that Spinoza saw the rabbis of Amsterdam (and their colleagues elsewhere in the Diaspora) as being the heirs of the Pharisees, whom he assumed had exercised the same kind of arrogant theological-political power as did the priests in the days of the First Temple.⁶⁴ In all three cases, Spinoza saw the results of this "clericalism" to be politically disastrous, and philosophically disastrous because this kind of clergy inevitably dictated belief. They thereby threaten what Spinoza saw to be the essential freedom the philosopher needs to think as he sees fit to think (*libertatus philosophandi*).⁶⁵ Moreover, because Spinoza wrote the *Theological-Political Treatise* in Latin for a Christian audience, one can infer that he had the Dutch Calvinist clergy in mind as another item on his list of dangerous *theocrats*, even though he couldn't explicitly attack them and expect his book to be published in the Netherlands. And, in fact, we know Spinoza was involved to a certain extent in anticlerical efforts to change Dutch politics, especially after the assassination of Johan de Witt, the "Grand Pensionary of the States of Holland," by religious fanatics acting in the interest of clerical hegemony, which they saw as threatened by de Witt's political power and agenda.⁶⁶ (However, to a much larger extent, Spinoza retired to a life of privacy and, indeed, this is the image of Spinoza as the lone philosopher working quietly in his workshop in Rijnsburg, the solitary intellectual, who has captured the imagination of those who think the life of the mind and the life of the polity cannot be lived in tandem.) Finally, Spinoza no doubt inherited much derision of the inquisitional Catholic clergy in Iberia, whose political power had forced his family to flee Portugal for the Netherlands.

---

⁶³ See Chapter 4.
⁶⁴ TTP, chapter 18, pp. 231–32.
⁶⁵ TTP, chapter 20, pp. 250–59.
⁶⁶ See Nadler, *Spinoza*, 254–59, 304–9.

Spinoza and the Zionist Dilemma

Finally, we might ask what Spinoza's Zionism has to say to the dilemma of all Zionists: What would make a state of Jews (*medinat yehudim*) a truly Jewish state (*medinah yehuydit*)? Contrary to the views of his secularist admirers (*hilonim* in modern Hebrew), Spinoza seemed to be convinced that a reestablished Jewish state could be "Jewish" only if its character was "theocratic" in the sense that God and His law (however mediated by human reason and experience) must be sovereign. But contrary to the views of religio-nationalist Zionists (*datiyyim l'umiyyim* in modern Hebrew), Spinoza was very much opposed to any clerical class having governing power in this Jewish state. And, contrary to the views of what we now call "ultra-Orthodox" Jews (*haredim* in Hebrew), Spinoza was clearly not in favor of waiting for a supernatural Messiah to reestablish the Jewish state. In short, then, if Spinoza is to be taken seriously as a Zionist prophet of sorts, then he must be taken as one whose "prophecy" is yet to be realized in history. Certainly, his Zionism corresponds with the outlook of none of the three groups of Zionists just mentioned. Nevertheless, I do not think it is unreasonable for Zionists to hope for what Spinoza seemed to have suggested, that is, if they also believe what he suggested is politically possible. Moreover, Spinoza's suggestion is, to my mind, morally more attractive than the hopes of the secularists, the religious-nationalist Zionists, and the ultra-Orthodox.

Whether Spinoza is part of the Jewish heritage or not is an endlessly debated question. In fact, as a positive answer to this question, in 1927, some 270 years after Spinoza's excommunication in Amsterdam, the first professor of Hebrew Literature in the recently established Hebrew University of Jerusalem, Joseph Klausner, staged a pageant on Mount Scopus.[67] At the conclusion of the pageant, Klausner – the self-appointed representative of the Jewish people no less – publicly embraced a man dressed like Spinoza with the cry: *ahinu attah! ahinu attah!* –

---

[67] See Schwartz, *The First Modern Jew*, 113–16; also, Novak, *The Election of Israel*, 44–49.

"You are our brother! You are our brother!" However, even if we think Spinoza did leave the Jewish people and Judaism for a kind of theological-political anonymity, he very much left modern Jews with a cogent theological-political vision. Spinoza not only predicted the reality of the Jewish state Jews now enjoy, but he gave Zionism as the idea of the Jewish state a cogent philosophical expression. That expression can be accepted, rejected, or modified. Surely, though, it cannot be ignored or dismissed, not on philosophical grounds and not on Jewish grounds either. Nevertheless, in the next chapter, let us look at two late nineteenth and early twentieth century Zionist thinkers, whose thought Spinoza made possible, but who were far inferior to him philosophically.

3

Secular Zionism: Political or Cultural?

Secular Zionism

The modern Zionism that emerged in the late nineteenth century was clearly a secular nationalist movement. The most extreme secularists were openly contemptuous of Judaism or the Jewish religious tradition, thinking that Judaism had turned the Jews into a passive apolitical people, which is a state of mind from which Zionism should liberate the Jews. For these extreme secularists, the Jewish religious tradition was not even owed any thanks, not even retrospectively, as they thought it had made the Jews a passive, apolitical people for far too long. Others, such as the influential Zionist theoretician Jacob Klatzkin (d. 1948), acknowledged that Judaism had performed the great nationalist task of protecting the Jewish national identity of Diaspora Jews from dissolution and assimilation in the past, without which there wouldn't be any Jews left in the world to actually found a Jewish state when the opportunity to do so did arise in the present. However, with the Enlightenment's devaluation of all traditional religion (especially Judaism) for modern men and women (especially the Jews), Klatzkin thought that Judaism had done its job for Jewish identity in the past, but is no longer capable of even doing that in the present. What is now needed, he thought, is for Judaism to be replaced by modern Zionism as

Secular Zionism

true Jewish nationalism itself. So he writes: "To regain our land is for us an end in itself – the attaining of a free national life."[1] Most tellingly, concerning Judaism, Klatzkin insists: "God has no heir (*yoresh*)."[2] He then goes on to speak of "a new criterion for Judaism, a nationalist criterion [*behinah l'umit*] for departing from Judaism."[3]

Even many religious Zionists affirmed the primacy of nationalism for the Jewish people. Thus Chaim Hirschensohn (d. 1935), an American rabbi and the author of significant *halakhic* responsa and theological essays, nevertheless wrote: "The Jewish religion is a national religion [*dat le'umit*], but Jewish nationalism [*le'umiyut yisra'el*] is not only religious nationalism ... religion is only one of the conditions of the life of the people ... [but] Jewish nationalism is not contingent on our religion."[4] It would seem, therefore, that whereas the most radical Zionists thought Judaism played a detrimental role for the Jews even in the past, and whereas Klatzkin thought Judaism had played a constructive role for the Jews in the past, Hirschensohn thought Judaism still has a constructive role to play for the Jewish people in the present and into the future. So, on the occasion of the Balfour Declaration of 1917, promising "the establishment in Palestine of a national home for the Jewish people," Hirschensohn stated: "From now on the rabbis of Israel are obligated [*hayyavim*] to research the *halakhah* [for sources] for the establishment of a state according to Torah foundations."[5] Yet it is clear that the difference between the religious Zionism of someone like Hirschensohn and the Zionism of someone like Klatzkin is one of degree rather than one of kind. In kind, both thinkers are primarily nationalists, even though Hirschensohn's nationalism

---

[1] Trans. Arthur Hertzberg in his *The Zionist Idea* (New York: Atheneum, 1959), 319.
[2] *Domains* [Heb.] (Berlin: Dvir, 1925), 83.
[3] Ibid., 95. For a critique of Klatzkin's anti-Judaism, see Yehezkel Kaufmann, *Exile and Estrangement* 1 [Heb.] (Tel Aviv: Dvir, 1930), 402.
[4] *Malki Ba-Qodesh* 1, no. 42 (St. Louis: n.p., 1923), 242; quoted in David Zohar, *Jewish Commitment in a Modern World* [Heb.] (Jerusalem: HaKibbutz Hameuchad, 2003), 63.
[5] Ibid., 25.

seems more like an historical development of Judaism itself, whereas Klatzkin's nationalism is openly revolutionary.

Because of the prevalence of secular nationalism even among religious Zionists, secular Zionism that doesn't claim to be religious needs to be examined before I can propose a religious Zionism that takes Jewish nationhood to be rooted in Judaism, not the other way around. This religious Zionism will eschew nationalist ideology altogether, because even Jewish nationalism inevitably makes the Jews *a* nation among all other nations *of* the world rather than being what the Jews have always considered themselves to be: *the* unique people in the divine scheme *in* and *for* the world. Nationalism does not and cannot provide either Judaism or Zionism with a sufficient purpose for its survival, let alone its flourishing. Yet that is no way denies that the ability of the Jews to survive and flourish as that unique people in and for the modern world, which now seems to require that they have a nation-state of their own in the land of Israel. Recognizing the importance of modern nationhood for the Jewish people, though, does not require a nationalist ideology for its justification.

When it came to determining purposes for Zionism, not all secular Zionism was of one mind. For there are two kinds of purposes: one, negative purposes that motivate reaction; two, positive purposes that inspire action. A negative purpose has been espoused by what has come to be known as "political Zionism." A positive purpose has been espoused by what has come to be called "cultural Zionism." Let us begin with political Zionism, not because it is older (which is debatable), but because it is better known, and is still the basis for much of the Zionism espoused today by Jews, and even by some of the non-Jewish friends of the Jewish people.

Political Zionism

In his most famous written work, the pamphlet entitled *Der Judenstaat* (usually but inaccurately translated as "The Jewish State"), the pamphlet that led to the convening of the First

Zionist Congress in 1897, Theodor Herzl (d. 1904), considered the founder of Zionism as a modern political movement, put forth a basically negative reason for the Jewish nationalism he was proposing.[6] After proclaiming, "We are a people [*ein Volk*]; one people," Herzl went on to proclaim: "we are a people: without our willing it – the enemy has made us that."[7] In other words, a people's self-definition is not theirs to determine for themselves; instead, that is done for them by a "negative other." Fifty years later, very soon after the lethal power of Nazi racism had been defeated, the thesis that a person's ethnic identity is determined by an enemy or negative "other" was more thoughtfully put forth by the non-Jewish French philosopher Jean-Paul Sartre in his 1947 book, *Anti-Semite and Jew*.[8]

In the precarious political climate of the Jews in the 1890s, the most prominent enemies of the Jews were the French antisemites, the so-called anti-Dreyfusards. They were the ones who charged that the treason imputed to the French-Jewish military officer Captain Alfred Dreyfus proved that he was a typical Jew, who not only could not assimilate into the French nation, but was like all the other Jews: a member of an alien nation that posed a great threat to France. (Other European antisemites condemned the Jews in their countries in much the same way.[9]) Moreover, the French antisemites concluded that it was a mistake to have granted the Jews equal citizenship rights in the wake of the French Revolution a century earlier, rights the Jews never had in the old French kingdom (*l'ancien régime*). Now a people can face such a political threat in one of two ways.

---

[6] Actually, *Judenstaat* literally means a "state of the Jews," though all the English translations I have consulted call the book *The Jewish State*. See, for example, the translation of S. D'Avigdor (London: Pordes, 1972). But the official Hebrew translation is correctly titled, *Medinat ha-Yehudim* (Jerusalem: Ha-Sifriyah ha-Tsiyonit, 1973).
[7] *Der Judenstaat* (Vienna: Breitenstein, 1896), 12.
[8] Originally published as *Réflexions sur la question juive* (Paris: Paul Morihien, 1947). Eng. trans. G. J. Becker, *Anti-Semite and Jew* (New York: Schocken, 1948).
[9] See Jacques Kornberg, *Theodor Herzl: From Assimilation to Zionism* (Bloomington, IN: Indiana University Press, 1993), 190–200.

On the one hand, a people can basically accept that kind of negative definition of who they are, and then retreat into passive submission, bowing to what the outside hostile world has decreed for them. In fact, there have been such Jews then (and even now there are some such Jews) who have seen the supposedly "new" modern political antisemitism to be the return of the old medieval "Jew-hatred." Moreover, they have actually agreed that the political emancipation brought about by the French Revolution was a mistake, the only difference being that the antisemites thought it was mistake that harmed France, while these modern Jewish traditionalists have thought political emancipation was a mistake that has harmed the Jews. For the emancipation thrust the Jews as vulnerable individuals into a secular political and cultural environment while simultaneously destroying the true political and cultural security they had enjoyed when the ancient, privileged Jewish communities (the *qehilot*) enjoyed quasi-autonomy. For these Jews, and especially for the traditionalist rabbis who saw how the emancipation of the Jews was undermining their authority as the leaders of communities that were governed by Jewish law that they interpreted and applied, nineteenth century antisemitism proved that political emancipation was a sham. It didn't deliver on what it promised the Jews who were so eager to embrace it; it only took away the great communal independence and quasi-autonomy the Jews until recently had enjoyed. In this view, the Jews should, therefore, accept their fate and return to the ghetto, in a figurative sense though, as there was no real ghetto anymore for the Jews to return to. And, it was these antimodernist rabbis who were in the forefront of opposition to Herzl's political Zionism, regarding it to be yet another attempt of some Jews to think they could be like all the other nations.[10] (There are still such rabbis and their followers today, who are antimodernists in general, and anti-Zionists in particular.)

On the other hand, a people can react to their political alienation, not resigning themselves to it as their inevitable fate, but

---

[10] See Gideon Shimoni, *The Zionist Ideology* (Hanover, NH: Brandeis University Press, 1995), 136–39.

rather taking this new alienation to be a challenge. Indeed, it was a challenge Jews should actively react to, making that reaction their political task of the hour. This was Herzl's response. In effect, he seemed to be saying in the name of the Jewish people: "If you gentiles have rejected us because we are a separate, unassimilated people, we shall actually become that people in spite of you! We will be as happy to be rid of you as you will be happy to be rid of us! But our political departure from your control will be on our terms, not yours!" For Herzl, this political response was to be *the* task of the Jews here and now. This task seemed to be the only real task for the Jews at this juncture of history. Everything else was to be secondary, if not negligible altogether. And that might explain why Zionism as Jewish politics became Herzl's religious-like passion, and why he seemed to have seen no need to incorporate any of the cultural and religious aspects of Judaism into his personal or familial life.[11]

A political purpose, and a negative one at that, for the Jews and for himself as their self-appointed political leader, was all Herzl seemed to have needed and wanted. What Herzl saw as his purpose in wanting to found *the* Jewish state was basically to react to the sorry, vulnerable political condition of European Jews, whether in Western Europe or in Eastern Europe. He wasn't really concerned with Jewish religion or Judaism, other than as some kind of cultural ornament, something that played an essentially ceremonial role in the life of a secular state. So, in fact, *Der Judenstaat* does not mean "the *Jewish* state" in the sense that the state or polity he envisioned was to have a uniquely Jewish character. If that was what Herzl meant, the German title would have been *Der Jüdische Staat*. Instead, *Der Judenstaat* means "the state of the Jews," which is what Herzl envisioned irrespective of what gives the Jews their unique identity in the world. That is because, in his view anyway, the negative identity of being *that* perpetually alien people is given to them, or rather, Jews are thrown into it by their enemies willy nilly. Their identity

---

[11] The best biography of Herzl is still Amos Elon's *Herzl* (New York: Holt, Rhinehart, and Winston, 1975).

is not really *theirs* at all, because it is not something the Jews give themselves, nor is it something given to the Jews from an external (and friendlier) source. For Herzl, their identity as a people is not a gift at all. Their identity, for Herzl, is their reaction to their rejection by their antisemitic enemies. It is, then, their active rejection of their rejection.

Needless to say, all this is very different from the passive acceptance of the rejection of the Jews by the gentiles advocated by the traditionalists, most of whom became anti-Zionists. In fact, it was only the liberals, rather than either the traditionalists or the Zionists, who refused to accept the antisemitic judgment of the Jews as an alien people. It was only the liberals (then and now) who did not want the Jews to be designated as "a people dwelling apart and alone, not to be counted among the nations" (Numbers 23:9).

Along these lines, I remember a *Yom ha`Atsma'ut* sermon delivered a few years ago by the former Ashkenazic Chief Rabbi of Israel, Israel Meir Lau, in the Great Synagogue of Jerusalem. At that national celebration, he asserted that Jews, and especially Israeli Jews, should not be satisfied with a mere "state of Jews" (*medinat yehudim*), meaning a country where Jews happen to be in the majority. Rather, Lau implored the congregation that Jews should be striving for a truly "Jewish state" (*medinah yehudit*). Considering Lau's rabbinical position in Israel, we can assume by a "Jewish state" he meant a religiously Jewish state, one governed according to traditional Jewish law (*halakhah*). Yet when a similar task seems to have been suggested or implied one way or another by some of Herzl's rabbinical contemporaries, he rejected it outright. For Herzl knew quite well that the only positive identity the Jews as a people have had throughout our history is a religious one. As such, if the state of the Jews was to have a positive political purpose, one identifiably Jewish, what else could that purpose be but the establishment of a religious state? Therefore, Herzl counters that suggestion with the rhetorical question: "Will we in the end have a theocracy?" And he answers his question by saying "No! While belief keeps us together, it is science that makes us free."[12]

---

[12] *Der Judenstaat*, 75.

By "theocracy" Herzl seems to have meant a clerical state, that is, a state governed by rabbis. (A better definition of "theocracy" is given in Chapter 4.) Yet, if I understand him correctly, he was not just rejecting the undemocratic possibility of the state of the Jews being governed by an oligarchy or small political clique, whether by rabbis or by any other group of self-interested politicians. Herzl was rejecting something much deeper than that. For what is implied by his use of the term "theocracy" is that the rabbis governing this state would be doing so according to the Jewish religious tradition and its law (*halakhah*). And he knew that the source of that law acknowledged by all traditional Jews is the God who traditional Jews believe governs the world He has created, who elects the Jews to be a singular people to receive and practice the law or Torah God reveals to them. And it is through this Torah that the Jews are able to actively express their special relationship with God, plus gain a land where they can do all that in the fullest way possible. Herzl's objections to all that were not just political; they were, more deeply, philosophical.

Though he certainly had abandoned even minimal Jewish religious observance in his own life and home, Herzl could no doubt remember how in the Jewish liturgy, God is called "our king" (*malkeinu*) and the Jews are called "His subjects" or "His servants" (*avadav*), who are chosen for that service. Unlike science that liberates us by giving us more control over our lives through the technology that appropriates the findings of science, religion subjects us to someone else's control. (Philosophers call that "heteronomy," i.e., being ruled by an *other*, rather than "autonomy," i.e., being ruled by ourselves.) Think of how I. N. Imber, the author of the Zionist anthem *Hatikvah*, whose words most Jews know by heart, spoke of the Jews wanting to be "a free people [*am hofshi*]," and like any other free people, to be that free people "in our own land [*b'artsenu*]." Contrast that with the talmudic teaching that only when a Jew is dead is that Jew free (*hofshi*), that is, now exempt from having to keep God's commandments.[13] When alive, however, a Jew is to obey God and

---

[13] B. Niddah 61b re Ps. 88:6.

be like a servant who must obey his or her master. Thus God is called "Master of the world" (*ribbono shel olam*), who has chosen the Jews to obey His decrees. Or, there is the rabbinic teaching that true "liberty" (*herut*) is being engaged in learning God's Torah, learning that brings a Jew to keep God's commandments intelligently, but obediently nonetheless.[14]

For Herzl, Judaism would be the official religion of the secular Jewish state he envisioned. But Judaism itself would play no major role in the conduct of that secular state; and, to be sure, that state would not take its warrant, its moral and political legitimization, from the Torah.[15] In a way, this is like the advice given to the Maccabean king Alexander Jannaeus (d. 76 B.C.E.) that he eliminate the Pharisees, whom the people looked to for practical religious instruction in all areas of life, because they were publicly questioning the king's taking more political authority for himself than warranted by the Torah. When it was asked (rhetorically): "So, what will happen to the Torah?," the king's advisor answered: "Let it be rolled up in a corner; whoever wants to study it, let him come and study it!"[16] Here, the double meaning of "Torah" is played upon. There is *Torah* as the ongoing interpretation of Scripture (*torah she-bi-khtav*: "the Written Torah"), whose continual application of that interpreted Scripture to all areas of life, especially to the nation's politics, is "the Oral Torah" (*torah she-b'al peh*). This is what the king thought would be too much religion for his realm, because it is a religion that looks to an authority infinitely greater than any king of flesh and blood. Then there is *Torah* as a scroll, Scripture alone, without any living interpretation and any application except for the Temple service, the place where the master copy of the Torah text was kept for safekeeping. Today, we might say the king wanted the Torah to be "in the closet," where it would not interfere, let alone judge, his own royal political authority.

---

[14] M. Avot 6.2 re Exod. 32:16.
[15] *Der Judenstaat*, 57. See Yoram Hazony, *The Jewish State: The Struggle for Israel's Soul* (New York: Basic Books, 2000), 138, for what could be taken to be a contemporary version of Herzlian Zionism.
[16] B. Kiddushin 66a.

Clearly, the king wanted these rabbis to be his lackeys, to be like the court prophets of Israel in the days of the First Temple, who were there to give official religious approval and endorsement of political policies that were based on decidedly nonreligious, secular considerations. But, when challenged about his religious critique of the political policies of the king of Israel, the prophet Amos retorts: "I am neither a prophet [*lo nav'i*] nor a member of the prophet guild [*ve-lo ven nav'i*]" (Amos 7:14), meaning I am not a professional prophet; I am not on the royal payroll. Therefore, I can say what God has commanded me to say, irrespective of the king's and his ministers' objections to my challenge of their unwarranted authority. Finally, it could be said that the Israeli Chief Rabbinate (*ha-rabbanut ha-rash'it*), in effect, is functioning today as King Alexander Jannaeus wanted the rabbis of his time to function, perhaps even functioning the way Amaziah the priest (perhaps the royal chaplain) and King Jeroboam II wanted the prophet Amos to function.[17] In our time, that has been most rigorously and bravely charged by the Israeli philosopher Yeshayahu Leibowitz (d. 1994), himself both a strictly observant Jew and a loyal citizen of the State of Israel from its inception.[18] Nevertheless, according to Herzl's view of state religion, there is no real basis for criticizing the rabbinical establishment in Israel today, except, of course, when the rabbis seem to be promoting certain political views outside their ecclesiastical mandate, or when the rabbis seem to be highly ambivalent about their loyalty to the secular state at all.

Though Herzl recognized how Jewish religion had kept the Jews together in the past, like most of his sophisticated contemporaries, he thought religion – anybody's religion – could no longer be adequate to deal with the new political realities of the late nineteenth century. For "science" (*Wissenschaft*) has convinced us all that a people's identity is "natural" (except those

---

[17] See Amos 7:10–17.
[18] See his *Judaism, Human Values, and the Jewish State*, trans. E. Goldman and Y. Navon (Cambridge, MA: Harvard University Press, 1992), 174–84.

Jews who insist on living and thinking a romantic fantasy about the premodern past they largely imagine). This natural identity is something a people learns from its history, which seems to constantly repeat itself. This natural identity is the identity of a species of human beings that regards itself to be a *specific nation* "naturally," that is, by virtue of common birth, which means having the same ancestors, having the same historical origins. Being a nation or "nationality" is a natural fact, or a "given," like being male or female, or like having a mother and a father. "Nationalism," then, becomes *the task* the nation takes upon itself from out of its past, absorbs in the present, and projects into the future. Thus the task is natural in origin, we are born with it. It is the natural drive of a species to survive in the world. Nationalism inevitably becomes the raison d'être of the state a nation has set up for itself.

In this view, we are also destined to carry what we are born with into the political world of nations in an historical trajectory. A nation grows up naturally, yet it has to willingly assert its independence or "sovereignty" (Herzl does use that political term) in the struggle for political existence in the world.[19] In that struggle, which is inevitable in the real world (of realpolitik), a nation has to face enemies who would deny them their natural identity, first in theory and then actually deny their collective existence in fact. The choice here is between national life and national death. An individual person, and even more so a nation, most often has to make that stark choice when faced with death, whether individual or communal. As the Talmud puts it, "we infer the positive from the negative."[20] In fact, most Zionist discourse has continued to make that choice of life against death the chief reason why every Jew should be a Zionist. Nevertheless, this radical political choice might well be uniquely modern, really beginning only in the late nineteenth century when Herzl, it seems, founded modern political Zionism. In fact, that might not have been the case before Herzl's time.

---

[19] *Der Judenstaat*, 61.
[20] B. Nedarim 11a.

When the challenge to unified Jewish identity in the premodern or medieval past was religious, that is, when European Christians wanted Jews to kill their identity as Jews by converting to Christianity, the response then had to be a reaffirmation of the religious identity of the Jewish people. Since biblical times, that identity has been proclaimed by the Jews to be the identity of the people chosen by God (*asher bahar banu* in liturgical Hebrew) for an everlasting covenant (*berit olam* in biblical Hebrew) with God.[21] Remaining within the traditional Jewish community (*kenesset yisrael* in rabbinic Hebrew) was (and still is, I think) the only way to remain faithful to the covenant (*ha-berit* in biblical Hebrew) with God.[22] (Whether that is the only way to remain Jewish coherently, i.e., whether there is "Jewishness" without "Judaism," is another question we shall return to.) Christianity, despite its connection to Judaism and the Jewish people, was not (and still is not) a covenantal option – at least not for Jews. A Jew who accepts the Christian religion and becomes part of the Church is still a Jew, but only in the sense that any such person is still considered to be married to his or her Jewish spouse (i.e., whom he or she had married before stepping out of Judaism), plus the fact that such an apostate (*meshumad* in rabbinic parlance) is always welcome to return to the Jewish fold with impunity. As the Talmud puts it: "Even a Jew who has sinned is still considered to be a Jew."[23] In other words, amnesty is readily granted in order to bring Jews home, where they truly belong. In every other way, though, that person is to be treated (no better and no worse, by the way) as if he or she were born a gentile (a *goy* in rabbinic parlance).[24] I mention all of this to show how serious the option of conversion to Christianity was taken by the Jews, especially in the Middle Ages when this was the only way a Jew could actually "check out" of the Jewish people (de facto, though still not de jure).

[21] See, for example, Gen. 17:7.
[22] See, for example, Deut. 28:69.
[23] B. Sanhedrin 44a re Josh. 7:11.
[24] See David Novak, *The Election of Israel* (Cambridge: Cambridge University Press, 1995), 192.

However, the options for the Jews radically changed in the late eighteenth century when the French Revolution began the process of the political destruction of traditional Jewish political identity by removing the quasi-autonomy communal identity the Jews had long possessed. It did that by making Jews citizens of a state that did not take its warrant from Christian revelation. The state became secular. But what did that mean for the state? And what did that mean for the Jews?

Whereas the medieval challenge to the Jews was religious, giving the Jews the choice of becoming full members of Christian societies *or* remaining parts of a vulnerable, barely tolerated, alien community, the new secular order gave the Jews a very different choice. And this new choice seemed much less onerous than the earlier one, because it seemed to involve much less of a loss of self-respect. The choice that Jews had was to either remain in the old ghetto *or* become equal fellow citizens of the new secular nation-state. Now, of course, no Jew could literally remain in the old ghetto since it had been destroyed or dissolved politically. (And where the ghetto literally remained, as it did in Eastern Europe throughout the nineteenth and into the twentieth century, there was no option of full citizenship in its place.) Yet, as we have already noticed, there were some Jews who saw the Revolution not to be emancipation, but anarchy. That became especially evident in the resistance by a number of Jewish traditionalists to the continuation of the political and cultural innovations of the French Revolution by Napoleon and his successors in Europe. Nevertheless, the vast majority of Jews in Western Europe, who did have the option of full citizenship in the new secular nation-states, willingly and gladly took it. For they believed the great slogan of the Revolution – *liberté, egalité, fraternité,* – was becoming a reality. That is, they believed themselves *liberated* from their old, marginalized, or ghettoized communal status; and they believed that this had made them truly *equal* to every other citizen of the new nation-state. They took as *the* great secular promise the seemingly harsh words of the French aristocrat, Count Stanislas de Clermont-Tonnere in 1789, the year of the Revolution, delivered before the New National

Assembly: "But, they [the adversaries of the Jews] say to me, the Jews have their own judges and laws. I respond that is your fault and you should not allow it. We must refuse to the Jews as a nation everything, and accord everything to the Jews as individuals."[25] And, when it came to *fraternité*, meaning "fellowship" or cultural integration with their French or German neighbors, these emancipated Jews assumed or hoped this "brotherhood" would eventually follow their liberation from the communal ghetto, plus accord them full political (and economic) acceptance in the state. Those Jews who still wanted some kind of identity over and above that of being simply a "citizen" could assemble with like-minded Jews as a private association of like-minded individuals, the same kind of *individuals* to whom Clermont-Tonnere had promised "everything."

Now many of us fail to consider, from the perspective of suspicious hindsight, that one of the main reasons many Jews at that time did not regard Count Clermont-Tonnere's proposition to be one sided was that the Revolution had given Christians the same choice. In the dissolution of the *ancien régime* through a process of secularization (what the French call *laïcité*), the Catholic Church, which previously had been the source of the legitimacy of the kingdom, now became an essentially private association (as did the much smaller and less powerful Protestant churches) in the new modern regime.[26] (So, if the old fashioned rabbis felt the Revolution had robbed them and their Jewish community of their ancient privileges, you can imagine how the Catholic bishops and their community felt about being robbed of their considerably greater ancient privileges!) So, it seems, *both* Jews *and* Christians had their old status taken from them, and had been given a new equal status that was strangely new to them both. As such, everybody's public status changed radically; and the privacy that had been that of the domestic domain (of "home and

---

[25] Quoted in *The French Revolution and Human Rights*, trans. L. Hunt (Boston and New York: St. Martin's Press, 1996), 88.
[26] See J. McManners, *The French Revolution* (Westport, CT: Greenwood Press, 1982), 61–105.

hearth") became the domain of both Church and Synagogue – at least in theory. Those few who resisted this secularization by refusing to embrace their new public identity, whether they were Jews or Christians, would wind up as "sectarians," like the Hasidim or the Amish, that is, living on the outermost fringes of a world that almost everybody else wanted get into. Moreover, the "science" that had made them "free" (which Herzl said with such certainty) could well be the new "political science." It talked about polities or states that humans make for themselves anew in the present, rather than their inheriting their political warrant from their ancestors through tradition, or receiving it through revelation from God.

However, despite the communal emancipation and the political equalization (the *liberté* and the *egalité*) that did come more or less, the cultural fellowship (the *fraternité*) did not come, even though it seems to have been promised by the Revolution, and hoped for by most of the Jews, who were the only significant minority in Europe at the time. That came to a head at the time of the public debate in the 1890s (and into the twentieth century) over the patriotic loyalty or disloyalty of Alfred Dreyfus. Then it became quite clear to Herzl that the anti-semites were right, albeit for the wrong reason: the Jews were and never would be true Frenchmen. Because many Frenchmen (and other Europeans) believed that about the Jews, the political equality of the Jews was therefore in great jeopardy, and their hard-won *egalité* was in great danger of going down with the ship called *fraternité*, a ship that had been barely launched before it was sinking in port. Thus the Jews were now presented with a very different choice than the medieval religious choice and the eighteenth century political choice. The choice now was whether the Jews would become a *nation* like the other nations, that is, a people striving for a *nation-state* like all the other nations either had already or wanted to have imminently. The only other option was for the Jews to assimilate, and that was not a real option inasmuch as the non-Jewish majority, who were becoming increasingly anti-semitic, were in no mood to accept the Jews as either a community or even as individuals, that is, as their "brothers." Compare that fact with the great eighteenth century poem by Schiller – the favorite poet, by the way, of acculturated German Jews in the nineteenth century – his "Ode to Joy" (which Beethoven famously set to music in the chorale of his Ninth Symphony): *Alle Menschen werden Brüder*: "All men are becoming brothers."[27] Alas, it didn't happen![28]

What motivated Herzl to found a Jewish national movement was the fact that "the enemy," that is, modern secular anti-semitism (as distinct from medieval anti-Judaism), made any choice of another identity out of the question for Jews, or for any other nation, but especially for Jews as the most conspicuous minority or "foreign" nation in Europe (and farther west into North America). Moreover, because this concept of "nationality" became a concept of racial identity, it denied that anybody had a choice to choose his or her nationality any more than one could choose his or her race or gender. As such, assimilation was now deemed to be impossible. So, there seemed to be no self-respecting option available or desirable other than this nationalistic option. Without it, Herzl was convinced that the Jews would disappear as a people in the modern world altogether. One could say that Herzl smelled how the Nazis, about thirty years after his own death, would extend the communal disappearance of the Jews into the disappearance of the Jews as individual bodies in the smoke of Auschwitz.

However, does this "negation of a negation," that is, this *reaction against* the negative assault on the legitimacy of the survival of the Jews as a people, lead to any positive purpose for Jewish communal or ethnic survival, of which Zionism is meant to be the chief facilitator? Although it is true that in mathematics minus times minus equals a positive number ($-1 \times -1 = +1$), the same does not seem to be true in real life and in human history. I don't think a negative reaction in real life leads to any truly positive end or purpose, precisely because the reaction never loses its need for the negativity that elicited its response in

---

[27] *Schiller: Selected Poems* [Ger.], ed. F. M. Fowler (London: Macmillan, 1969), 2.
[28] See Kornberg, *Theodor Herzl*, 8–10.

the first place. So, despite my admiration for Herzl as a political visionary – O' how I wish we had a political visionary like him now! – I can't accept his idea of Zionism nonetheless. And, along the same lines, despite my admiration for the Canadian-Jewish philosopher Emil Fackenheim (d. 2003), I don't think that his famous maxim that we are "not to give any posthumous victories to Hitler" is a sufficient reason why the Jewish people ought to survive and individual Jews ought not assimilate (which, by the way, is much easier to do than it was in Herzl's day).[29] It certainly doesn't give a reason for the existence of the State of Israel. Resistance to evil, here the evil of anti-semitism or anti-Zionism, should intend or point to some transcendent end that attracts it. Without that kind of end attracting it, the whole project in the end is only reactionary. Jews need much more in the world than the world's rejection of them and Jews' rejection of the world in return.

We need also consider the only kind of reaction that could be more negative than that of political Zionism of Herzl and his disciples. I mean the Zionism that takes the primary purpose of Jewish political activity to be a war against the anti-semites on their own turf, "fighting fire with fire," as it were. Unlike the reaction of the political Zionists to the negativity of anti-semitism, which was to escape it so as to create an alternative polity for Jews, the reaction of some radicals to anti-semitism was not to flee *from* it, but rather to fight *against* it. Now, of course, that was a political impossibility in Europe, even in places like Poland where Jews comprised as much as 10 percent of the population. So, in fact, that kind of reactionary negativity was more likely to be embraced by Jews who, for all intents and purposes, severed any real connection they might have had to the Jewish people. They were the kind of rebellious Jews, who joined (even led) non-Jewish (even anti-Jewish) revolutionary movements such as Anarchism (think of Emma Goldman) or Communism (think of Rosa Luxemburg or Leon Trotsky). But I mention them only in

---

[29] *God's Presence in History* (New York: Harper Torchbooks, 1970), 84. See also idem., *To Mend the World* (New York: Schocken, 1982), 201–50.

Political Zionism

passing, as all of them in one way or another were quite explicitly, often vehemently, anti-Zionist in both word and deed, plus had contempt for Judaism that no doubt preceded their anti-Zionism. And that is so despite the fact many of these Jewish anarchists and communists claimed that their initial attraction to either Anarchism or Communism was because it seemed to be the only real way to overcome the antisemitism they themselves had suffered, along with their fellow Jews whom they tried to bring along with them into these non-Jewish political movements. In the end, though, this kind of anti-Jewish, anti-Zionist reaction became nihilistic, going so far as to deny the Jewish people and Judaism any place at all in the new world order they envisioned. It led to nothing positive for the Jewish people or, indeed, for anybody else.

Finally, to be honest, some of this kind of radical negativity seems to be found in the "Revisionist Zionism" of Ze'ev Jabotinsky (d. 1940), Menahem Begin (d. 1992), and now Benjamin Netanyahu, the current prime minister of Israel. However, these "revisionists" have not made fighting enemies of the Jewish people their primary raison d'être. They have still made that negative struggle a means to the positive end: the establishment and survival of the Jewish state in the land of Israel. That fact has made of those who are not their followers refuse to tarnish them as nihilists. And, the fact that Menahem Begin especially, when he had real political power, was willing to compromise belligerence for the sake of a more positive and realistic Israeli foreign policy shows that a seemingly radical negativity was tempered in reality for a greater positive end. Therefore, it seems after all is said and done, there is no real difference in kind between the "revisionists" and the other "political" Zionists, just a difference in degree regarding political tactics. Happily, such radical negativity among Jews – what is certainly nihilism – has been confined to such fringe groups as the "Stern Gang," a breakaway group from Begin's Irgun, who during World War II actually tried to make common cause with the German Army under Rommel to fight the British, despite the fact that the British were fighting the Nazi murderers of the

Jewish people at the same time.[30] At present, such negativity seems to be confined to the few followers of the deceased Meir Kahane who are still active.[31] Nevertheless, even though political Zionism cannot be tainted with nihilism, we are still led back to the question of whether political Zionism isn't still too negatively motivated to provide enough of a positive purpose for the State of Israel, and for our support of the State of Israel as Zionists.

The Jewish reaction of the political Zionists was basically: "If they don't want us in their state, we'll create a state of our own!" Of course, there is the clear implication that if "they" – the anti-semitic gentile nationalists – hadn't rejected us Jews, would we have any motivation to propose a nationalism of our own? Do the Jews really need the anti-semites to motivate them to become what they ought to become, and would probably better become were there no anti-semitism at all? – Enter what came to be known as "cultural Zionism."

Cultural Zionism

The chief theorist of cultural Zionism was the Russian-Jewish essayist Asher Ginzberg (d. 1927), known by his pen name "Ahad Ha`Am" (literally, "one of the people").[32] The populism that his pen name seems to proclaim is rather ironic, because Ahad Ha`Am was anything but "one of the people." He certainly was not an ordinary Jew, and he certainly did not act like an ordinary Jew, something of which he was quite self-conscious. Instead, he was very much an intellectual elitist, a rather aloof (often reclusive) thinker and writer (of superb modern Hebrew) who was not so much articulating an old culture he had inherited as he was attempting to devise a new culture for the Jews to replace *their* old one. The vehicle for that cultural innovation was Zionism.[33] And, right from the start, Ahad

---

[30] See en.wikipedia.org/wiki/Lehi_(group).
[31] See his *They Must Go* (New York: Grosset and Dunlap, 1981).
[32] The term appears in Gen. 26:10.
[33] See Jacques Kornberg's introductory essay in *At the Crossroads: Essays on Ahad Ha`Am*, ed. J. Kornberg (Albany, NY: State University of New York

Cultural Zionism

Ha'Am wanted to distinguish his kind of Zionism from political Zionism, arguing that the political Zionists were well intentioned assimilated Jews, who "love the members of their people, their brothers in distress [*be-tsarah*], but they do not love their people [*amam*], its historical soul."[34] It was the cultivation of the "historical soul" of the Jewish people" as an end in itself that Ahad Ha'Am took to be the essentially positive task for his kind of Zionism. This was the goal Ahad Ha'Am envisioned for the Jewish people, and for himself as a Zionist theorist. This was what his goal-oriented discourse was all about. But the goal is internal, not external, that is, it is the goal *of* the Jewish people, not the goal *for* the Jewish people that has been imposed *upon* them by some outsider, not even by God (as we shall soon see).[35]

Ahad Ha'Am was concerned that his secularly educated Jewish contemporaries were fast losing interest in keeping, let alone developing, their Jewish identity, because they saw no purpose in it or for it. But hasn't classical Jewish theology *always* provided the Jews with their purpose? Don't the Jews exist, and shouldn't the Jews continue to exist, for the sake of the everlasting covenant for which the transcendent God has elected them irrevocably, and given them the Torah as their fiduciary responsibility? Yet that Torah is not beyond human acceptance and application of it. "It is not in heaven" (Deuteronomy 30:12), even though the Torah orients the Jews here on earth toward the transcendent God by pointing them in the direction of a purpose that is not immanent, that is, it does not come from anything in the world, not even from the Jews themselves. Nevertheless, the Torah has proven itself still quite capable of functioning effectively in the world. The Torah is *for* the people, even though it is not *from* the people. What comes from the people is the interpretation and application of what they have received.

Press, 1983), xv–xxvii; see also Steven J. Zipperstein, *Elusive Prophet: Ahad Ha'Am and the Origins of Zionism* (London: Peter Halban, 1993).

[34] "Renewal and Creation," *Complete Writings of Ahad Ha'Am* [Heb.] (Tel Aviv: Dvir, 1949), 292–93.

[35] For the influence on Ahad Ha'Am's thought of the antimetaphysical ideas of Darwin and Herbert Spencer, see Shimoni, *The Zionist Ideology*, 270.

All that notwithstanding, Ahad Ha'Am was firmly convinced that no truly modern Jew believes that kind of religious doctrine anymore, most of all himself.[36] The American-Jewish historian Arthur Hertzberg (d. 2006) was quite insightful when he went so far to call Ahad Ha'Am an "agnostic rabbi."[37] Indeed, the most Ahad ha'Am could honestly say about traditional Jewish faith in God was: "Even somebody who doesn't believe in divine existence [*be-metsi'ut ha'elohut*] per se, still cannot deny its existence as a real historical force."[38] However, isn't it virtually blasphemous to suggest that the God revealed in the Torah can be looked upon as some immanent force within *human* history? Surely, no such "force" could possibly choose to make a covenant with anybody, with any people, and no such force could possibly judge a people for their faithfulness or lack of faithfulness to the constitution of the covenant: the divinely revealed Torah. Nevertheless, Ahad Ha'Am did not shy away from pursuing his radical, secular "Judaism," better called "Jewishness" (which is actually closer to the medieval Hebrew term *yahadut*; "Judaism" being more accurately a synonym for *Torah*). If classical Judaism was lost forever, there was no point in trying to resurrect it. What the Jews desperately needed, in his view, was a spiritual replacement for what had been permanently lost. History, in this case the situation of the Jews in modernity, is like nature; it abhors a vacuum.

The question Ahad Ha'Am grappled with in all his writings is: Do modern Jews need some new purpose to inspire them? And, if so, what is that purpose, and how are modern Jews to attain it? What are the appropriate means to this end? As we shall soon see, Ahad Ha'Am is not like Herzl, who if anything

---

[36] See ibid., 292.
[37] *The Zionist Idea*, 249–51.
[38] "Torah from Zion," *Writings*, 408. The Zionist theoretician, Aaron David Gordon (d. 1922), precisely because he was a pantheist, understood that the Divine (*ha'elohut*) had to be more than an "historical force," but rather a universal, cosmic Reality, since historical forces (plural) are always particular and partial. Hence he avoided the ontological superficiality of Ahad Ha'Am's rhetoric. See the collection of his writings, *Nation and Labor* [Heb.], eds. S. H. Bergman and A. Shochet (Jerusalem: Ha-Sifriyah Ha-Tsiyonit, 1956), esp., 1:175, 219, 255, 260; 2:112, 148, 277.

marginalized traditional Jewish religion in his Zionist thought while leaving it more or less intact nonetheless. Ahad Ha`Am was more radical, for he thought Zionism could well be a replacement for traditional Jewish religion altogether. Now for his Zionist replacement to be acceptable to the Jews, it had to do what Jewish religion had been able to do in the past, yet could no longer do in the present. His Zionism had to provide the Jewish people with a purpose inspiring enough to make them want, even desire, to remain Jews actively rather than merely being passively resigned to a fate heaped upon the Jews by the gentiles. With steady persistence, Ahad Ha`Am thought the brand of Zionism he was developing to be up to this great task. This new Jewish ideology would and could provide the Jews with an inspiring purpose, one that is consistent with modern nationalist aspirations, and also consistent with nineteenth century faith in natural science, especially Darwinian biology's teaching about the survival of living species. To Ahad Ha`Am, the Jews are such a living species, and Zionism and nothing but Zionism could teach them how to live their own being successfully in the modern world.

In keeping with the rise of nationalism in the late nineteenth century, with its concern with what "spiritual" factor made one people different from other peoples (best known by the German term *Volksgeist*, meaning "the spirit of a nation"), Ahad Ha`Am saw "feeling," rather than either classical Jewish "faith" (*emunah*) or eighteenth century "reason," to be the medium through which a Jew could sense his or her purpose. (Through faith you *accept* the purpose God has *given* you, and through reason you *discover* the purpose that *attracts* you, yet neither of which originates in human souls.) The feeling Ahad Ha`Am is writing about, though, is not primarily individual; it is collective or national. Thus he writes: "We feel [*margishim*] in our heart our Hebrew nationalism [*l'umiyutenu ha`ivrit*] ... which is felt by us inwardly, unmediated."[39] And what does this national feeling intend? It intends

---

[39] "This is Not the Way," *Writings*, 11. For a more nuanced secular notion of "national[ist] feeling," see Kaufmann, *Exile and Estrangement*, 1:145, 196–97; 2:279.

what Ahad Ha`Am thinks has always been the intention of the Torah, which was suppressed by too much Diaspora theology.[40] For him, there is "only one purpose [*takhlit ahat*] … the general success of the nation [*ha'ummah*] in its ancestral land."[41] And, though he sometimes sees "the land and laboring for it [*avodatah*] beloved in and of itself," the Jewish connection to the land of Israel is primarily historical.[42] That connection to the land is a major component of Jewish national feeling. It is what Jews feel when they include themselves *within* the history of *their* people, which is what each of them does or should do, that is, to internalize that collective feeling in each and every Jewish heart. This feeling is not individual, but rather collective; and it is not spontaneous but rather it regularly manifests itself in Jewish history. Yet this feeling needs to be attached to a particular land to which the Jewish people have a continual historical connection. And, modernity at the dawn of the twentieth century seemed to be providing a unique opportunity for the Jews to reconnect to their ancestral land.

A land is what any self-respecting, self-asserting people needs to be the center of its national life. (The question of whether this national life needs to be totally contained within one place or not will be dealt with in Chapter 6.) But that national life is historical, not simply natural or biological. The national life of the people is primarily in time. Being a temporal phenomenon, it moves in a direction, history being the trajectory of a people's journey in the world through time. Secondarily, but necessary nonetheless, is that the historical journey or progression of this people through time needs a spatial location in the world. In this

---

[40] The founder of the religious-Zionist movement, *Mizrahi*, Isaac Jacob Reines (d. 1915), also spoke of "national feeling" (*regesh ha`amamut*), yet he insisted that traditional Jewish religion (*ha-dat*) is the indispensable element (along with race, language, and land) in Jewish nationalism, both in the past and in the present. *Mizrahi Book* [Heb.], ed. J. L. Maimon (Jerusalem: Mosad Harav Kook, 1946), 4, 25–27.
[41] *Writings.*, 12. See, also, "Truth from the Land of Israel," ibid., 23.
[42] Ibid., 25.

case, the Jews need a place of our own. The Jews are not and ought never be nomads.

This is important to emphasize because, if the connection of the Jewish people to the land of Israel were primarily "natural," then the Jews would have lost their connection to this land when physically expelled from it by their conquerors and then replaced there by other peoples. The Jews would be like all the other peoples who have been exiled from the land that they simply "grew up in." Like an uprooted tree, the Jews would have had to sink roots elsewhere or die. But, then, if these roots are sunk into foreign soil, the tree will inevitably grow up to be like the other trees that grow there in that "strange ground" (Psalms 137:4). So, were Jewish identity primarily determined by location in space rather than through history, the Jews would be like those other peoples who have no history (or not enough history) to sustain them when they have been driven out of their land. The Jews would have no history to give them sufficient memory of their time in their own land to maintain hope for an eventual return to "the land" (ha'arets).

In fact, the Torah teaches that the Jews were not indigenous to the land of Israel, but that they were *sent there* by God at a certain time, and that they will be *returned there* at a certain time. And because for Ahad Ha`Am, "God" is to be looked upon as an "historical force," he would say that their connection to the land (qesher), whether coming to it originally or finally returning to it, is essentially historical.[43] Thus he resists any kind of romantic naturalism, insisting that the centrality of the land of Israel depends on the ongoing history of the Jewish people. Zionism, then, needs to be historical before it can become territorial. Accordingly, Ahad Ha`Am writes that the Zionist task is "to create [li-vro] in the land of Israel a healthy settlement [yishuv bari] ... the external natural [tiv`i] base for the revival of our spirit there ... the national, spiritual centre [ha-merkaz]."[44]

---

[43] "Renewal and Creation," *Writings*, 293.
[44] "The Way of the Spirit," *Writings*, 181.

This sounds like the words of the old Zionist song: "We have come to the land to build it up [*li-vnot*] and to be built up by it [*le-hibanot bah*]."[45] However, the "pioneers" (*halutsim*) who sang this song were mostly socialists, who were more interested in the material reconstruction of a Jewish society in the land of Israel than they were in that society being primarily a "spiritual" or cultural center there.

One main historical reason, it seems, why Ahad Ha`Am thought Jewish creativity has to be separated from religion is that the religious Jews, especially their rabbis, were not interested in, and were even notably opposed to, building a "new" Jewish anything. Their slogan, in fact, became "what is new [*hadash*] is prohibited by the Torah." Even though this slogan was coined (actually appropriated) by the Hungarian Orthodox rabbinical authority, Moses Schreiber (better known as "Hatam Sofer," d. 1839) and directed against the Reform movement (which itself would become mostly anti-Zionist), this slogan was, nevertheless, directed against any Jewish movement that claimed to be innovative.[46] As such, the slogan and its clearly implied condemnation were easily applied to Zionism, especially the cultural Zionism that was trying to displace religion among the Jews. It would seem that these rabbis wanted Jews to continue living a "sectarian," ghettoized political and cultural life apart from the modern world as they had been apart from the medieval world. In fact, it was charged that while Reform Judaism tries only to assimilate individual Jews into the modern world, Zionism tries to assimilate the whole Jewish people into that world. After all, the plea "let us now become like the [other]nations, like the families of the [other] lands" (Ezekiel 20:32) was made by "you" (*attem*, plural), that is, the plea was made by the Jews collectively. And, of course, the theological problem with this new Jewish "creativity" is that in classical Judaism, creativity is exclusively divine; it is a uniquely divine prerogative. Conversely, Ahad Ha`Am used the verb *bar'o*, "create" to describe what Jews can do, whereas in

---

[45] See Gordon, *Nation and Labor*, 1:150.
[46] See *Encyclopedia Judaica*, 2nd ed., 18:742–43, s.v. "Sofer, Moses."

the Bible only God creates, and hence only God could be the subject of this verb. There is no doubt that Ahad Ha`Am, coming as he did from an intensely religious background, was fully aware of how radical his break with the Jewish tradition had become.

Now, if national creativity is to replace the Torah, that is, to replace Judaism as the religion of the Jewish people, then it seems to follow that Ahad Ha`Am's new religion will have to replace the God who creates the world and who gives His Torah to His chosen people. Indeed, Ahad Ha`Am was quite willing to go that far, writing: "The ancient God [*eloah ha-qadmoni*] makes room for what is better than him ... and becomes a pure and exalted ideal, which stands before man in its splendid glory [*be-hadar ge'ono*] and commands him [*u-metsaveh alav*] to choose good."[47] Promoting this idealism, though, raises two problems, which Ahad Ha`Am seems to struggle with.

The first problem is philosophical. It concerns Ahad Ha`Am's *idealism*. An "ideal" is a human creation. An *ideal* stems from an *idea* of perfection thought up by human minds, which these same humans then turn into the task or project of perfecting themselves according to the idea.[48] When that project involves human practice and not just human thought, our human task is to morally perfect ourselves. An ideal, then, is an idea turned into a purpose or goal by those who thought of the idea. The process of turning an idea into an ideal is idealization; those who do this are "idealists," whose general theoretical approach is "idealism." The humanly conceived idea of perfection is thrown ahead as the practical aim or purpose, the *ideal* we humans are to perpetually strive to reach or attain. In today's psychological parlance, this is "choosing our goals." In traditional Judaism, conversely, our goals are chosen for us by God.[49]

Like other idealists, however, Ahad Ha`Am could not explain just how an ideal as a human creation – even *the* most exalted

---

[47] "The Way of the Spirit," *Writings*, 161.
[48] See Kant, *Critique of Pure Reason*, B596–97.
[49] For Ahad Ha`Am's rejection of any transcendent teleology, whether chosen by God or even the apex of external nature, see "Servility in Freedom," *Writings*, 68.

human creation – can "command" its human creator to act at all. Isn't the human creator of some *thing* – even an ideal projected by a human mind – superior to *what* has been produced, because he or she can speak and be spoken to? As the Psalmist put it: "their idols of silver and gold are the work of human hands [*ma`aseih yedei adam*]" (Psalms 115:4). As such, unlike their human makers, these idols "have mouths but they don't speak; they have eyes but they don't see" (Psalms 115:5). This comparison of "idols" and "ideals" is more than a pun, because "silver and gold" are like ideals, that is, they are valuable to humans because of their capacity to be made into articles that humans admire rather than just use. They are put on a pedestal. Thus idealization is the modern version of idolatry.[50]

However, only a person can command another person. When the commanding person is a fellow human creature, the commandment is relative, that is, in certain situations I have the right to command you to act in a certain way; in other situations you have the right to command me to act in a certain way. Thus in a democracy, elected officials have the right to command me to act in a certain way, but that way must be consistent with the mandate that I among the other citizens who voted for them have given them. But, when there is no opportunity for me to ever command you to act in a certain way, then you have either made yourself or have been made by somebody else into a god. (The most basic Hebrew term for "god," i.e., *elohim*, means "a person who has authority"; and the word is used to name both divine and human authorities.[51]) Now, such modern "idols" frequently claim they have a right to command absolutely because they are acting in the name of a great ideal, plus they have devised the most powerful technological means to realize that ideal. We, their subjects, become disposable parts in that technologically manipulated project. Is it any accident, then, that Marxism, which epitomizes this whole ideological approach, became so attractive to many Zionists, both of the political and cultural variety?

---

[50] See MR: Leviticus 33 re Deut. 4:28; Jer. 27:8; Dan. 3:9.
[51] See, for example, B. Sanhedrin 56b re Exod. 22:7, and 66a re Exod. 22:27.

Furthermore, we can accept the commandments of our Creator, because the very fact we are commanded by God with "just laws and ordinances" (Deuteronomy 4:9) is evidence that God cares for us, taking responsibility for us by showing us how to live purposeful lives in the world. No human authority could possibly have this kind of cosmic responsibility. Who else but God could we request to "deal kindly with Your servant, so that I might live to keep Your word" (Psalms 119:17)? Could we be so commanded by anyone but the one transcendent God? This philosophical problem becomes Ahad Ha`Am's problem inasmuch as he is advocating *national moral autonomy*. The question that he seems to have no satisfactory answer to is: How can an ideal projected by the Jewish national spirit – which unlike the biblical God no one has ever heard speak to them – how can what functions autonomously or "on its own" actually command the very people whose national spirit created it?

The second problem with Ahad Ha`Am's cultural Judaism is that his "national spirit" (*ruah le'umi*) seems to suggest *polytheism*: the assertion that there are many gods. For when he asserts that the Jewish national spirit projects an ideal, he is aware that there are other national "spirits," that each nation has its own spirit, each has its own motivating historical force (its own *Volksgeist*), each has its own national ideal.[52] That national spirit creates a moral ideal that is projected to spur humans to realize it through their own moral action. As such, that means each nation has its own morality, its own norms governing how the transactions or interactions of the members of that nation among themselves are to be conducted. Indeed, Ahad Ha`Am's nationalism requires him to say that, because the liberal opponents of Jewish nationalism argued that the reason why the Jews now liberated from the ghetto *ought* to remain with Judaism (their traditional communal religion) and not assimilate, is because it is their historical task to promote a *universal* moral ideal. They do that by teaching all humankind how best to approximate that universal ideal (if not actually to fully attain it). Along these lines, the

---

[52] "The Way of the Spirit," *Writings*, 162.

German-Jewish philosopher Hermann Cohen (d. 1918) – who was himself a formidable anti-Zionist – argued that because the other nations have not even approximated this universal moral ideal, and because the Jews have preserved universal morality in a very special way, the Jews should work to bring the nations of the world up to *their* more ideal moral level rather than going down to the less moral worldly level of the other nations.[53]

Ahad Ha`Am criticized these Jewish "universalists," arguing that it is bizarre, if not absurd, to think that the survival of a particular nation's way of life is to be primarily for the service that nation is supposed to perform for others. Surely, a nation's cultural survival, let alone its cultural flourishing, is first and foremost for itself, and whatever moral instruction or influence it can provide the other nations (what the rabbis called *ummot ha`olam*: "the nations of the world") is secondary.[54] To influence "the world" is not the nation's primary purpose. For Ahad Ha`Am, the Jews live to realize their national ideal, their national spirit. They are not responsible for the rest of the world. Whatever international influence the Jewish people might have can only be what the non-Jewish nations of the world can't help but notice about Jewish national existence in its own land, that is, when the Jewish people are not an isolated tribe living apart from the world.[55] Nevertheless, whatever the nations notice about the Jewish people in their own land and admire, even if they want to emulate the Jewish people, that is still not something the Jews should intend to be their primary purpose for being a nation in the world. (Along these lines, it used to be noted with pride how the kibbutz movement had inspired some other, non-Jewish, collectivist or "socialist" movements, even though most of the early "kibbutzniks" were primarily Jewish nationalists and only quite secondarily, if at all, internationalists.)

---

[53] See his *Religion of Reason Out of the Sources of Judaism*, trans. S. Kaplan (New York: Frederick Ungar, 1972), 359–63. For a critique of Cohen, see Novak, *The Election of Israel*, 64–77.
[54] "The Way of the Spirit," *Writings*, 156.
[55] See "Priest and Prophet," *Writings*, 92.

But, if the Jews' primary, indeed essential, purpose is not just their physical survival, but much more their approximation of their own national ideal, and if *their* national ideal has taken the place of their God for Ahad Ha`Am, doesn't this then imply that just as the Jews have their own "ideal/god," every other nation has its own "ideal/god"? In other words, isn't Ahad Ha`Am implying there are many gods? Therefore, isn't Ahad Ha`Am not just a cultural pluralist; isn't he a radical metaphysical pluralist as well?

I think, however, Ahad Ha`Am tried to head off this conclusion by contrasting monotheism – the idea of the one God who transcends the world – not with polytheism, which would surely be abhorrent to just about anybody who has any religious connection to the necessarily religious Jewish tradition. Instead, he contrasts classical Jewish monotheism with "pantheism," which is the idea that God pervades the whole world, that is, all of "nature" (*ha-tev`a*), like the soul is thought to pervade the entire body. Writing about what he calls "national pantheism," Ahad Ha`Am contrasts it with the classical Jewish monotheism that asserts (in his words): "Nature is only the agent of God, the instrument of the Master of the universe (*ribbon ha`olamim*), who made it according to His will and who stands over it [i.e., to govern or control it]."[56] (This "Jewish" monotheism, by the way, was accepted virtually intact by Christianity and Islam, which explains why medieval Jewish, Christian, and Islamic philosophers could talk about God in a remarkably similar way.)

Nevertheless, no clear thinking pantheist, neither Spinoza nor Goethe (whose respective pantheisms have many differences between them), could advocate "national pantheism."[57] Indeed, *national pantheism* is an oxymoron; for "national" is

---

[56] "Renewal and Creation," *Writings*, 292. Cf. Gordon, *Nation and Labour*, 1:353; 2:96, 122.

[57] Actually, the pantheism of Ahad Ha`Am (and even more so that of A. D. Gordon) shows more of the influence of Goethe's romantic pantheism than that of the more ontological pantheism of Spinoza. See *Goethe: Wisdom and Experience*, ed. and trans. H. J. Weigand (New York: Frederick Ungar, 1964), 73–79.

a *particular* term just as the Jewish nation is *a* nation among a plurality of nations: *this* nation, not *that* nation or not *those* nations. "Pantheism," on the other hand, coming from the Greek *pan* meaning "all," and *theos* meaning "God," is necessarily about what is *universal, unitary, and absolute*. "Particular" and "universal" are opposite adjectives; they cannot cogently modify or describe the same noun. To be sure, Ahad Ha`Am's preference for pantheism over monotheism could suggest to his intellectually sophisticated readers (and, unlike Herzl, he was more of an introvert writing for his readers than he was an extrovert speaking to his audience) the pantheism of Baruch Spinoza (d. 1677). In fact, some of the early Zionists were attempting to rehabilitate Spinoza as a Jewish thinker, despite the ban (*herem*) placed upon him by the Amsterdam rabbinate. (And that was because they saw Spinoza to be a proto-Zionist, something discussed in Chapter 2.) But Spinoza, who was certainly not advocating many gods, would also consider himself to be a monotheist because he is a "monist," that is, he continually insisted that God who is Nature and Nature that is God is essentially one universal substance that includes everything we know and even what we don't know.[58] Spinoza, like the classical Jewish tradition he seemed to have abandoned, was as much opposed to polytheism as were the rabbis, advocates of the classical Jewish tradition, from whose community and yeshivah he willingly departed. Therefore, when Ahad Ha`Am's notion of a "national spirit" is taken to be a metaphysical concept – and, what talk of "spirit" is not "metaphysical"? – that notion has to be taken to be *polytheistic*, whether he could admit that or not.

This is the aspect of Ahad Ha`Am's ideology that his cultural Zionist followers either didn't understand or, if they did, didn't want to deal with its very radical implications. Surely, just about every Jew who has ever said the *shema* (Deuteronomy 6:4) and who knows what he or she is saying, that is, "the Lord God alone is our God" (*adonai elohenu … ehad*), knows that Judaism, the religion of the Jewish people, affirms one and only one God.

---

[58] *Ethics* IV, preface.

And every great Jewish thinker, whether Maimonides in the twelfth century or the Israeli philosopher Yehezkel Kaufmann (d. 1963) in the twentieth century, teaches that at the core of Judaism is the affirmation of the one and only God, coupled with the rejection of any other "gods," both in theory and in practice.[59] Jews might give up classical Judaism for a variety of other "isms." Yet, very few such departed Jews have left the tradition for polytheism or anything like it. Even otherwise secular Jews who might be atheists still want to deny *one* God rather than embrace *many* gods.

Instead of being concerned with these philosophical and theological questions, Ahad Ha`Am and the cultural Zionists were more concerned with the question of how this national feeling expresses itself. How does this national feeling actually lead to concrete action in the world? Ahad Ha`Am's answer is "culture." It is for the Jews to create a culture, for which he still uses the Russian word *kultura* (rather than the Hebrew term *tarbut* that soon supplanted it).[60] And as we all know, there are still today a number (even a growing number) of Jews who will say of themselves, "I am a *cultural* Jew," meaning: "I am not an adherent of the Jewish religion. I either ignore it or resist its claims upon me." In other words, instead of seeing "culture" as an expression of "religion" (after all "culture" and "cult" do come from the same Latin root), most "cultural Jews" want there to be a total separation of the two.

However, if "culture" means a coherent body of practices that positively identify the members of a particular people, and negatively distinguish them from the members of any other people, then don't the Jews already have a culture? Haven't the Jews had a culture since their very beginning as a people when they were taken out of Egypt to be given the Torah at Mount Sinai? And doesn't the "Oral Torah" (*torah she-b`al peh*) mean their ongoing *cultural* development of what was given to them at Sinai? And,

---

[59] MT: Yesodei ha-Torah, 1.7; Kaufmann, *The Religion of Israel*, trans. M. Greenberg (Chicago: University of Chicago Press, 1960), 60–69.
[60] "The Way of the Spirit," *Writings*, 181.

aren't their distinctive cultural practices the positive commandments (*mitsvot ma`asiyot*) of the Torah? Aren't the traditional cultural practices of the Jews more than what Ahad Ha`Am's American disciple, Mordecai Kaplan (d. 1983), called "folkways"?[61] And (as we shall see in Chapter 6) isn't the essential connection of the people Israel (the Jews) to the land of Israel, which is the fundamental concern of Zionism, concretized in a divine commandment the Jews are to keep? Moreover, isn't all that because Jewish sacred acts are more than "natural" practices like pagan nature rites, and aren't they more than ancient customs that have somehow or other cropped up in Jewish history? Isn't that because these commandments are considered to be the content of the covenant between God and Israel, that is, with the God who has created nature and directs or judges history? As such, that covenant is more than natural, more than historical. The covenant is *meta-physical*: it is beyond natural or historical facts. As Maimonides pointed out, the Torah, the constitution of the covenant, is not natural, even though it enters into the created natural world to govern it and direct it toward God.[62] The covenant is *metahistorical*: its truth (*torat emet*) is beyond historical processes. The covenant comes from a transcendent source beyond the confines of nature or history, that is, it comes from *the Source whom* neither nature nor history can escape into any real independence of their own, because the God who creates nature and directs history will not be indifferent to them and to what humans, especially God's chosen people, do with them.

Even though all that religiously rooted *culture* might well fulfill the tentative, phenomenal definition of "culture" I have just put forth, Ahad Ha`Am would have surely rejected it. It doesn't, indeed it cannot, fit the Jewish culture he wants. Why? It's because he cannot acknowledge a God who does all this. Thus he speaks of culture as "an objective acquisition [*qinyan*],

---

[61] *Judaism as a Civilization*, enlarged ed. (New York: Reconstructionist Press, 1957), 431–59.
[62] *Guide of the Perplexed*, 2.40.

Cultural Zionism

an existing creation [*briyah*] that stands on its own, which in every age concretizes the best inner powers of the people."[63] In other words, culture is the collective creation of the Jewish people throughout their history. Furthermore, Ahad Ha`Am clearly understands that the old religious-practical content of Jewish culture cannot simply be repackaged and made secular, precisely because nobody who practices that religious content consistently and intelligently would do so if these deeds weren't taken to be commanded by God. In other words, culture and religion are at loggerheads: the kind of culture he wants must be severed from any religious roots; the kind of religion he rejects cannot recognize any human praxis that claims to be independent of revelation and the tradition rooted in it.

In fact, the only essentially religious practice Ahad Ha`Am actually endorses is the Sabbath, about which he famously said: "More than Israel has kept [*shamru*] the Sabbath, the Sabbath has kept [*shamrah*] Israel."[64] Yet even here, it is not clear whether the Sabbath, like other traditional Jewish religious practices, *did keep* Israel, in the sense of guarding Jews in the diaspora (*galut*) from assimilation by making these Jews distinctive in the way they kept time in the world; or whether the Sabbath *has kept* Israel in the sense of still having the power to spiritually rejuvenate the Jews from physical and mental exhaustion, even the inevitable fatigue involved in the labor of rebuilding the land of Israel. (If the latter, though, Ahad Ha`Am's idea of the Sabbath had virtually no effect on the secular kibbutzim who practiced "Hebrew culture," for virtually all of them were notorious for their *hillul shabbat* or "desecration of the Sabbath.")

It seems that the only real, concrete cultural creation Ahad Ha`Am can point to is the revival of the Hebrew language, in which he was a major influence. Hebrew was now meant to be a language in which anything pertaining to the Jewish people

---

[63] "The way of the Spirit," *Writings*, 175. For a critique of "culture" as a Jewish reality, see Ernst Simon, "Are We Israelis Still Jews?, *Commentary* 15 (1953), 358.

[64] "The Sabbath and Zionism," *Writings*, 286.

could be expressed. (Herzl, by the way, had ridiculed the idea, just as he couldn't see why the Jews couldn't have another place for their state, as the land of Israel was presently unavailable for the taking.) This is what makes Hebrew's revival (some used to call it "Neo-Hebrew") something new, since, for the most part, Hebrew in the Diaspora was confined to strictly religious matters. In fact, speaking and writing Hebrew, as well as making it able to express modern realities, became a passion of many of the cultural Zionists. And, no doubt, this has been a most impressive achievement, for which all Jews should be grateful. Nevertheless, how "Jewish" can Hebrew remain if it is not rooted in the Jewish religious tradition, regularly drawing on it for nurture and growth?

Along these lines, think of how artificial the Yiddish of the Soviet Jewish "protectorate" of Birobidzhan (set up for "secular Jews" by Stalin in 1934) became, because, to secularize it (and, also, separate it from Zionism's emphasis on Hebrew as the Jewish language) all its Hebrew content was intentionally removed. Artificial languages work only for computers, not for real people. Along these lines, think of several Israeli philosophers (whose essays I read and even enjoy sometimes) who happen to write in Hebrew because Hebrew is their mother tongue, yet whose work doesn't express or even reflect any uniquely Jewish content. They seem to be writing in a new language, one that uses Hebrew words, but not Jewish concepts. Nevertheless, there are those in Israel today who argue that all the Jewishness of the Jewish state needs is for the Hebrew language to be spoken by the majority of its citizens. But couldn't you be a Zionist, even a loyal Israeli citizen, with no Hebrew or a smattering of Hebrew? Indeed, couldn't you be a Zionist, or even a citizen of Israel, without having to be Jewish at all? Now that is no way denigrates Hebrew and its continuing role in authentic Jewish life. Hebrew was always meant to be the language of the Jewish people in *all* areas of their life, whether religious or secular. But, just as the sanctity of the land of Israel depends on the sanctity of the Jewish people (as we shall see in Chapter 5), so does the viability of Hebrew as *the* Jewish language depend on the viability

Hebrew Jurisprudence

of the Jewish religious tradition, of Judaism. Certainly, Hebrew depends on Judaism for its continued viability and vitality.

Hebrew Jurisprudence

Finally, there is another kind of secular Zionism (although its first manifestation was before the rise of either political or cultural Zionism) called "Hebrew Jurisprudence" (*mishpat ivri*).[65] This is the attempt to see Jewish civil law as a body of law that can be studied, and applied in a Jewish state, apart from its historical manifestation as a department of traditional Jewish law (*halakhah*), all of which is rooted in divine revelation. And, because traditional Jewish law governs all aspects of human life, most especially including the God–human relationship, the secularization of a part of that law is a radical move, even though almost all the advocates of Hebrew Jurisprudence have been religiously observant Jews. Moreover, this school of thought is "political" Zionism inasmuch as law is a political institution; yet it is also "cultural" Zionism insofar as it draws on probably the most important aspect of traditional Jewish culture: its law. It is more cultural than political Zionism, and it is more political than cultural Zionism. However, it might also be said that Hebrew Jurisprudence combines the error of political Zionism plus the error of cultural Zionism. That is, it marginalizes the Jewish religion as political Zionism does, and it distorts the Jewish tradition as cultural Zionism does.

To be sure, there are many aspects of Jewish civil law, especially, that seem to be no different than any other system of civil law, like the systems of law in modern European states that have severed any connection they might have had in the past with Canon Law. And, in fact, there is some basis in rabbinic tradition for legally effective recognition of the commonalities between Jewish and non-Jewish civil law.[66] Nevertheless, despite

---

[65] See Menachem Elon, *Jewish Law* 4, trans. B. Auerbach and M. J. Sykes (Philadelphia: Jewish Publication Society, 1994), 1898–1946.

[66] See S. Shilo, *The Law of the State is Law* [Heb.] (Jerusalem: Jerusalem Academic Press, 1974).

such commonalities, even Jewish civil law has still been taken to be *Torah*. One important practical effect of that assertion is that Jewish civil law, like any other department of Jewish law, is to be administered by judges (*dayyanim*) who are publicly reputed to be personally committed to and observant of all of Jewish law, even those departments of Jewish law an individual judge is not appointed to administer.[67] Indeed, because of the entire law's inextricable connection to the religious tradition and the divine revelation upon which the tradition is founded, some Israeli legal scholars are opposed to this whole movement to make it the basis of the legal system of the secular state of Israel. The secularist (*hilonim*) opponents fear that its overall religious character makes it ultimately uncontrollable by the government of a truly secular state. The religious (*dattiyyim*) opponents fear that the essentially religious character of Jewish law, even Jewish civil law, would be desecrated and hopelessly distorted by most irreligious (if not antireligious) officials appointed by the necessarily secular government of an explicitly secular state. That is probably why fewer and fewer Israelis are interested in Hebrew Jurisprudence. In a society ever more polarized into religious and secular communities, Jewish civil law cannot be a bridge between the two communities, because it is too secular for the religious, and it is too religious for the secularists. And the proponents of Hebrew Jurisprudence have no good answer (as far as I know) to either group of their opponents, probably because they have not adequately examined the theological roots of Jewish law.

What I do think emerges from our examination of secular Zionism, both the political kind and the cultural kind, whether that of Herzl and his followers or of Ahad Ha`Am and his followers, is that Zionism needs to be thought of and formulated as a specific manifestation of Judaism in general in and for the modern world. On that score, I think, both Herzl and Ahad Ha`Am, and their epigones, "have been weighed in the balance and found

---

[67] MT: Sanhedrin, 2.7 re Exod. 18:21.

wanting" (Daniel 5:27). In the end, about both kinds of secular Zionism it could be said: "They have forsaken the source of living water to dig for themselves wells that are broken, which hold not water" (Jeremiah 2:13) So, it would seem, the only cogent kind of Zionism to be developed is "religious," stemming from a some kind of theological-political Jewish worldview.[68]

---

[68] See Leo Strauss, *Spinoza's Critique of Religion*, trans. E. M. Sinclair (New York: Schocken, 1965), pref., 5–7.

4

Should Israel Be a Theocracy?

What Is Theocracy?

To even suggest that the Jewish state of Israel be constituted according to religious criteria seems to most people now to be advocating that it be a *theocracy*. But, "theocracy" has long been a dirty word for most of us who consider ourselves to be "modern." Indeed of late, "theocracy" has become an even dirtier word when we look at the actions of such "theocratic" regimes as Saudi Arabia and, especially, Iran (even if Iran were not threatening the existence of the State of Israel). So, a Jewish theocracy seems to mean a state governed according to a law the majority of the people haven't accepted to be authoritative, and to be governed by rabbis whom even a majority of those Jews who do accept this law to be authoritative haven't elected to govern them. Moreover, to be instituted, such a theocracy would surely require some sort of rabbinical *coup d'état,* that is, a revolution when a minority of a minority seizes state power and imposes itself on the majority of unwilling people.

Furthermore, it is important to bear in mind that almost all the Jewish "theocrats," who seem to many of us to want a Jewish version of Saudi Arabia or Iran, are actually anti-Zionists. For these Jews, now called *haredim* or "trembling ones" (because of their very public religious fervor), the present Zionist State of

Israel, even if it did adopt traditional Jewish law as its official legal constitution, would never suffice to be the theocracy they hope and pray for. Even those *haredim* or "ultra-Orthodox" who have made their peace with the Zionist State of Israel (and many of them have not made their peace with it) have done so only for pragmatic reasons like getting subsidies from the state; hence this "peace" is more like a temporary truce at best. In fact, some of them would like the State of Israel to be a fully secular state, one that makes no attempt to be "Jewish," thus leaving Judaism to those Jews who have totally separated their Judaism from nationhood in the modern sense.

The task for religious Jews who are Zionists (now called *datiyyim* as distinct from *haredim*), who want the integration of Jewish religion and Jewish statehood, is to articulate what we mean by the old slogan, "the land of Israel for the people Israel according to Israel's Torah" (*al pi torat yisrael*). And this vision of the Jewish state (*medinah yehudit*) must be carefully differentiated from the kind of "theocracy" proposed by anti-Zionist "theocrats." It is also important to note that the anti-Zionist theocrats are almost all anti-democratic as well, regarding both Zionism and democracy to be antireligious Western ideologies. Indeed, the need to avoid the charge that any *theocratic* religious state would have to be anti-democratic must be countered by any Zionist thinker who knows that Western democracy is the only form of modern government that has been good *to* Jews, and is also considered by most Jews to be the best kind of government *for* Jews when the Jews do govern themselves.

However, that is not the most basic challenge to a religious Zionism, as *theocracy*, which literally means "God's rule," is not primarily a political matter. Politics deals with human, not divine rule.[1] Theocracy is also not primarily a legal or "halakhic" matter, because *halakhah* has true authority only when it is continually connected to its religious foundation in the *Torah*: God's normative revelation to the people Israel. Without constant inquiry into

---

[1] See Michael Walzer, *In God's Shadow: Politics in the Hebrew Bible* (New Haven, CT: Yale University Press, 2012).

this religious foundation, *halakhah* becomes but the program of a particular political party, which happens to call itself "religious" or *dati*. Perhaps the prophet's words apply to them: "Their reverence for Me [God] is but a commandment of men [*mitsvat anashim*] learned by rote" (Isaiah 29:13). Or, "they who grasp [*tofsei*] the Torah do not really recognize Me." (Jeremiah 2:8). So, before theocracy becomes a legal or political matter, it is first and foremost a religious matter, to be investigated by *theology* as the method of enquiry into essentially religious matters, which is best conducted by those thinkers for whom these religious matters are of ultimate importance in our own lives. The legal and political ramifications of theocracy should be dealt with subsequently. The fundamental theological questions concern God's rule of the world, God's rule of humans, God's rule of the Jewish people, and God's rule of the land of Israel.

Let us now look at the term "theocracy" in its original meaning and thus see how different that original meaning is from the pejorative meaning the term has been given in modernity.

The very term "theocracy" is a neologism, admittedly coined by the first-century Jewish historian Josephus, who wrote: "Our lawgiver [Moses] ordained the [Jewish] polity to be a 'theocracy' [*theokratian*], assigning sovereignty [*tēn archēn*] and dominion [*to kratos*] to God."[2] But note that Moses is called "lawgiver" (*nomothetēs*), not "prophet," which means that God's normative authority for this Jewish polity is the authority God has given to the Law revealed to the people Israel. God's rule is the rule of God's irrevocable and immutable Law, which is very different from an ad hoc prophetic ruling. In fact, one could call such rule a "nomocracy," that is, "the rule of the Law."[3] *Nomos* is the Greek word for "man-made law"; but the earliest Greek rendition of the Bible translated the Hebrew word *torah* as *nomos*,

---

[2] *Contra Apionem*, 2.164 (Cambridge, MA: Harvard University Press, 1926), p. 358.
[3] See Isaac Halevi Herzog, "The Israeli State According to the Outlook of the Tradition and Democracy," *Complete Writings of Rabbi Isaac Halvey Herzog* [Heb.] (Jerusalem: Mosad Harav Kook, 1989), 8.

thus giving this word the new meaning of "God-given law."[4] And most importantly, this law is the law the people Israel have willingly accepted to be ruled by.[5] (Indeed, there is a striking Talmudic discussion of how even God could not force the people to willing accept the Torah, the implication being that even though the authority of the law depends on God's will, not human will, the effective application of the Law to all areas of life does depend on the people's willing, even loving, acceptance of it.[6]) Furthermore, this law is made known to the Jewish public regularly by being read aloud in synagogues on a weekly basis. That means nobody who is making a legal ruling could do so by his own authority, that is, if that ruling either contradicted the Written Torah, or if that ruling's reason seemed to have no basis at all in the Written Torah.

Now it is true that Josephus does see the administration of the Law, in all aspects of life, to be in the hands of the priestly caste (i.e., the *kehunah* into which he himself was born).[7] Nevertheless, the rabbinic tradition, which developed the idea of "theocracy" to a far greater extent than did Josephus, saw the administration of the Law to be in the hands of anybody (i.e., any non-priest) who had the ability to administer the Law intelligently, and who had the support of both his rabbinical colleagues and, especially, the people for whom he would be administering the Law. Moreover, this administrative office was neither one that the administrator necessarily inherited from ancestors, nor was it one the administrator could necessarily bequeath to his descendants.[8] Therefore, when looking at the original meaning of "theocracy," especially as developed by the Rabbis, we see that it does not designate the program of a human interest group, that it does not designate the rule of a law imposed upon a people who haven't accepted it,

---

[4] Cf. B. Niddah 73a re Hab. 3:6.
[5] See Simon Federbush, *The Nature of Kingship in Israel* [Heb.], 2nd rev. ed. (Jerusalem: Mosad Harav Kook, 1973), 26–34.
[6] B. Shabbat 88a-b re Exod. 19:17 and Prov. 11:3 and Rashi, s.v. "de-saginan" thereon.
[7] *Contra Apionem*, 2.185–87. See also *Antiquities*, 14.41.
[8] M. Avot 2.12; B. Nedarim 81a re Num. 24:7.

and that it does not designate a law administered by an unelected oligarchy of clerics. In other words, "theocracy" is almost a homonym when one compares its original denotation with its current connotation. Therefore, the theocracy Josephus praised and the theocracy that Herzl rejected (as we saw in the previous chapter) are decidedly two different things. In fact, Spinoza (of all people!) gave the best definition of theocracy: "This state could be called a theocracy, since its citizens were bound by no law but the Law revealed by God."[9]

However, whereas we have some idea of what it means for us humans to be ruled by other humans, we do not have a clear idea of what it means to be ruled by God, that is, to be ruled by a God-given law. Indeed, in the aspect of Torah law with which we are most concerned here, that is, the "Zionist" commandment – "You shall inherit the land and settle it" (Numbers 33:53) – we are dealing with a "religious" matter, that is, it pertains to the relationship "between humans and God" (*bein adam le-maqom*). Now in all aspects of Jewish law it is to be assumed that the law is *from* God (*torah min ha-shamayim*).[10] Jews who deny that dogma place themselves outside the domain of normative Jewish discourse (even though there is considerable leeway as to what that dogma actually means).[11] However, the relationship with God is only the subject matter of those commandments that are to be observed "for God's sake" (*le-shem shamayim*), that is, for the sake of the covenantal relationship *with* God.[12] When dealing with these commandments, the theological component is very much in the forefront and not just in the background, unlike what might be termed the more "secular" commandments that pertain to interhuman relations. Whereas in commandments whose subject matter is what is "between one human and another" (*bein adam le-havero*), it is only important to affirm

---

[9] *Tractatus Theologico-Politicus*, chapter 17, trans. M. Silverthorne and J. Israel (Cambridge: Cambridge University Press, 2007), p. 214.
[10] See the magisterial work on this subject by Abraham Joshua Heschel, *Heavenly Torah*, trans. G. Tucker and L. Levin (New York: Continuum, 2005).
[11] M. Sanhedrin 10.1; see B. Baba Metsia 59b re Deut. 30:12.
[12] M. Avot 2.12.

(or at least not deny) *that* the commandment is from God, in what might be called "covenantal commandments" the question of *how* God rules us is paramount.[13] It cannot be overlooked or bracketed without making it less important in Jewish existence than it truly is and must continue to be. The commandment to settle the land of Israel, which is Zionism in action, is such a covenantal commandment. It directly bears on the relationship between God and the people Israel.

The Primacy of Theology

In all of these questions about ruling, it must be assumed that we are inquiring about God's choices told to us in the Torah, because ruling can only mean that the person ruling has freely chosen to rule, that a ruler could just as easily have chosen not to rule, or could have chosen to rule altogether differently from the way that ruler in fact does rule. No one can be forced to rule, for otherwise the one who forced you to rule would be the true ruler, and you would be an unwilling follower. But what do these choices mean, both for God who chooses to rule and for the creatures whom God chooses to rule over? We shall speculate here about the meaning of four such choices: (1) What does God's choice to create the universe and rule it mean? (2) What does God's choice to create humans in God's image and rule humans mean? (3) What does God's choice to covenant with the Jewish people and rule mean? (4) What does God's choice of the land of Israel for the Jewish people mean? In other words, what are the reasons for these choices? Why were they made? Why were these options chosen instead of others?

These four questions are essentially theological. They are certainly not essentially political in the ordinary sense of politics. Even to make these questions essentially legal or *halakhic* does not go deep enough.

Now there are religious Jews who definitely do not consider their Zionism to be secular. They regard their active participation

[13] M. Yoma 8.9; MT: Berakhot, 11.2.

in and support of the Jewish state in the land of Israel, their "religious Zionism," to be directly mandated by Jewish religious law (*halakhah*). The purpose of their Zionism is usually the establishment of a polity there for which that law will become the official law of the state. Nevertheless, these "panhalachists" (to use the term coined by my late revered teacher Abraham Joshua Heschel, in his critique of what he called "religious behaviorism") or Jewish legal positivists cannot claim that their Zionist praxis is *religious* unless they can intelligently articulate the theological roots of the law they themselves live by and advocate all Jews live by.[14] Law needs to be constantly informed by the ideas that the action it mandates in order to be intelligent human action instead of mindless behavior. Theology for religious Jews, especially those who are Zionists too, needs to be much deeper than dogmatic assertions, legal pronouncements, homiletical hyperbole, or obsequious apologetics.

Although *halakhah* is the legal structure the system of Torah commandments (*mitsvot*) needs to be coherent, it cannot be taken to be the sufficient ground of commanded Jewish praxis (including Zionism as integral Jewish praxis here and now). To identify such sufficient grounding is the task of theology. Thus the most important doctrine put forth in the rabbinic writings is "the Torah is from God" (*torah min ha-shamayim*).[15] This doctrine is the most basic justification of all the specific norms or precepts of the Torah. It functions like the preamble of a constitution.[16] That is, it gives the most basic general reason why the law is to be obeyed, that is, the law is to be obeyed *because* it comes from God. Thereafter, in logical sequence, theology deals with the specific reasons or *why* it seems likely God commanded us to do what we are commanded in the Torah to specifically do.

Not to deal with Zionism as a theological question is to miss how deeply Jewish is the Jewish attachment to the land of Israel.

---

[14] *God in Search of Man* (New York: Farrar, Straus, and Cudahy, 1955), 320–35.
[15] M. Sanhedrin 10.1.
[16] *Mekhilta*: Yitro, sec. 5 re Exod. 20:2, ed. Horovitz-Rabin, p. 219. See David Novak, *Law and Theology in Judaism* I (New York: KTAV, 1974), 136–50.

The Primacy of Theology

After all, the very name of the Jewish people, "Israel," means "striving with God" (Genesis 32:38). Jews got that name when Jacob returned to his father's house in "the land of Canaan" (Genesis 31;18), the land that eventually became known as the "land of Israel." In other words, the land of Israel wouldn't have gotten its name were it not for its relation to the people Israel; and the people Israel wouldn't have gotten their name were it not for their relationship with God. Only through that theological engagement will "theocracy," which is the kind of society the Jewish people are commanded to set up in the land of Israel, be restored to its original meaning. That is its most defensible meaning, even today. Only through that theological engagement will it be shown that theocracy properly understood is the true raison d'être of the Jewish state in the land of Israel, hence the best reason for anybody to be a Zionist. This meaning of *theocracy* is altogether different from its usual meaning today. Theocracy properly understood is certainly not a dictatorship of rabbinical clerics, nor is it the special interest of a particular party that promotes the political power and welfare of a group of people who happen to be "religious" or *dati*. True theocracy today is a theological desideratum, but it is not yet a political reality in the world.

Even though our present concern is with how theocracy provides a reason for the Jewish state in the land of Israel, we must nevertheless begin this enquiry with the question of God's first choice of which we are told in the Torah, that is, God's choice to create the universe. Only thereafter can we properly deal with the question of God's choice to create humans in God's image, and only thereafter can we properly deal with the question of God's covenantal election of the Jewish people. Finally, only after dealing with these three prior questions in their correct logical sequence can we properly deal with the last question, which asks about God's election of the land of Israel for the Jewish people. Each subsequent question follows from the question before it. We must, therefore, begin at the beginning, because the depth of each question can be appreciated only when the questions are asked in proper sequence. We shouldn't "jump the queue" in our questioning lest we become confused.

To be properly understood, Zionistic theocracy requires theology as we have been seeing heretofore. But what is "theology," and what makes it an authentically Jewish enterprise? At the outset, though, we should be aware that the word "theology" names both a method of enquiry and the content about which that method inquires. Theology as method means what we now call "God-talk" (*theologikē* in Greek).[17] Theology as content is God's word, that is, the content of revelation (*dvar adonai* in Hebrew).[18]

As method, theology is a way of thinking about the fundamental principles of a religious tradition to which the thinker is personally committed. As such, theology is "religious philosophy" insofar as this is the philosophy of a religious person about the fundamental principles of the religion he or she is personally committed to. Philosophy seems to provide the best method for thinking about such fundamental principles, especially about the fundamental principles of a religious tradition like Judaism that claims to be founded in the revelation of the Creator of the universe. As such, Judaism presents itself to be a matter of ultimate importance. That is what makes Jewish theology as method a philosophical enterprise that is concerned with matters of ultimate importance. Like the classical philosophers – Socrates, Plato, and Aristotle – rationalist Jewish theologians such as Philo, Saadiah, and Maimonides, were concerned with questions having cosmic significance, and not just historic significance for Jews. In fact, it was that common cosmic or universal concern that enabled rationalist Jewish theologians to learn much of their methodology from the classical philosophers. These thinkers, whether Jewish or not, were personally committed to pre-philosophical traditions, however novel their respective approaches to them became. In our case, because we take Zionism to be an indispensable modern manifestation of the Jewish religious tradition, a

---

[17] The term was coined by Aristotle when talking about what we now call "ontology," that is, discourse about *being*, whose prime subject for premodern ontologists or metaphysicians is God. *Metaphysics*, 6.1/1026a20.

[18] See, for example, LXX on Ezek. 1:3.

cogent Zionist thinker or philosopher should be somebody who is committed to the Jewish tradition and its goals, and who is then committed to Zionism as an integral part thereof. When properly understood, theocracy is Zionism's true goal.

Theology as content is what theology as method thinks about. No method of thinking, and that includes theology as method, creates its own subject matter. Thinking needs something to work on.[19] Moreover, philosophy, which could be regarded as the most serious kind of thinking, is not primarily about "things" in the world. Rather, it is primarily about "praxis" or the way humans interact with each other in the world. (That praxis or transaction inevitably involves such nonpersonal "things" as the land of Israel.) That praxis is already there in the world before philosophy thinks or inquires about its fundamental principles. It is like law, which is already operating in the world before ethics enquires about its fundamental principles.[20] Clearly, "Judaism" or the *Torah* presents itself as a "life form," that is, a way of life informing human interaction in the world.[21] Zionism as the praxis of being actively committed to the Jewish state in the land of Israel is one way Jews interact with one another Jewishly. Like any authentic Jewish praxis, Zionism is grounded in and given its content by revelation, which is transmitted, interpreted, and augmented by the Jewish tradition. Revelation (*mattan torah* in Hebrew; literally "the gift of Torah") presents itself mostly as a "given" (a *datum*) to be actively *received* and applied wherever and whenever its recipients find themselves.[22] Revelation and its attendant tradition, then, comprise *theology* as practical content. It is the "Torah of the living" (*torat hayyim*), without which the Torah as a book would only be a "dead letter."[23]

---

[19] See Edmund Husserl, *Cartesian Meditations*, sec. 16, trans. D. Cairns (The Hague: Martinus Nijhoff, 1960), 33.
[20] See Hermann Cohen, *Ethik des reinen Willens*, 5th ed. (Hildesheim and New York: Georg Olms Verlag, 1981), 227.
[21] See Ludwig Wittgenstein, *Philosophical Investigations* I, 2nd ed., no. 23, trans. G. E. M. Anscombe (New York: Macmillan, 1958), 11.
[22] *Sifrei*: Devarim, no. 33 re Deut. 6:6, ed. Finkelstein, p. 59.
[23] See B. Kiddushin 66a.

Theology as content must be intelligible enough and profound enough to be the subject matter of theology as philosophical method; and theology as philosophical method must be intelligent enough to be able to plumb the depths of theology as content, itself the product of divine wisdom. Because all of Judaism (Zionism included) is about praxis, and because authentic Jewish praxis is doing the commandments of the Torah, it is the task of a Jewish theologian to inquire into the reasons or purposes of these commandments (*ta`amei ha-mitsvot*) given by an all-wise God.[24] That is, he or she must search for the "why" of the commandments, and how doing what is commanded actually does intend these purposes. Theological method is akin to the method of ethics as inquiry into the principles that underlie the law and that give it purposeful direction. But ethical reasons or purposes of laws can only be the benefits (called "the common good") that humans can reasonably assume will accrue to their law-abiding community. That is why the reasons we discern for commandments that pertain to interhuman relations are almost always ethical reasons.[25] But, is there something more here?

In the case of keeping the commandment to settle the land of Israel, the ethical reason might be: the Jewish people need a homeland in which to be able to govern themselves rather than being governed by non-Jews elsewhere. Now there is nothing that is not true here. This ethical reason is as good as far as it goes. Nevertheless, what difference does it make whether this is God's commandment or not? A nonbeliever like Herzl or Ahad Ha`Am could say the same thing. So, it seems, to make the commandment to settle the land of Israel have theological and not just ethical significance, we must try to imagine why our keeping this commandment benefits God. Why does this commandment serve God's own interests? How does our keeping this commandment enable us to make God's own interest our own interest?[26] Here we need more than ethics.

---

[24] Maimonides, *Guide of the Perplexed*, 3.26.
[25] See, for example, B. Gittin 36a re Deut. 15:9.
[26] M. Avot 2.4.

The Primacy of Theology

Whoever perceives that theology needs more (but not less) than ethics is best able to speculate about or imagine the meaning of freely chosen divine acts. These divine acts are what humans can imitate when we speculate about or imagine what choices God has made, the results of which we are told of through revelation. And to those who would say such imaginative, metaphysical speculation is "un-Jewish," I would point to rabbinic and kabbalistic *aggadah* (best translated as "theological narration") that deal with divine action.[27] In fact, this method of imaginative speculation is quite similar to the method of hypothetical conjecture often employed in the Talmud called *haveh amina*, meaning: "I might have thought *that would have been* the law were it not for the fact that Scripture ruled *this is* the law."[28] In other words, this kind of hypothetical conjecture deals with the options that the divine Lawgiver *could have* chosen, but didn't choose. So, this metaphysical speculation is about the options that might have been behind the divine acts actually revealed in Scripture, and possibly why God chooses to act one way rather than otherwise.[29] This kind of theological method is akin to the method of classical metaphysics as speculation about the principles that possibly underlie nature and give it purposeful direction. The difference, though, is that classical metaphysics deals with mute nature by expressing for nature what nature cannot express by itself. Moreover, because true expression can only be the choice of a person to express him- or herself, we cannot attribute free choice to what is mute. And, because free choice can be made only when there is more than one possibility before it, in classical metaphysics one cannot talk of "what could have been but wasn't" because it does not deal with possibilities. Instead, classical metaphysics deals with a universe assumed by premodern natural science, which is an atemporal universe,

---

[27] *Sifrei*: Devarim, no. 49 re Deut. 11:22, ed. Finkelstein, p. 115: "If you want to recognize the One who spoke the universe into existence, learn theology [*haggadah*]. From out of that, you will recognize the One who spoke the universe into existence, and you will cleave to His ways."
[28] See, for example, B. Baba Kama 3a.
[29] See, for example, B. Berakhot 7a; 61a re Gen. 5:2 and 9:6; B. Menahot 29a.

eternal and immutable. (In what passes for the metaphysics now done by some contemporary philosophers, though, "what might have been" and "what might have been said about it" are only a set of logical possibilities, not a set of cosmological options; as such, they are only scenarios in a "mind game.")

A theological metaphysics of Scripture, on the other hand, has the advantage of speculating about spoken data, *bespeaking* what is implied by what God chooses to do in the *speech-acts* that were subsequently written down in the Torah text. That is, it speculates about the *practical* divine thought or wisdom (*mahshavah*) that seems to underlie God's revealed acts, even though "My thoughts are not your thoughts" (Isaiah 55:8). The highly imaginative character of this kind of theological speculation makes it akin to poetry (even when its expression is quite prosaic). Only theology as speculative metaphysics can plumb the depth of God's original preference for the land of Israel and why that should also become the subsequent preference of God's preferred or elected people Israel. Zionism's true depth, then, is metaphysical. We might call it "meta-theology." In fact, without this kind of speculation, Zionism quite easily becomes authoritarian dogmatics, shallow apologetics, or devious propaganda.

Jewish theology ("all the way down" so to speak) is most deeply concerned with election: the choices God makes and their significance for human thought and action. These choices seem to be (1) God's choice to create the world as God's total possession; (2) God's choice to create humans as the unique "image of God" (*tselem elohim*), that is, for a singular mutual relationship with Godself; (3) God's choice of Israel/Jewish people (*am yisrael*) as the optimal community for the God–human relationship (the *berit* or "covenant") to develop in; and (4) God's choice of the land of Israel (*erets yisrael*) as the optimal earthly locus of the God–Israel relationship. Finally, there is a fifth choice: a human choice, that is, the political choice of the Jewish people, primarily living in the land of Israel, to choose the kind of polity (or *medinah* in Hebrew) they judge to be the best means for keeping the divine commandment to settle the land of Israel as the earthly center of the covenant between God and the people Israel. Only

The Primacy of Theology

that political choice, it seems, does the Jewish tradition leave to the Jewish people to decide by themselves for themselves voluntarily. In fact, Jewish history shows several different options have been tried by the Jewish people.[30]

Accordingly, theocracy is a theological concept that properly characterizes God's governance of the universe, God's governance of the human world, God's governance of the Jewish people, and God's governance of the Jewish people in the land of Israel. Only the people's choice of what kind of government they want to administer their communal existence is not and should not be considered a theocratic enterprise, even though it is devised for the sake of the theocratic enterprise.

The Torah teaches the four aforementioned choices are all made by God. Indeed, one could not speculate about the options not chosen had the actual choices and their results (*desiderata*) not been explicitly revealed in the Torah. Humans could know nothing of what God does in the world had not God revealed in the Torah what God does in and for the world, plus what God expects our human responses to these divine activities to be.

In this chapter we shall now think about the first two choices, that is, God's choice to create the universe and God's choice to create humans in His image. Thinking about these two choices first enables us to appreciate the ontological significance of the last two choices, that is, God's choice of the Jews and God's choice of the land of Israel for the Jews. In other words, the election of the Jews and the election of the land for us are consistent with the way we can think about God's relationship with the universe and with humankind. With this ontological grounding, these latter two choices seem to be less capricious than would be the case were we to think about them in a more mundane way. These last two choices are discussed in the next chapter. Readers who are anxious to get to the point about Zionism more quickly might want to skip this kind of metaphysical discussion and proceed to the next chapter directly. If

---

[30] See David Novak, *The Jewish Social Contract* (Princeton, NJ: Princeton University Press, 2005), 124–56.

you do so, I don't think the overall thrust of the argument of the book will be lost.

Let us now look at these first two choices more closely.

God Chooses to Create the Universe as God's Possession
First, let us distinguish between "the universe" and "the world." The universe is everything God has created. The world is the earthly part of the universe humans can experience, know, and inhabit, which is not even all of the earth (*ha'arets*). It is what the Rabbis called "the habitable world" (*yishuvo shel olam*) or what we would call "civilization," and what the philosopher Edmund Husserl (d. 1938) called *Lebenswelt* or "human life world."[31] What the Rabbis also called "this world" (*ha'olam ha-zeh*) is preceded by the creation of the universe (and it is succeeded by a radical future, a presently unknown *olam ha-ba*: "world-yet-to-come").[32] When the universe as a whole is taken to be more than its earthly part, it is called "the heavens" (*ha-shamayim*). Thus the School of Shammai emphasizes the syntax of the first verse in Genesis (1:1), which could be translated as "When God began to create the heavens (*ha-shamayim*), and then the earth."[33] That means God initially (*bere'sheet*) chose to create a universe, the vast majority of which is beyond human experience, knowledge, and habitation. As the Psalmist puts it: "The heavens are for God; the earth he gave to humans [*li-vnei adam*]" (Psalms 115:16).

Accordingly, the context of God's next three choices regarding humankind, the people Israel, and the land of Israel is *the world*, not the universe. The meaning of the universe for the world is

---

[31] B. Sanhedrin 24b; Husserl, *The Crisis of European Sciences and Transcendental Phenomenology*, sec. 28–29, trans. D. Carr (Evanston, IL: Northwestern University Press, 1970), 103–14.

[32] B. Berakhot 34b re Isa. 64:3; MT: Repentance, 9.7-8.

[33] B. Hagigah 12a. Even though the Talmud states that the opinion of the School of Hillel is to be followed rather than that of the School of Shammai, that applies only to practical options (B. Eruvin 13b). But when it comes to theoretical options, you may agree or disagree with any rabbinic opinion, that is, as long as you don't deny any basic Jewish dogma (such as the divine revelation of the Torah). See Maimonides, *Commentary on the Mishnah*: Sotah 3.3.

The Primacy of Theology

that God has freely chosen to create the universe in such a way that a habitable world can arise *therein*. It is where humankind, the people Israel, and the land of Israel could be chosen by God. "The Lord creator of the heavens, He is the God who forms the earth, who makes it and establishes it; He created it to be a habitation [*la-shevet*], not chaos [*tohu*]." (Isaiah 45:18) God's choice to found the world as the place of human habitation, though, presupposes that God has first chosen to create a universe where the three choices just noted are all of cosmic or universal significance. They are not, therefore, cosmic flukes. Responsible election lies at the core of reality. Nevertheless, God's chosen interest in the world is not confined here any more than God's chosen interest in the entire universe is confined there. So, even when King Solomon is asking God to take interest in the humanly built temple he is dedicating, he still proclaims: "Would God really dwell [*yeshev*] with humans [*et ha'adam*] on earth?! For if even the farthest heavens do not contain you [*yekhalelukha*], how could this house [i.e., the temple] I have built?!" (II Chronicles 6:18) Unlike all of His creatures, the world (even the surrounding universe) is not God's place. "Blessed be God's presence [*kvod*] coming from his own place [*mi-mqomo*]" (Ezekiel 3:12). Unlike all of his creatures (even human creatures), God comes and goes in the world as God pleases.[34] There are no spatial limitations on God's freedom.[35]

Along these lines, we can say that the doctrine of "creation from nothing" (*yesh ma'ayin* or *creatio ex nihilo*) is an affirmation of God's transcendence of the universe. That means the universe is not an emanation *from* God, which would make the difference between God and the universe one of degree rather than one of kind.[36] It also means that there are no preconditions

---

[34] See Jer. 14:8; Est. 4:14; MR: Genesis 68.9 re Gen. 28:11.
[35] God's limitations are self-chosen; they are not due to external factors limiting God's infinite freedom. See David Novak, "Self-Contraction of the Godhead in Kabbalistic Theology" in *Neoplatonism and Jewish Thought*, ed. L. E. Goodman (Albany, NY: State University of New York Press, 1992), 299–318.
[36] See Gershom Scholem, *On the Kabbalah and Its Symbolism*, trans. R. Manheim (New York: Schocken, 1965), 66–67.

of God's creativity, no primordial substance, that would limit what God could do, like the nature of the building materials limits what the builder can do with them when building a house. Before God created the universe, there was nothing except God. And after God created the universe, there is nothing beside God; hence God and the universe are not two substances, for that would mean God is limited by God's own creation.

God's purpose in creating the universe is, as Maimonides taught, the purpose God created *for* the universe. The purpose of the universe or "Nature" is not immanent within the created universe itself (as it is for Aristotle).[37] So, choices are considered to be rational when they are made for a purpose; choices are capricious or arbitrary when they are made for no purpose. It would be an insult to God to presume that God's choices are made for no purpose, that God is capricious, arbitrary, and thus irresponsible.[38] For us, the purposes or ends for which we choose to act one way rather than another are *already there* before our choice or rejection of them (they are a priori), eliciting our response to them.[39] But God's creative choosing or electing creatures is also God's creation of the purposes that ultimately structure or inform these creatures; hence they are what God creates *for* the universe *while* God simultaneously creates their substance (they are a posteriori). "The Lord makes it [*osahh*], forming [*yotser*] it to be structured [*le-hakhinahh*]" (Jeremiah 33:2).[40] These purposes, though, are not what God finds *already within* the universe. To presume that would be to assign the universe itself (or its intelligible "nature") priority over God himself.[41] God's choices, then, are infinitely more radical than our own.

The creation of the universe, being an option God chose, means that elected creation is an event in the life of God. Now all events could occur or happen only in time. All choices and their products, then, are temporal events, which are the realization

---

[37] Maimonides, *Guide of the Perplexed*, 2.19, 22.
[38] Ibid., 3.25–26.
[39] See Aristotle, *Nicomachean Ethics*, 3.2/1111b30.
[40] See Commentary of David Kimhi (Radaq) thereon.
[41] Cf. Plato, *Timaeus*, 27C–29C.

The Primacy of Theology

of possible options.[42] As such, creation has a temporal beginning (*terminus a quo*) and a temporal end (*terminus ad quem*). And, whereas these events take place *in time* or *immanently*, which means they are finite or limited, time itself transcends them at both their start (*archē*) and at their finish (*telos*). Time per se being understood to be infinite or unlimited must be also be understood as coequal or coeval with the limitless duration of God's life. "I am He: before me there is no creature [*notsar*], and after me none will ever be" (Isaiah 43:10).[43] The universe and everyone in it has been born and is going to die, because everlastingness is not built into it.[44] Indeed, were that so, the universe would not be transcended by God subsequently.

---

[42] Cf. Spinoza, *Ethics* 1,P32–36 and Appendix. For Spinoza, there are no possibilities in Nature; everything is and always has been what it is necessarily. See Chapter 2.

[43] See Commentary of David Kimhi (Radaq) thereon.

[44] I use the awkward term "everlastingness" rather than "eternity," because *eternity* usually means what is both everlasting and immutable. But, if one follows Scripture by assuming that God makes real choices, then God does *change* from who God *was before* that choice into who God *is after* that choice has been made (*factum est*). God's choices are different from human choices inasmuch as God's options are infinite in number and God has an infinite amount of time to make them. This, then, doesn't compromise God's everlastingness. Moreover, God, like any person who chooses, remains the same person *throughout* all of the changes He has made in His own life. See David Novak, *The Election of Israel* (Cambridge: Cambridge University Press, 1995), 200–207. The difference between our time and God's time comes out in some of the best translations of Exod. 15:18, which in English is usually rendered as "The Lord shall reign forever [*l`olam*] and ever [*va`ed*]." LXX translates the last two Hebrew words as *for eternity and more* (*ep' aiōna kai eti*), followed by Vulgate: *in aeternum et ultra*. In their translation of the Pentateuch, *Die Fünf Bücher der Weisung* (Cologne: Jakob Hegner, 1954), p. 193, Martin Buber and Franz Rosenzweig render these words as *in Weltzeit und Ewigkeit* (which is close to Martin Luther's *immer und ewig*). *Weltzeit* could mean what Einsteinian physics calls "space–time," where "space designates physical entities' three spatial dimensions of height, width, and depth, whereas "time" designates their inseparable fourth dimension. The transcendence of *Weltzeit*, which is limited to physical entities, by *Ewigkeit*, means that God's limitless/infinite time is not a dimension or attribute of created spatial-temporal entities. God's time is not tied to them. See Franz Rosenzweig, "Der Ewige," *Kleinere Schriften* (Berlin: Schocken Verlag, 1937), 182–98 (his last essay, written in 1929, the year of his premature death). There Rosenzweig wants to drop the term "eternal" from contemporary Jewish theological discourse.

However, to say that time itself is created would mean that creation itself wouldn't be the result of God's choice, because there would be no dimension *in which* God could make a choice. (Once again, this shows a theological ontology that sees choice to be of ultimate cosmic significance challenges a number of other ontologies that, in effect, ascribe free will, but not free choice, to God.)

Of course, because free choice requires more than one option before it can be chosen or else it wouldn't be free, God could have just as easily chosen not to create the universe, that is, to remain in and by Godself. Creation, as the modern Jewish philosopher Franz Rosenzweig (d. 1929) taught, is God's coming out of God's self-satisfied disinterest in anything else.[45] So, why did God create the universe? Even though we can only surmise why, we first need to assume that God's action has a purpose, nonetheless. To presume God acts capriciously, without a purpose, would make God unworthy of our desire to have a personal relationship with Him by imitating him. How could we imitate a capricious God?[46] Why would any intelligent person want to imitate a capricious God? Moreover, the fact that God has a purpose in creating the universe and everything in it means that God has created a criterion for creation He promises to adhere to. Yet that criterion is not preexistent; it too is a creature (*ens creatum*).[47] Indeed, this is what God promised after almost destroying the world through the Flood: the natural order will continue with regularity, and it will continue to be hospitable to its human inhabitants and their animal companions. "This is My covenant [*beriti*] with you and your descendants after you,

---

[45] *The Star of Redemption*, trans. B. Galli (Madison: University of Wisconsin Press, 2005), 31–48. This is contrary to what Hermann Cohen (Rosenzweig's teacher) wrote in *Religion of Reason Out of the Sources of Judaism*, trans. S. Kaplan (New York; Frederick Ungar, 1972), 86: "Creation is the logical consequence of God's unique being, which would have no meaning if it were not the presupposition of becoming."

[46] See Ludwig Wittgenstein, *Tractatus Logico-Philosophicus*, 3.031, 5.4731, trans. D. F. Pears and B. F. McGuiness (London: Routledge and Kegan Paul, 1961), pp. 18–19, 94–95.

[47] Y. Rosh Hashanah 1.3/57b re Lev. 22:19; MR: Leviticus 35.5 re Lev. 19:32.

The Primacy of Theology

and with every living being that is with you ... there will not be another flood to destroy the earth" (Genesis 9:9–11).

In regard to the universe as a whole, God's justice consists of the criteria whereby the universe has sustainable continuity, what philosophers came to call "laws of nature." As the Psalmist says: "The way of the Lord is straight [*yashar*], and all His doing is trustworthy [*b'emunah*] ... through the word of the Lord were the heavens made ... for He spoke and it came to be; He commanded and it endured [*va-ya`amod*]" (Psalms 33:5–6, 9). This is Scripture's way of saying: God created both the content and the structure of nature. But what could the purpose of this just or righteous Creator-God be?

Perhaps God desired there be something other than God, which could be the object of God's continuing concern. To fulfill this desire could be God's purpose in creating the universe, a universe different from God, and a universe that is not part of God. To be the object of God's continuing concern, though, means that the universe is meant to always stand *before* God, that is, to face God [*lifnei*] rather than turn "away from [(*mi-lifnei*] God" (Genesis 4:16). That is, the universe cannot transcend God like God transcends the universe. The universe has no life of its own independent of God, but God has a life independent of the universe and His concern for it. That wouldn't be so, however, if God had chosen to create a truly self-sufficient, absolute, autonomous universe, a universe turned loose, as it were, to run on "automatic pilot." Were that so, to assert that the universe *was* created by God to be independent of God would make God Himself superfluous by the time such an assertion could be made by any creature. If the Creator *is* indifferent to His creatures once the creatures have been created, don't the creatures have good reason to be similarly indifferent to their Creator thereafter?

If cosmic independence were what a created universe means, transcendence would be symmetrical: God and the universe could stand totally apart from each other; each would transcend the other. However, as a prophet proclaimed in God's name: "To whom could you compare Me that I be equal [*ve-eshveh*]?!" (Isaiah 40:25). And, were two such independent entities to face one another, it seems that their confrontation would inevitably be oppositional conflict. As the Talmud puts it: "Can two kings wear one crown?!"[48] This is evident in the modern confidence in the autonomy of the world. This has resulted in the loudly proclaimed "death of God." So, if God and the universe are to be related to one another, to enjoy some commonality, the universe cannot be thought of as being autonomous, and God cannot be thought of as being indifferent to the cosmic other, leaving the universe to its own devices. Surely, if the relation of God and the universe is to be true to God and to the universe, it must be asymmetrical.

This ontology has a practical corollary. If God and the universe were totally independent of each other, we humans might think we too could transcend or escape from God's concern for us. To this temptation the Psalmist speaks: "Where can I go away from Your spirit; and where can I flee from Your gaze [*mi-panekha*]? Even if I could climb up to the heavens [*ha-shamayim*], You are still there [*sham*]" (Psalms 139:8). As Adam and Eve learned, there is no place for any creature to hide from God; God always asks "where are you [*ayekka*]"? (Genesis 3:9). God will not ignore us, even when we unsuccessfully try to ignore God. This follows from the fact that the God–universe relation is asymmetrical: the universe is not related to God like God is related to the universe. God is not correlated with this universe or with any other possible universe. No matter what relation God has to the universe or any of its parts, there is always a divine surplus.

This ontology has another practical corollary. God's autonomous relation to the created universe is radically different from the universe's contingent relation to God. So, when humans presume (like the ancient Epicureans) that even if there is a God (or gods) "out there," presuming that "God" has no concern for our world, there is no reason to abhor idolatry, the process whereby we humans ascribe ultimate authority to some entities within *our* world. After all, a world thought to be independent of God will inevitably be regarded to be autonomous by its human

---

[48] B. Hullin 60b.

The Primacy of Theology

inhabitants, and hence they will be fully capable of designating their own gods here. Weren't the first human couple tempted to disobey God because they thought themselves "to be like gods" (*ve-heyyitem k'elohim* – Genesis 3:5) in our little world? That seems why the Jewish tradition considers idolatry to be prohibited to all humankind. It is based on a lie that everybody knows is a lie.[49] Even those who doubt God's reality still know what is not-God.[50] Furthermore, it is a widely held opinion in the Jewish tradition that the founding patriarch, Abraham, would not have been chosen by God for the covenantal relationship had he not first totally repudiated the idolatry that was his patrimony.[51] Finally, that seems to be the reason why the Jewish tradition regards the presence of idolatry to be especially abhorrent in the land of Israel, the chosen land promised to Abraham and his descendants.[52]

The universe that could or could not have come to be ("why something rather than nothing?" as the eighteenth century philosopher Leibniz famously asked), requires God to will it into being, even though God does not have to will anything at all.[53] Without this theological affirmation of God's free choice to create a universe, the existence of the universe is ultimately absurd.

---

[49] Maimonides, *Commentary on the Mishnah*: Avodah Zarah 4.7; MT: Kings, 9.2; *Guide of the Perplexed*, 2.33.
[50] See David Novak, "Defending Niebuhr from Hauerwas," *Journal of Religious Ethics* (2012), 40:288–92.
[51] MT: Idolatry, 1.3.
[52] Ibid., 7.1.
[53] "On the Ultimate Origination of Things," trans. G. H. R. Parkinson and M. Morris, *Leibniz: Philosophical Writings*, ed. G. H. R. Parkinson (London: J. M. Dent and Sons, 1973), 136–44. Cf. T. F. Torrance, *Divine and Contingent Order* (Oxford: Oxford University Press, 1981). Actually, the question is not "Why is there something rather than nothing?" but rather "Why is there something other than God?" And that is a question only God could ask and answer, as we are the "other" God has willed into existence; hence only the Creator can answer why He created what he created. Thus the question "Why is there God?" is a pseudo-question, as that would imply that God is willed into existence as an effect of a cause greater than God. However, a God who is not "that which nothing greater can be conceived" is no God at all by definition of the name "God." So, we can only imagine why God created, that is, freely willed, the universe and all that it contains into existence.

That is, the universe has no meaning or purpose, not having been made by anyone for it. As such, it is a universe in which our human choices, which cannot be avoided, would also be ultimately absurd, ultimately meaningless. In fact, living absurdly might be the most rational choice a human person could make under these circumstances. However, the idolatry we have just noted is usually what is brought in to fill this unbearable existential vacuum.

God's choice to will *that* the universe come-to-be (its existence), plus God's willing *what* the universe is-to-be (its essence or nature), like all choices takes place in time with its possibilities. Thus the universe itself was once only a possibility for God. The universe is a temporal reality in which choices, both divine and human, can take place, because there are always possibilities *as yet* unrealized. An essentially temporal universe has an open future. Thus the eighteenth century Jewish exegete and theologian Hayyim ibn Attar argued that because free choice presupposes a free, undetermined future, God chose not to know in advance what choices humans would make, because any such divine foreknowledge would destroy the open future free choice requires to be truly free.[54] An essentially temporal universe is not one that is wholly determined by strict causal laws from top to bottom, so to speak. In such a universe, human choices are as undetermined as are divine choices. Nevertheless, there is an essential difference. Divine choices involve an infinite range of possibilities, whereas human choices are confined to a quite finite range.

Because the temporal universe always has unrealized possibilities, God can insert Himself into the natural order at will, whenever God wants, to realize what for is us a highly remote possibility, one that is not part of our accustomed experience of nature (what the Rabbis called *minhago shel olam*: "the customary world").[55] When the intended divine intervention is a public

---

[54] *Or Ha-Hayyim* on Gen. 6:5. See B. Rosh Hashanah 16b re Gen. 21:17; Y. Rosh Hashanah 1.3/57a and Moses Margolis, *Pnei Mosheh*, s.v. "yotser" thereon.

[55] B. Avodah Zarah 54b.

The Primacy of Theology

event proclaimed by a prophet, it is a "miracle," which becomes an event whose practical corollary is that it is to be regularly celebrated by the whole people. Passover is the prime example of this. Without that prophetic proclamation, all such unusual events are still assumed to have been purposefully caused by God. Yet they are taken to be only manifestations of general divine providence to happily thank God for, or they are manifestations of general divine judgment to be sadly accepted.[56] It is that general and usual divine governance of the world called "nature" on which we rely for our coherent action in the world.[57] It is also the presupposition of natural science; that is, nature is usually describable and predictable.

What actually occurs in the universe, whether miraculous or only unusual, is neither accidental (i.e., uncaused) nor necessary (i.e., self-caused).[58] Therefore, even the behavior of impersonal entities or "things" is the result of a personal choice made by God or made by humans. Humans are responsible only for the events in the world they have caused, whereas God is responsible for the events in the entire universe that He has caused.[59] In rabbinic thought, everything in the universe is either made "by God's hands" (*bi-ydei shamayim*) or made "by human hands" (*bi-ydei adam*).[60] But because God knows everything humans have done and why, whereas humans know virtually nothing of what God has done and why (except when informed by a prophet), God can judge humans whereas humans cannot judge God. As God reminded Job: "Will you deny My justice [*mishpati*]; will you indict Me in order to justify yourself (*le-ma`an titsddaq*)?!" (Job 40:8). Humans cannot judge God; they can only complain to God. A complaint, however, unlike a judgment, has to wait for

---

[56] M. Berakhot 9.5.
[57] B. Pesahim 64b.
[58] Nahmanides called these unusual occurrences "secret miracles" (*nissim nistarim*), because they are experienced and understood only by saints. See his *Commentary on the Torah*: Gen. 17:1 and Exod. 6:2; also, David Novak, *The Theology of Nahmanides Systematically Presented* (Atlanta, GA: Scholars Press, 1992), 61–75.
[59] B. Hullin 7b re Ps. 37:23 and Prov. 20:24.
[60] M. Kelim 9.8, 17.12; B. Hullin 55b.

an answer, like Job had to wait for God to answer him out of the whirlwind. A complaint about God that answers its own question negatively is blasphemy.[61]

Contrary to the prevalent opinion about the supposed irresolvable antinomy between "religion and science," such divine intervention does not "break the laws of nature." These laws are only generalities, and our knowledge of them does not predict how innumerable particular possibilities will in fact be realized. Miracles do not defy the very general laws of nature we do know. They only defy those who think that every event in the universe could be predicted, or those who think everything that is customary is as unchanging as are the few general laws of nature that we do know. When these possibilities are *now* realized by persons, they are realized through these persons choosing to realize one possibility rather than the other possibilities before them. (When these possibilities are close at hand to humans, we call them "probabilities.") After a chosen possibility has been realized, the person who realized it is responsible for that reality, that is, for what he or she caused to occur in the past. Choices are thus made in the present, toward the future, and then their results become part of the immutable past. In an essentially temporal universe, the past, the present, and the future remain distinct occurrences. They do not merge into an unchanging eternity.

Now even after God makes a choice, God is not correlated with what God chooses, that is, God has a life of God's own not only *before* creation, but also *outside* and *alongside* creation (and maybe even *after* the created universe has run a finite temporal course). Yet what that pre-universal/extra-universal life of God is, that cannot even be known by anyone other than God. Thus Maimonides, somewhat similarly, argued that humans can think of only what God *does* in, through, and for the universe, but not what God *is* beyond God's relation to the universe.[62] We can only affirm that "beyond"; we cannot say what it is because that would require us to go beyond the horizon of this

---

[61] Job 2:9–10.
[62] *Guide of the Perplexed*, 1.54.

The Primacy of Theology

worldly experience of ours. What cannot be experienced cannot be described. Even what we know of the universe is limited to what we can experience of it from our worldly perspective. So, here and now we humans need to affirm that *beyond*, so it might function for us here and now as a limitation of the metaphysical pretension of confining God to a total correlation with His creation, thus making God as dependent on creation as creation is dependent on God.

From all of the preceding we derive the following seven points: (1) The "universe" is all that God has freely and purposively chosen to create, not from out of Himself, without any preconditions. There is no divine a priori, at least none we humans could possibly know by ourselves. The "world" is the purposeful human habitation therein, made possible by the way God has created the universe. (2) Having a purpose means God is not capricious, and that God creates a criterion by which to run the universe, a criterion God chooses and promises to adhere to. These are the laws of nature. (3) Like all choices, God's choice to create the universe is made in time; hence the universe itself is a temporal phenomenon, having a history that starts in time and develops through time. The past only has facts (that is, coming from *factum est:* "what has been done") but no possibilities; the present only has possibilities to be chosen, but no facts; the future is where only some possibilities will be realized, that is, there some of them will be turned into facts. The present with its possibilities is a continual locus of choices, therefore. (4) God transcends the universe, but the universe does not transcend God; hence God is autonomous or independent of the universe in a way that the universe is not autonomous or independent of God. The created universe is only different from God. (5) The practical corollaries of this ontology are that nothing can escape God's concern anywhere in the created universe, and that idolatry is the primal human sin, which falsely presumes that the world can be independent of God's concern. Idolaters presume that humans can take charge of their own world and make their own gods here. (6) The rejection of idolatry is the necessary precondition of the election of the people Israel and the land of

Israel, that is, from the side of the human recipients of this election. (7) God's transcendence clearly implies that God has a life of His own, which we can only affirm but not even imagine what that life per se is, because it is in no way correlated with anything outside Godself.

God Chooses to Create the Human Person

Humans are distinctly different from all other creatures, so Scripture clearly describes our creation differently. Throughout the creation narrative in the first chapter of Genesis we are told that God "made" this or that by speaking it into being, and that immediately afterward God *approved* what He made, for example, "God saw the light that it is good [*ki tov*]" (Genesis 1:4). "Good" here seems to mean: God was pleased with what He made, as it turned out the way God wanted it to turn out. (We shouldn't be wary of attributing an emotion like pleasure to God, because God's creation of an "other" in which God is concerned means that God has chosen not only to create or *effect* that other, but also to be *affected* by that other.) However, when it comes to the creation of "man" or humans (*adam*), it says: "Let us make [*na`aseh*] man in our image [*be-tsalmenu*] like us [*ki-demutenu*]… male and female He created them" (Genesis 1:26). Moreover, it does not say that God was pleased or happy with this human creation: God did not conclude that his human creatures are "good" (*tov*). That absence of approval seems to be because God is not the sole maker of humans; instead, it seems as though God made us humans His partners in our own making. That is, interacting together with God we humans make our lives. God does not yet approve or disapprove of this human life, that is, the life of every single human person, because we and God are not finished working with each other. As Franz Rosenzweig (d. 1929) taught, this explains the "we" in "let *us* make man."[63]

At this point, we must distinguish between the creation of living human *beings* and the creation of human *persons*. As "living

---

[63] *The Star of Redemption*, 200–201. Cf. Aristotle, *Nicomachean Ethics*, 1.10/1100a10–1100b20.

The Primacy of Theology

beings," humans are no different from the other living beings in the world. "The Lord God formed human beings [*ha'adam*] from the dust of the earth [*adamah*]" (Genesis 2:7). And like all other living beings, when the course of our earthly life is over, as "dust" we become again the "dust of the earth as it was" (Ecclesiastes 12:7). But human personhood is different; it is not coequal with human being. It doesn't manifest itself at birth when human being becomes fully manifest; and it often ceases to manifest itself before the actual death of a human being. That is because human personhood becomes manifest only when a human being is able to engage in intelligent speech.[64]

We see this in the interpretation of the scriptural verse: "He [God] blew the breath of life [*nishmat hayyim*] in his [the human being] nostrils, and he became a living animal [*nefesh hayah*]" (Genesis 2:7). Now it would seem that that the "breath of life" of a human being is not different from the "breath of life" of any animal. In fact, in Jewish law, the cessation of breathing is considered to be the point of demarcation that indicates this non-breathing body lying before us should now be treated as a corpse rather than as a living human being.[65] However, in an ancient

---

[64] See, for example, M. Baba Kama 8.4.

[65] B. Shabbat 151b. Human being is a body of having form (M. Niddah 3.2 and Maimonides, *Commentary on the Mishnah*, ed. Kafih, p. 366 thereon; B. Niddah 22b). Nevertheless, even when this human body doesn't yet have or never did have the intelligent characteristics of human personhood, that human body may still not be violated and must be nurtured (B. Sanhedrin 58b re Gen. 9:6; B. Shabbat 151b). Moreover, even when it becomes a corpse, that body is still not to be violated because it still has a trace of having been made in the image of God. See B. Berakhot 19b-20a re Num. 6:7; *Sifre*: Deuteronomy, no. 221, ed. Finkelstein, p. 254; T. Sanhedrin 9.7and B. Sanhedrin 46b re Deut. 21:23; also, B. Berakhot 18a re Prov. 17:5. This respect also extends to a miscarried human fetus that could have become a human person. See B. Ketubot 20b; L. Greenwald *Kol Bo al Avelut*, 3.2(New York: Philipp Feldheim, 1965), pp. 199–200; also, David Novak, *The Sanctity of Human Life* (Washington, DC: Georgetown University Press, 2007), 35–50, 122–35. One might say that human bodily being is the passive object of God's concern for *what* has been specially created by God ("in our image"); and one might say that human personhood is the active subject *who* can reciprocate God's concern for him and her ("male and female He created them"), plus imitate ("like us") God's concern for all life (Ps. 145:9, 15). Both human being and human personhood, body and soul, always function in tandem. Each requires

Aramaic version of this verse, we find the words "there came to be in the human being [*b'adam*] a speaking spirit [*le-ruah memalela*]." Picking up on this point, the medieval exegete Rashi notes, commenting on Genesis 2:7, that over and above all the animals, the human being was given "intelligent speech" (*de`ah ve-dibbur*). In other words, the human being or animal becomes a human *person* when acquiring the ability to speak intelligently. This seems to explain what "our image like us" (*be-tsalmenu ki-demutenu*) means: *The human person is like God, sharing with God the attribute of intelligent speech; and human persons can become like God when we speak and act intelligently.*[66] But, in what does "intelligent speech" consist, and how does it enable us to have a relationship with God?

The ability to speak intelligently can be exercised by humans only when we have first been spoken to. Human speech is initially elicited by our hearing what somebody who is near us initially has to say by addressing us, and who expects a response in kind. That kind of speech, intended to reach a particular listener, who is summoned by his or her personal name, is essentially prescriptive. As such, that kind of speech is originally evocative: it makes a claim upon those being so addressed: minimally, to listen to what is being said to them; maximally, to do what is being

---

the other (MR: Leviticus 4.5 re Lev. 4:2, ed. Margaliot, pp. 87–90), even though there can be passive human being without active human personhood, but not vice-versa. This is like saying that a human being can have a brain without exercising a conscious mind, but he or she cannot exercise a conscious mind without having a brain.

[66] B. Shabbat 133b re Exod. 15:2 (the view of Abba Saul). Human personhood is actualized human being just as human being is potential human personhood. Indeed, one might say that a living human person is an "ensouled" human body (Gen. 2:7), whereas a dead human being is a "de-souled" human body (B. Shabbat 151b re Ps. 88:6), that is, a body that has lost its potential for human personhood in this world (Ps. 30:10; 115:17). So, when an active human person violates bodily human being in him or herself or in anybody else (M. Baba Kama 91b), that person is guilty of rejecting the necessary embodiment of anybody's own personhood. And when a human being doesn't properly actualize his or her personal potential in this world, that person will be judged in the world-beyond for not having developed the potential God gave him or her to actualize in this world (B. Shabbat 31a).

asked of them.[67] Accordingly, the "speaking spirit" in humans was awakened to respond to the speaking spirit of God, who is the same speaking spirit who began the creation of the universe ("heaven and earth") by calling light into existence: "Let there be light!" (Genesis 1:2–3). The difference between the creation of light (and everything that came thereafter) and the creation of humans is that light automatically did what God wanted it to do, whereas humans were told what to do by God. God's first contact with humans is prescriptive speech; it is God's explicit choice to make a claim on His human creatures. "The Lord God commanded [*va-yitsav*] the humans [*al ha'adam*]" (Genesis 2:16).[68] Being addressed this way means that humans have the capacity to choose to respond to this prescriptive speech freely. This response is done *deliberately*, that is, humans think of what they have been told (thought being internalized speech), and then decide whether or not to do it. As Maimonides pointed out, the fact that God relates to humans normatively, that is, through commandments, presupposes that humans have the capacity to choose to either obey or disobey God. If humans did not have this capacity for free choice, God would have related to them like He relates to the rest of creation, that is, as a cause operating on essentially inert objects.[69]

Humans are responsible or answerable to God only for acts that are freely chosen explicit responses to God's commandments. Thus, in what seems to have been the first crime, that is, the murder of Abel by his brother Cain, God does not accept Cain's claim "I didn't know!" (Genesis 4:9). And that follows from the rabbinic view that God not only addressed commandments *to* humans, but that one of the first of those commandments was *about* how humans are to treat each other.[70] The fact that all humans are privileged by God to be addressed by God,

---

[67] *Sifra*: Vayiqra, ed. Weiss, 3a re Lev. 1:1 (and Rashi, *Commentary on the Torah* thereon). See David Novak, *Jewish-Christian Dialogue* (New York: Oxford University Press, 1989), 145–48.
[68] T. Avodah Zarah 8.4; B. Sanhedrin 56b.
[69] MT: Repentance, 5.1–5.
[70] B. Sanhedrin 56a–b.

as the objects of God's special concern for us, indicates that we humans are to respect each other's lives (hence a prohibition of murder), each other's bodies (hence a prohibition of incest), and each other's property (hence a prohibition of robbery). God chooses to create the human person to be God's partner in the governance of the world.[71] We are therefore responsible *for the world* entrusted to our care, and we are answerable *to* God as to our actions in this world.[72] But what might the options not chosen be?

God could have just as easily remained in relation to the universe as its possessor and ruler, choosing not to create anybody in God's image. We humans have no primordial claim on God. God did not *have to* create us in God's image (which means our having the unique capacity for a mutually free relationship with God) any more than God *had to* create the universe. We humans, on the other hand, *had to* be created; we had no choice in the matter. As the Mishnah puts it: "You were born involuntarily [*b'al korhekha*]."[73] Human *being* is not chosen by us. Only acting human *personhood* involves the choice of how we are going to activate it, that is, by either cooperating with God as God's personal partners in the development of the world, or resisting God and becoming instead thing-like *beings* who are mere instruments in God's hands for governing the world.

God's special concern seems to be God's purpose in creating humans in His image to be like Him, that is, God's concern intends an object *with whom* to be in a relationship. God's purpose in creating humans in his image seems to be that God desired companions to whom God could speak and who could respond accordingly. Thus God calls Abraham "My beloved friend [*ohavi*]" (Isaiah 41:8). And, about Moses, the Torah says: "And the Lord spoke to Moses face to face, like a man speaks to his companion [*re`ehu*]" (Exodus 33:11). Unlike us, though, God can live without companions. To imply that God

---

[71] B. Shabbat 10a and 119b re Gen. 2:1.
[72] B. Shabbat 31a.
[73] M. Avot 4.22.

The Primacy of Theology

cannot live alone by Godself impinges upon God's transcendence of everything and everybody who is not-God. Unlike our desires, however, God's desires for what is not-God are themselves chosen; God could have other desires or none at all. God has the freedom to transcend everything, even His own desires.

We humans, though, cannot transcend our desires nor can we successfully suppress them, because they define our nature. We can only decide which desires are to be acted on with moral and theological justification, and which desires need to be sublimated into morally and theologically justified desires. Our will is basically our capacity to direct our desires to their proper objects, and these proper objects are discerned by our intellect. God, conversely, wills creatures into existence. "O' Lord, by Your will [*li-retsonekha*] You have set up the mighty mountains" (Psalms 30:8). God then decides which creatures He desires to rule without their cooperation, and which ones He desires to rule with their cooperation. So, in the Talmud, it is taught that nobody should "partner" (*meshattef*) God with anything in the world (*davar aher*).[74] Yet it is also taught that a human person who cooperates with God in effecting justice in the world is considered God's "partner" (*shuttaf*).[75] The difference is: we cannot choose God's partners; only God can choose us to be His partners.

God could have chosen some sort of *symbiosis* with God's human image, that is, to reduce Godself to a correlation with humankind alone. But that would make God as answerable to humans as humans are answerable to God. Thus God declared to Job: "Where were you when I founded the earth? Tell it if you have any insightful understanding!" (Job 38:4). "Do you know the laws of heaven [*huqqot shamayim*]; could you apply their governance [*mishtaro*] on earth?" (Job 38:33). God's concern with the human world is not exhausted here. God is still concerned with what lies beyond the human world, just as God's concern with the universe doesn't disable God from having his own life totally independent of his being the Creator of the

---

[74] B. Sukkah 45b re Exod. 22:19.
[75] B. Shabbat 10a re Exod. 18:13.

universe. Just as God's transcendence of the universe is affirmed when God is not reduced to God's creative relation to the universe, so God's transcendence of the world is affirmed when God is not reduced to only being the "Master of the world" (*ribbono shel olam*). Even God's relation to the universe is more complex than simply making the earthly part of the universe fit for life and human habitation.

The question now is: Why isn't God's relationship with every human person, for which every human person has a capacity, sufficient? Isn't the election of humankind enough for God? Why does God want to choose Israel, and choose the land of Israel for His people to settle there? We shall deal with these two subsequent questions in the following chapter.

5

Why the Jews and Why the Land of Israel?

We are now ready to deal with the two most important theological questions regarding Zionism, that is, why did God choose the Jews, and why did God choose the land of Israel for the Jews? In the previous chapter we dealt with the metaphysical questions, Why did God choose to create the universe, and why did God choose to create humans in His image? These two questions seem to be presupposed by the two questions we shall now deal with in this chapter. Nevertheless, these latter two questions can be dealt with more or less independently of their metaphysical presuppositions. Hence readers who skipped much of the previous chapter will not have lost the thrust of this book's overall argument if they pick up following the overall argument of the book in this chapter.

Let us now attempt to answer the first of the last two questions about God's choice of the Jews.

God Chooses Israel

From the creation narrative in Genesis, we learn that from the beginning God first relates Godself to humans in community, that is, as *humankind*.[1] So, before we can properly understand

---

[1] Hence *ha'adam* (Gen. 2:7, etc.), usually translated as "the man," actually means "humankind," which is a generic term. See B. Yevamot 61a and Tos.,

why God is related to *this* people Israel, we need to understand why God would desire to relate to *any* people, that is, to any specific human community in the world.

The first such human community is the marital union of a man and a woman. That union is a union of living bodies, whose chief (though not exclusive) purpose is to extend that present bodily union into the future by having children. Thus Scripture states: "Therefore a man [*ish*] shall leave his father and his mother and cleave to his wife [*ishto*], whereby they shall become one flesh." (Genesis 2:24) The great medieval commentator Rashi, in his Bible commentary, interprets "become one flesh" to mean: "the child [*vlad*] molded by the two of them, and there [i.e., the site of their genital union] their flesh [*besaram*] is made one." Commenting on the same verse in his Talmud commentary, he also notes: "Seed [*zera*] coming from them is what makes the flesh of the father and the mother one."[2] So far, though, humans are no different from other mammals who procreate through sexual intercourse.

Nevertheless, it seems that the human marital union is essentially different inasmuch as the first man is attracted to the first woman, wanting her to become his mate because he can speak with her, which he cannot do with any other creature.[3] The key factor of speech means that this union is not just one of biological necessity, but it is an essentially political union.[4] Bodies come to together through touch; but what philosophers used to call the "body politic" comes together through interactive speech or conversation. The domestic body is the beginning of the body politic. Humans need each other's bodies for such basic needs as food, clothing, and shelter; but we need each other's spirit for more than that. Humans also want somebody to converse with for a purpose that is more than instrumental for some bodily

---

s.v., "v'ein"; and B. Sanhedrin 59a and Tos., s.v. "ela" (the interpretation of Rabbenu Tam).

[2] B. Sanhedrin 58a, s.v. "mi she-na'aseh."
[3] See B. Yevamot 63a re Gen. 2:23; B. Bekhorot 8a; MR: Genesis 17.4 re Gen. 2:19.
[4] Cf. Aristotle, *Politics*, 1.1/1252a25-1252b17.

need. The speech that brings humans together is itself more than a bodily need; it has to be something humans want to know expressly. As such, a speaking relationship has to be one that the two speakers choose to enter into freely. It has to be more than necessary; it has to also be desirable. Humans are communicative animals. In fact, as Aristotle astutely noted, humans are political animals because they speak with one another; and humans speaking with one another thereby constitute their common political world.[5]

But what is the content of this political communication? If the primary topic of communication in the community is economics, that is, how to fulfill bodily needs by means that surpass the ability of a single family to fulfill them, the difference between animal herds and human communities, then, is only one of degree. The fulfillment of bodily needs is the same purpose of both animal and human collectives. It is just that human collectives fulfill these bodily needs more skillfully. For most humans, though, there should be more to life than the fulfillment of bodily needs, even the bodily need for aesthetic pleasure and amusement. Most humans need a purpose to inspire us, not just necessities to motivate us and amusements to entertain us. To be sure, as sentient beings we have much in common with animals. That is why we can sympathize with their bodily suffering and attempt to relieve it. Nonetheless, we do not share a common purpose with them, because animals are not intelligent persons; they do not choose (as far as we know) to pursue a nonphysical purpose. That is why we really don't communicate *with* them; we can only care *for* their bodily needs when they depend on us (i.e., when they are domesticated or "brought into our house" in one way or another for our use or our enjoyment). Their cries have an emotional pull on us; but they don't make an intelligent claim on us, one that we must intelligently deliberate about in order to respond to it in kind.[6] The fact is, we humans want a

---

[5] Ibid., 1.1/1253a1–5.
[6] Maimonides, *Guide of the Perplexed*, 3.17 re B. Shabbat 128b.

trans-bodily purpose, and we want to communicate about that purpose and the means to attaining it.

The content of intelligent conversation or dialogue is "teleological" or purposeful. Indeed, these purposes become known when we know with whom we are speaking and ourselves as the addresses of that speech. As we have seen, speech emerges in the world from two speech situations. First, God speaks to the human person, commanding us (him and her) to act a certain way in the world that is pleasing to God, who is the master of our world (*ribbono shel olam*).[7] Second, the man speaks to the woman, inviting her to build up the world we have been placed in by God. In both situations, the parties to the conversation have freely chosen to participate in it. In the first situation, God freely chooses to address humans; and humans freely choose whether to respond to God's address either positively or negatively. In the second situation, the man freely chooses the woman he wants to marry, and the woman freely chooses to accept his marriage proposal.[8] Moreover, in both situations, any coercion on either side could easily invalidate the mutual relationship.[9] It is significant, therefore, that in the rabbinic tradition, the covenantal relationship between God and Israel and a marriage between a man and a woman are analogous.[10]

The first speech constituted relationship is what obtains between humans and God (*bein adam le-maqom*). The second relationship is what is between humans themselves (*bein adam le-havero*). The two relationships are themselves interrelated. We humans are ultimately interested in God because God has created each of us and all of us for a free normative relationship with Godself. And we humans are ultimately interested in each other because we are all participants in the common world God has created for the divine–human relationship to be conducted

---

[7] T. Avodah Zarah 8.4; B. Sanhedrin 56a–b re Gen. 2:16.
[8] B. Kiddushin 2b and 41a.
[9] B. Baba Batra 48b and Rashbam, s.v. "Mar bar Rav Ashi" thereon; Moses of Coucy, *Sefer Mitsvot Gadol*, pos. no. 48 re Deut. 24:2; Jacob ben Asher, *Tur*: Even Ha`Ezer, 42.
[10] MR: Song of Songs 1.14 re Song of Songs 1:2.

God Chooses Israel

coherently therein. So, the essential purpose of the interhuman relationship is to enable the human community to be related to God insofar as we are to be ruled by God. And the optimal divine–human relationship can be conducted only in a human community who have freely accepted this to be their transcendent purpose, their raison d'être. (There are numerous examples in the Jewish tradition of how these interrelated relationships operate, and how conflicts between them are resolved.[11]) We humans are both the divinely oriented image of God and political beings oriented to each other. However, when our "religious" nature is reduced to our "political" nature, we become the servants of political idolatry or the divinization of the state. And, when our religious nature is separated from our political nature, it is like when Plato urged us "to fly from the world and become like God."[12] Then, the world either ignores us or, more usually, it banishes us. Thus each aspect of our nature checks the excesses of the other.

This is what human community per se is supposed to be: one community under God and living for the sake of God. Thus, after humankind is restored in the world after the Flood, when humans are reminded of the first communal commandment, which is to effect justice in the world among its human inhabitants, we humans are commanded: "Whoever sheds human blood [*dam ha'adam*], his blood shall be shed by humans [*ba'adam*], because humans [*ha'adam*] are made in God's image [*be-tselem elohim*]" (Genesis 9:6). In other words, injustice, of which murder is the worst example, is what offends both the inter-human community and the divine–human community.[13]

Already before the Flood, the interrelation of the divine–human and the interhuman realms began to unravel. Humans established societies apart from their relationship with God. About Cain, who had offended God by murdering his brother Abel, it is

---

[11] See B. Baba Metsia 30a-b and Tos., s.v. "ela"; B. Shevuot 30b and Tos., s.v. "aval."
[12] *Theatetus*, 176A–B.
[13] *Zohar*: Yitro, 2:90 re Exod. 20:2 and 13.

said: "Then Cain went away from the Lord [*mi-lifnei adonai*] ... Cain knew his wife and she conceived and gave birth to Enoch; and he then built a city, and called the city by the name of his son Enoch" (Genesis 4:16–17). Yet, in the scriptural narrative, about another man also named "Enoch" (*hanokh* or "dedicated one"), it is said: "Enoch walked with God and he was no more, for God took him away [from this world]" (Genesis 5:24). In a number of rabbinic speculations about this enigmatic character, Enoch is portrayed as a man whose devotion to God could not be correlated with involvement in contemporary politics. Therefore, he had to leave his polity and become a virtual recluse.[14] Apparently, religious commitment and political commitment were incompatible; hence Enoch had to choose between the two. He chose devotion to God over political involvement. So, the first Enoch, son of Cain, is dedicated to the polity his father established "away from the Lord," while the second Enoch, son of Jared (Genesis 5:18), is dedicated to God away from his polity. Surely, loyalty to God and loyalty to the state were on a collision course; one would inevitably try to displace the other. In ancient Israel, on the other hand, the political institution of kinship and the religious institution of the priesthood could function harmoniously together, at least in principle, because both human institutions were under the rule of God, who transcends any human institution, a point loudly proclaimed by the prophets.[15]

Political estrangement from God comes to a head when humankind does come together, but not under God's kingship. Instead, they come together in order to storm heaven and displace God altogether, replacing God's kingship with their own international authority. Thus the verse, "The whole earth had one language [*safah ahat*] with similar words" (Genesis 11:1), has been interpreted to mean that all humankind conspired together for one purpose: to wage war against God, replacing

---

[14] See M. M. Kasher, *Torah Shelemah* 1 (Jerusalem: Beth Torah Shelemah, 1992), pp. 358–60.
[15] See Amos 7:12–17; also, Shalom Spiegel, *Amos versus Amaziah* (New York: Herbert H. Lehman Institute of Ethics, 1958).

God with the Tower of Babel, the product of their own industrial ingenuity. "Let us build for ourselves a tower [*migdal*] whose head goes up into heaven; so let us make a reputation [*shem*] for ourselves" (Genesis 11:4).[16]

God's response to this universal human audacity is to undo such perverse human unity by scattering now divided humankind "all over the earth" (Genesis 11:9). Moreover, God undoes their stated desire for political unity, which could be constituted only by linguistic unity, by causing that elusive unity to unravel into linguistic/cultural diversity. Without a common project, there is no longer any need or desire for any unifying communication, thus making realistic communication the pragmatic negotiation of disparate religious, cultural, political, and economic interests. There is no unity among such radical, antagonistic divergence. Therefore the desideratum of humankind truly united for the sake of a transcendent goal, that is, to be united under God's universal sovereignty, becomes in scriptural teaching the eschatological desideratum only God can and will realize. "For then I [God] shall turn to the peoples with clear speech [*safah berurah*], to call all of them in the name of the Lord, to serve Him with one consensus [*shkhem ehad*]" (Zephaniah 3:9).[17] For humans to presume that unity is ours to achieve with us, or that it even lies on a visible horizon, is itself dangerous utopianism. In other words, the true and final unity of humankind will come only when God chooses to reestablish the universal authority He exercised at creation. "On that day the Lord will be one, and His name one" (Zechariah 14:9), which is interpreted to mean that the God who is now worshiped by Israel alone will be worshiped by everybody later; and the God who now rules Israel directly through His Torah revealed to Israel will directly rule everybody later.

Because of universal political estrangement from God, the only human relationship with God possible under these

---

[16] *Mekhilta de-Rabbi Ishmael*: Mishpatim, sec. 20 re Gen. 11:6, ed. Horovitz-Rabin, p. 332.

[17] See Kasher, *Torah Shelemah*, 1, no. 64 re Gen. 11:7, p. 515; also, MT: Kings, chap. 11 (uncensored ed.).

circumstances becomes God's relationship with lone individuals, who have either separated themselves or who have been separated from political life, as we have just seen. Thus in rabbinic speculation about the life of Abraham before his election by God, Abraham (or "Abram" as he was called before his election by God) is portrayed as a lone God-seeker in a society essentially hostile to God. And, in such a society hostile to God, it is inevitable that there will be violence and oppression among the human inhabitants who, lacking a truly equal commonality, have no real basis for seeking justice and peace among themselves. Abraham is both are a religious and a political rebel.[18]

Nevertheless, instead of being commanded to become a sort of hermit in an uninhabited wilderness (which would be a utopia, there being no such place on earth), Abraham is commanded to go to a particular land, one already inhabited and therefore inhabitable, there to found an altogether new sort of human community. Hence this new community is a theological-political entity, one where the religious and political sides of human nature are interrelated, and where neither is neglected for the sake of the other. This community is founded through a covenant between God and this particular people, who become "the unique nation [*goi ehad*] on earth" (I Chronicles 17:21), that is, they are uniquely related to "the singular [*ehad*] God" (Deuteronomy 6:5).[19] The election of Abraham, then, makes the God-human relationship in this world a *specific public* relationship instead of a *private* one with *particular* individuals outside human society. Nevertheless, that relationship is not yet the actual kingdom of God on earth (*malkhut shamayim*) with *universal* humankind.[20]

The present state of God's relationship with humans in the world is better than the relationship with lone individuals outside the world. Moreover, this *communal* relationship is not one we humans ourselves could have established with God any more

---

[18] See Louis Ginzberg, *Legends of the Jews* 1 (Philadelphia: Jewish Publication Society of America, 1909), 185–206.
[19] B. Berakhot 6a.
[20] MR: Genesis 59.8 re Gen. 24:7 (and Rashi's comment on Gen. 24:7).

than individual humans could have established the God–human relationship by themselves. How could we do so, as nothing in the world tells us that God is concerned with us at all, that God wants a relationship with us at all, that God desires us? That information can only come from God. (That also explains why humans cannot really love God unless we are convinced that God loves us first.) And God did just that when God called Abraham into the covenant, and then commanded Abraham and his descendants to live in a way that gives the covenant structure and content. "I set up [*ve-haqimoti*] My covenant between Me and you, and between your descendants after you for their generations, to be your God and your descendants' God after you" (Genesis 17:7).

God's choice of a particular people, who become a people because of God's election of them for a covenantal relationship, seems to be the best choice God could have made under the circumstances. The other options would have been to leave the divine–human relationship at the level of a divine–individual relationship, or to redeem all of humankind by making the covenant become truly universal. The first option is similar to what is called today the "privatization of religion," which makes living a religious life ultimately untenable politically, as religion, like language, is an essentially public matter.[21] The theological-political realm does not function as a public-private relation. The second option, that is, the redemption of the whole world sounds best; nevertheless it seems that God did not think humankind is ready yet for the end of history this ultimate universality entails.

This only tells us, though, *that* God's desire to elect *a* people is in God's best interest; it does not tell us, however, *why* God actually chose *this* people Israel. Now the answer to this question could be either retrospective or prospective. (The election of the covenanted people, like any divine choice as we have seen, should not be taken to be capricious, which would impugn God as irrational and unjust.) Now the Torah rules out a retrospective

---

[21] See Ludwig Wittgenstein, *Philosophical Investigations* 1, nos. 242–46, trans. G. E. M. Anscombe (New York: Macmillan, 1958), pp. 88–89.

answer: "Not because of your great numbers did God desire [*hashaq*] you to choose you, for you are the least of the nations. It is because of the Lord's love [*me'ahavat adonai*] for you, and his keeping the promise [*ha-shevu`ah*] he made to your ancestors ...." (Deuteronomy 7:7–8). Hence whatever the people Israel are able to accomplish is not due to their own meritorious efforts in the past, but rather because God "upholds His covenant [*brito*] that He promised your ancestors" (Deuteronomy 8:8). And that promise is not a promise of payment for services rendered to God by Israel. Instead, it is a promise of divine grace or charity. "You should not say in your heart ... because of my righteousness [*be-tsidqati*] the Lord has brought me to inherit this land" (Deuteronomy 9:4).

It seems better to assume that the answer to the question "Why Israel?" is prospective rather than retrospective. Israel's election is not because of what the Jews have been in the past. It is because of what they will be in the future, a future only God can truly anticipate. But, were this future to be revealed to us by God in the present, it would cease to be an open possibility, as we saw in the previous chapter. Were that the case, then we humans would have to do nothing in the present, because there would be nothing we could change, there being no possibilities to be chosen here and now. The future would not be dependent on anything we could do; everything would have already been done. Our freedom of choice would be pointless. So, it is only when God brings about the radically transcendent future that we will know why and how the deeds of this particular people contributed to it especially. That knowledge will *then* be retrospective, but it will be a retrospective knowledge that no creature has the capacity to know as yet. It is what "no eye but God's could see" (Isaiah 64:3).[22] But as of now, this world is not yet ready for the optimal God–human relationship, which is with all humankind and the whole universe along with us, the fulfillment of the covenant being the purpose of all creation. "Were My covenant [*briti*] not by day and by night, I would

---

[22] B. Berakhot 34b.

not have established the laws of heaven and earth" (Jeremiah 33:25).[23] However, as we shall see in Chapter 8, that is an eschatological matter; it is for God not us to bring about in the world. Our task is to actively wait for that end by living the life of the covenant prescribed by God in the Torah. "The hidden matters [*ha-nistarot*] are the Lord our God's; but what has been revealed [*ve-ha-niglot*] are for us and our children to do all the words of this Torah" (Deuteronomy 29:28).

One cannot assert an explicit reason why God chose *this* people Israel, as that would require one to locate some unique natural or historic factor in the life of the people that they possess and that they know they possess. If the people knew that it is *because* of *that* factor they were in fact chosen, then their chosenness would become their worldly possession rather than their task to fulfill in the world. But their task in the world is to show God, themselves, and the world that God did not make a mistake by choosing this people in the first place. That task always lies before them; it is never a *fait accompli*. So, when we Jews blatantly reject the task of actually proclaiming the sanctity of God's name or reputation (*qiddush ha-shem*) to the world or to themselves, the reputation of God in the world is tarnished (*hillul ha-shem*).[24] Nevertheless, even though the knowledge of some unique factor they already possess would deprive them of any incentive to fulfill their task in the world of being "My [active] witnesses and my servant whom I have chosen" (Isaiah 43:10), there could still be some precondition for the election of Israel, without which it seems the Jews would be in no position to actively accept their being chosen and to act accordingly. (This is what philosophers call a *conditio sine qua non*.) In other words, though God *could* choose any people, it is unlikely God *would* have chosen a people who lacked the capacity to understand what it means to be ruled by God directly when they do not even understand what it means to be ruled by God indirectly through natural or universal moral law.

---

[23] B. Pesahim 68b.
[24] See, for example, MT: Robbery and Loss, 11.7.

This comes out in a famous rabbinic legend about God offering the Torah to other peoples before He actually offered it to the people Israel (who accepted it without question).[25] Now you might have thought that when the various peoples asked what is in the Torah for them to do, God would have told them some of the commandments unique to the Mosaic Torah like the dietary restrictions or the Sabbath. In fact, that is what Jews are supposed to tell gentiles who are considering conversion to Judaism and thereby full membership in the Jewish people.[26] Instead of that, though, God tells them about the prohibitions of murder, incest, and robbery. These prohibitions are not unique to the Mosaic Torah; they are the core of the Noahide commandments (to be discussed more fully in Chapter 7), which all humans are obligated to keep, because all humans are expected to know them due to their being rationally evident to everybody.[27] Even though the Jews did accept God's full Torah unquestioningly (unlike the other peoples), the legend seems to assume that the Jews had *already* accepted these basic moral laws; indeed, it is this prior acceptance of them that made it possible for the Jews to accept the full Mosaic Torah intelligently and willingly. Thus it could be said that this prior acceptance is a necessary but not sufficient condition of the Jews having been elected to receive the full Torah.

Perhaps there were other peoples as well for whom this acceptance would have been possible, so we cannot say the Jews were the only such morally earnest people in the world. We cannot say God couldn't have chosen one of them rather than the Jews. The Jews were probably not God's only option. Nevertheless, the Rabbis seem to be saying that although we cannot know for sure why God did choose *this* people Israel ("from out of all the other peoples" as the liturgy puts it), we can be more certain of why God didn't choose some of Israel's neighbors at the time of

---

[25] *Sifrei*: Deuteronomy, no. 343 re Deut. 33:2, ed. Finkelstein, pp. 395–96.
[26] B. Yevamot 47a.
[27] See David Novak, *Natural Law in Judaism* (Cambridge: Cambridge University Press, 1998).

the elective giving of the Torah at Mount Sinai. For those lacking this basic moral commitment would be in no position to accept God's election of them to a higher level of sanctity.[28] The human acceptance of that more specific level of sanctity presupposes the acceptance of the more general level of sanctity below it that makes that ascent possible, but not necessary or automatic. In other words, without a solid foundation, you cannot build a solid house upon it, even though the fact of a solid foundation doesn't mean a house *has to* be built upon it at all. Moreover, that affirmation of the law does not mean the Jews were or were expected to be perfect in their observance of it.[29] After all, "the Torah [even the Noahide proto-Torah] is not given to ministering angels."[30]

Just as the acceptance of the Mosaic Torah doesn't necessarily have to follow from the acceptance of the more general Noahide law, so the acceptance of the Torah by the Jewish people does not mean the Jews have to try to get everybody else to follow suit. In my opinion, and in the opinion of almost everybody in the Jewish tradition for the past two thousand years, *this* chosen people should not expand into that optimal united humankind by actively bringing to the world the message and content of the Torah revealed to Israel by means of universal proselytization (though there is no actual prohibition of doing that). Whether Jews really did proselytize in antiquity or not, for the past two thousand years Jews have taken a decidedly different stance toward the world from that of Christianity and Islam. Moreover, I think that this aversion to proselytization, which is quite different from accepting gentiles who come on their own to a Jewish community to convert to Judaism, is not just because the Christians and Muslims under whose political rule Jews had to live for so long often forbade them from even

---

[28] See B. Yevamot 22a.
[29] For the difference between "affirmation" (*qiyyum*) of the law and total doing (*asiyyah*) of the law's commandments, see B. Baba Kama 38a and B. Avodah Zarah 2b re Hab. 3:6; Nahmanides, *Commentary on the Torah*: Deut. 27:26 (cf. Paul, *Galatians* 3:10 re LXX on Deut. 27:26).
[30] B. Kiddushin 54a.

accepting converts. I think Jews would still have this aversion to proselytizing even if it hadn't been politically dangerous for centuries. Instead, the Jewish people should wait for God to bring the world to them, that is, when the nations of the world want to become part of God's covenant with Israel. "It shall come to pass in the end of days when the mountain of the House of the Lord shall be firmly set at the top of the mountains, exalted above the hills, that all the nations [*kol ha-goyyim*] shall flow towards it. And many peoples [*ammim rabbim*] will go and say: 'let us go up to the mountain of the Lord, to the House of the God of Jacob, that He may instruct us of His ways so that we walk in His paths" (Isaiah 2:2).[31]

Furthermore, the type of proselytizing or quasi-proselytizing, which is often suggested by those who speak of the Jewish people being "a light to the nations," is based on their misreading a key scriptural text. The verse reads that God "will raise up the tribes of Jacob, to return the survivors of Israel; I shall make you a light of nations [*l'or goyyim*], that My salvation reach the ends of the earth" (Isaiah 49:6). When read in context, the verse does not speak of the Jews having some sort of mandate to go out and enlighten the gentiles (let alone conquer them), as the verse does not speak of the Jews extending, or being commanded to extend "light *to* the nations" (*or la-goyyim*). Instead, the verse speaks of what God *will do*, that is, when God redeems the Jewish people at the time of the future and complete redemption (*ge'ulah shlemah*). This very act of God will enlighten the gentiles, inspiring them to want to be part of this divinely effected redemption of Israel. This is what God promises to do for the Jews, one effect of which will be the enlightenment of the gentiles. It is what God promises to do Himself, not what God commands Israel to do on His behalf, let alone what the Jews can do or should do on their own behalf. The enlightenment of the gentiles is a divine project, not a human one.

Restraint from active proselytizing follows from the fact that God chooses Israel; Israel does not choose God. The Jews can

[31] See David Novak, "The Jewish Mission," *First Things*, no. 227 (2012), 39–43.

only choose to confirm or deny (though not with impunity) their election by God. Thus the Jews should only wait for God to elect the rest of humankind along with them in the transcendent future, which lies beyond our worldly horizon. In the meantime, Jews should strive to live their covenant with God as best they can, but without any progressive trajectory driving them. And just as Jews ought not act as if they elected God to be their Sovereign, so they ought not elect themselves to become God's regents over all humankind. Election is specific; only God can truly universalize it into completion, just as only God can initiate it.

The election of Israel is not due to any inherent properties, either biological (with their racist implications) or cultural (with their chauvinistic implications), by which Jews can claim to be inherently superior to the rest of humankind.[32] The Jewish people differ from the rest of humankind only because of God's claim upon them to live with God in what is a monogamous relationship, that is, on their side of the covenant. Thus the same prophet who says to Israel in God's name, "Only you have I intimately known of all the families of the earth" (Amos 2:3), also reminds the people that just as "I have brought Israel up out of the land of Egypt," God has also rescued "the Philistines from Caphtor and Aram from Kir" (Amos 9:7). Outside that covenantal relationship with God, the Jewish people are no different from any other people; hence they should not represent ourselves to be the only humans God is concerned with. Israel's unique relationship with God, which is essentially God's relationship with them, is a reality *between* Israel and God alone, not between the Jewish people and the world. Even despite the Holocaust, Jews have no

---

[32] Even when Jews are considered to have certain "traits" (*simanim*) or virtues (*middot*), like compassion, modesty, and kindness (B. Yevamot 79a re Deut. 13:18, Exod. 20:17, Gen. 18:19; MT: Forbidden Intercourse, 19.17 and Vidal of Tolosa, *Maggid Mishneh* thereon), all of them are the subsequent effects of a relationship with God, not the prior cause of that relationship. They are all acquired cultural traits, not ontological realities. In the kabbalistic tradition, though, Jews are considered to be a different species from the rest of humankind, thus possessing different specific properties. See *Zohar*: Ber'esheet, 1:20b; Emor, 3:104b, based on the view of Rabbi Simeon ben Yohai (assumed to be the author of the *Zohar*) on B. Yevamot 61a re Ezek. 34:31.

special claim on the world; they only have the claim any people has to be treated justly by the world, both as individuals and as a people. But the Jews do have a claim on God to redeem them, even though they have no right to set the date or even know it. "I know My Redeemer lives, though he be the last to arise on earth ... then from my own flesh I shall see God" (Job 19:25).

To cogently affirm that God chose the people Israel is to thereby deny that the Jews chose God. And, that affirmation thereby denies that the Jews chose themselves to be different from every other people as end in itself. That affirmation also denies that the Jews choose to be a conquering people (*Herrenvolk* in German), that is, a people dedicated to obliterating every other people's difference from them by absorbing these other peoples into the political and cultural domain of the Jews. That is a counterfeit universalism, for it makes one particularity universal by default (the covenant is certainly particular, being between the unique God and a particular or unique people). It becomes universal by obliterating in one way or another every other particularity. That is now what we call a "zero-sum game." Conversely, "Then I [God] shall turn to the peoples [including Israel] with clear speech, calling all of them [*khulam*] in the name of the Lord, to serve Him with one shoulder" (Zephaniah 3:9).

To affirm that the Jews chose God (as did Spinoza, as we saw in Chapter 2) is to assume that the Jews by their own rational powers discovered the one true God and, then, decided they wanted this God to be their sovereign, that is, they elected Him. (That also means they could unelect God and replace His rule with someone else, if they found a more politically effective alternative, as Spinoza thought.[33]) But that is not what happened in the scriptural account of the initiation of the covenant between God and Israel. Instead, the people only learn of the God who cares for them when that God reveals to them how He is electing them for this covenantal relationship. "I take you to be a people who is mine, and I shall be God for you" (Exodus 6:7). Before that

---

[33] *Tractatus Theologico-Politicus*, chapter 17, trans. M. Silverthorne and J. Israel (Cambridge: Cambridge University Press, 2007), pp. 213–19. See Chapter 2.

revelation, the people know nothing of God's real care for them, which is God's actively delivering on what were only promises to their ancestors about an unknown future.[34] (The most humans can surmise apart from revelation is there might be a God who makes them different from all other creatures.) In other words, humans are *elected by* God their Sovereign to be God's own people before they themselves could possibly *elect* anyone else to be their own sovereign. Once humans are elected by God, though, they have no right to elect anyone else to replace God. This is like our relationship with our parents: once they have chosen to bring us into the world, we cannot really replace them with others. (Other parental figures can perform the functions of a father and a mother only when the real parents are either unable or unwilling to be responsible for their offspring whom they have brought into the world.) The choice of who our God is to be is not ours to make any more than it is our choice to be born and who is to give us our birth.[35] "I am the Lord [YHWH] your God who has brought you out of the land of Egypt, out of slavery"; therefore, "You shall have no other gods [as sovereign] beside Me" (Exodus 20:2–3).

The people Israel only have the choice to either confirm or deny their election by God. When they do confirm that covenantal election, they are given much authority or voluntariness to interpret and develop the Torah, which is the constitution of that covenantal relationship, as they see fit.[36] But, when they attempt to repudiate their election by God, God does not accept their illegitimate autonomy to do so with impunity. When this happens (and

---

[34] MR: Exodus 6.2 re Exod. 6:3, ed. A. Shanan, pp. 184–85; *Midrash Leqah Tov*: Exodus (va'era) 3 re Exod. 6:3, ed. Buber, p. 15b.
[35] M. Avot 4.22.
[36] B. Baba Metsia 59a re Deut. 30:12. This text that speaks of the Torah as "not being in Heaven" (*lo ba-shamayim hi*) has been distorted by many liberal Jewish thinkers to buttress their argument that the Torah is, *de facto*, a human matter. However, in rabbinic teaching, both the *archē* and the *telos* of the Torah are divine. "The Torah from Heaven [a euphemism for the transcendent God]" (M. Sanhedrin 10.1) and the study and practice of the Torah are "for the sake of Heaven" (M. Avot 2.12). See David Novak, *The Jewish Social Contract* (Princeton, NJ: Princeton University Press, 2005), 65–81.

it happens regularly), God reiterates His covenantal claim over and over again, often through that minority of Jews, the "remnant of Israel" (*she'erit yisra'el*), who have always remained faithful to the covenant all along.[37] God does not allow them to unelect themselves and thereby nullify the covenant with Him, no matter how far they have strayed.[38] So they, as it were, do not let God unelect them and thereby nullify the covenant. That is because, even though God did not have to choose the people Israel, once God did choose the people that choice became irrevocable. God is responsible for the choice He has made, because that choice was not capricious. That choice was made by means of an oath (*shevuah*).[39] Were God to break His oath, He would thereby cease to have any moral authority over them, as a liar is no longer to be trusted, and all moral authority is based on trust.[40]

Some have said, in the words of the secular Israeli philosopher and Bible scholar Yehezkel Kaufmann (d. 1963), that the election of Israel (*behirat yisra'el*) is "an old religious idea the Jews thought of themselves as a holy race (*zer`a qodesh*)."[41] That seems to be saying that the Jews chose themselves. But how do people choose themselves? Isn't "choose" a transitive verb, describing an external relation between a subject who *chooses* and a separate object who is *chosen*? (This is what philosophers call the problem of "self-reference.") So, it would seem that to say a people choose themselves means that they choose to be different from every other people and make that differing (what some French philosophers call *la différence même*) their raison d'être, that is, their very purpose for being in the world. (In fact, this is what Spinoza accused the Jews in the Diaspora of.[42]) Nevertheless, difference for the sake of difference becomes a never ending process

---

[37] Isa. 46:3; Jer. 23:3–4; Ezek. 11:13–21.
[38] B. Sanhedrin 44a re Josh. 7:11; Novak, *The Election of Israel*, 138–43, 189–99.
[39] B. Berakhot 32a re Exod. 32:13.
[40] B. Makkot 4b re Exod. 20:13; B. Sanhedrin 29a re I Kings 21:10; MT: Testimony, 17.2.
[41] *Exile and Estrangement* 1 [Heb.] (Tel Aviv: Dvir, 1930), 217.
[42] *Tractatus Theologico-Politicus*, chapter 3, p. 55.

of negating everything and anything in Jewish life that seems to make Jews like the other peoples in the world, no matter how trivial that likeness really is.[43] In effect, it becomes national nihilism. So, to preclude this national nihilism, the people Israel need to know: *Who* chose them; *what* that covenantal election consists of; *how* that covenantal election is to be lived concretely; and *why* they have been elected. Their differences from the other peoples are the result of their affirmation of these realities, not the negation of them or their difference from them for its own sake. Hence their affirmation of *this* God entails their negation or denial of the reality of any other god; their affirmation of *this* covenant entails their negation or denial of the primary claim of any other covenant upon them; their affirmation of this covenantal way of life entails a negation or denial of any other way of life for them. And their affirmation that Jews' purpose in the world is to be faithful to the covenant entails their negation or denial of any other competing purpose for themselves in the world. In each case, then, negation presupposes positive affirmation, not vice versa.

Choosing to make the rest of the world like oneself seems to avoid the nihilism of difference for the sake of difference. Nevertheless, even though the unity of the world seems to be a positive end, and negating everybody else's difference from oneself seems to be only the means to that positive goal or end, does the end justify the means?[44] And, has that good end ever been attained in this world? So, isn't one left with the negative means alone when the end seems to be infinite and, hence, always beyond one's positive attainment of it? That is what inevitably happens when one believes oneself to be God's regent for the

---

[43] Those who endlessly seek to accentuate Jewish difference from the rest of the world (and often the rest of the Jewish world too) usually base this on the prohibition: "You shall not go according to their [the gentiles'] laws" (Lev. 18:3). However, this applies only to specifically religious practices of the gentiles. *Sifra*: Aharei-Mot, ed. Weiss, p. 86a; B. Shabbat 67a; Rashi, *Commentary on the* Torah: Lev. 18:3; MT: Sabbath, 19.13; Maimonides, *Guide of the Perplexed*, 3.37.

[44] B. Sukkah 30a re Mal. 1:13; also, LXX and *Targumim* on Deut. 16:20.

governance of the world. Instead, though, the Jews are chosen to be God's servants, not to rule the world as if they were God. Indeed, the recurrent fantasy of the enemies of the Jews is that the latter have chosen to conquer the world (which is often a projection of these enemies' own desires). One of the tasks in keeping the commandment to "sanctify God's name in the world" (*qiddush ha-shem*) is to demonstrate to the world how the Jews are the servants of God, not their would-be rulers.[45] Only doing that makes God's election of Israel truly different from the Jews electing themselves.

Finally, this intimate, intense, covenantal relationship with Israel notwithstanding, God still has a life of God's own before, after, and alongside the creation of the universe. Just as God is still concerned with the rest of the universe after and alongside God's creation of humankind in God's image, so is God still concerned with all other human beings (individually and collectively) after and alongside God's election of Israel.[46] That needs to be emphasized whenever the Jewish people try to confine God's concern to God's covenantal relationship to be with themselves alone. Indeed, the Jews need to be reminded of the asymmetry of the covenant: God is not contained or constrained by his covenant with Israel, unlike the people Israel, who are contained and constrained by their having been covenanted by God. The asymmetry of all three of these God–creation relationships: between God and the universe, between God and humankind, and between God and the people Israel, all of them must be regularly recalled lest any one of them is taken to be a symbiosis that eclipses the transcendent freedom of God.

However, being confined to the world, the people Israel need a place to call home in this world, a place in which to center the God–Israel covenant. As the most famous Israeli philosopher, Martin Buber (d. 1965), stated so well: "The unconditional relationship between a people and a land is to be taken up into the covenant [*Bund*] between God and the people."[47]

---

[45] B. Sanhedrin 74a re Lev. 22:32; Deut. 6:5.
[46] See, for example, Jonah 3:10–11.
[47] *Israel und Palästina* (Zürich: Artemis-Verlag, 1950), 34; see ibid., 161.

God Chooses the Land of Israel

It seems that Abraham was regarded by the people of Canaan to be a nomad, a designation even he accepted by calling himself a "transient resident" (*ger ve-toshav* – Genesis 23:4). But is that his permanent status and that of his people in the world or not? Now there have been both Jews and non-Jews who have thought that being "the Wandering Jew," forever homeless in any and all lands, is an essential strength of the Jewish people, one Jews should take special pride in. In this view, the Jews' strength is that they are not tied down to any land, thus making the real homelessness of all humans in this world an asset rather than a liability. But, if this were the true status of the Jewish people, they would have the same dichotomy we saw when considering what the God–human relationship would be like were it to be an essentially private relationship between God and some isolated individual humans. For if that were the case, the essentially political nature of humans would be left out of the God–human relationship, as the relation of a polity to a particular *territory* is a political necessity.[48] Even Bedouins are always dependent on some real political *location* they are wandering *around*. (A wilderness is always framed by the habitation it is outside of.) To be sure, even in exile, Jews can still retain their communal life, but they are still living *under* the political domain of some other people. The Jews would still be living as aliens in any society whose warrant comes from a non-Jewish historical revelation (like that of Christianity or Islam). Or, they would be living as anonymous individual citizens of a society whose warrant comes from a social contract among equals that does not directly stem from their different prior communal commitments. And in this type of liberal society, a Jewish community (*qahal*) can only be a private association of individuals. This is why the optimal existence of the Jewish people is in a special land of their own. Thus the Torah teaches that just as God chose the people Israel to be his

---

[48] See David Novak, "Land and People: One Jewish Perspective" in *Boundaries and Justice*, ed. D. Miller and S. H. Hashemi (Princeton, NJ: Princeton University Press, 2001), 213–36.

special covenanted people, so did God choose the land of Israel to be the locus of that covenant in the world, that is, the place (*maqom*) where the covenant is to be lived primarily. Thus a rabbinic comment compares the chosenness of the people Israel and the chosenness of the land of Israel: "God said to Moses that the land is precious [*havivah*] to me ... and [the people] Israel is precious to me ... I shall thus bring Israel who is precious to me into the land that is precious to me."[49]

It would seem that God's other options vis-à-vis the land for His covenanted people Israel would be to either let the people choose whatever land they wanted for themselves, or to let the people conquer one land to be the headquarters of the universal project to conquer the world for the Jews' covenant with God, or to let the people think of themselves as aboriginal natives of the land, that is, that the land is their natural location in the world.

The first option or possibility would be similar to the view rejected earlier in the previous chapter, that is, that God created the universe as a *fait accompli* and then turned it loose to function autonomously on its own. In this case, allowing the people to choose their own land to conquer would be like saying that God chose to create the people Israel then, but they are now on their own to do as they see fit for themselves. Contrary to this opinion, however, the Torah states: "You should know that it is not because of your righteousness [*be-tsidqatekha*] that the Lord your God gives you [*noten lekha*] this good land to inherit it [*le-rishtah*]" (Deuteronomy 9:6). This means the people Israel have no right or claim to take any land because of what they have made of themselves. Thus the verse concludes: "for you are a stiff-necked people." The land, then, is a gift to the people from God, not as recompense for their righteousness, but rather as a task for the people to fulfill: "to inherit it." In other words (as we shall examine more closely in the next chapter), Jewish settlement of the land of Israel is a divine commandment (*mitsvah*), a task the Jews are to fulfill for the sake of their communal covenant with God. So, it is not the land that is given to them as

---

[49] MR: Numbers 23.7 re Deut. 11:12.

passive recipients, but rather the commandment to settle the land that is given to them by God. The commandment is what God has chosen for them to do; the land of Israel is where God has chosen for them to do it.

Like all the divine commandments, this is not a task humans have chosen for themselves autonomously. (There are such voluntary tasks in the Jewish tradition, but they are thought to be for the sake of what we discern to be the overall purposes of the Torah.[50]) Were the choice of the land of Israel theirs to make autonomously, this autonomy could then lead them to pick any land they thought best for themselves here and now, or they could decide there is no land here and now that suits them. In fact, not having a theological foundation for his Jewish nationalism, Theodor Herzl thought that the offer of Uganda in Africa as a Jewish homeland, made by the British Government, was more in the interest of the Jewish people than was the land of Israel (i.e., Turkish-ruled Palestine at the time).

Having no good theological foundation, the historical argument against Herzl's preference for Uganda (i.e., the Jewish people were sovereign only in the land of Israel) made by Chaim Weizmann (who became the first president of the State of Israel in 1948) and others was also insufficient. For the "historic connection" of the Jewish people seems rather tenuous in the face of the Palestinian Arabs who make the same historical claim on the land, and it seems with much more history of living in the land on their side. So, if the Jewish people have a more cogent claim on the land, that claim should be the biblical one that pertains to the land of Israel alone, that is, it is because God chose this land for the Jewish people to settle there as permanently as is humanly possible.

Conversely, though, Israel's Declaration of Independence speaks of the "historic right" (*zekhut historit*) of the Jewish people to the land of Israel.[51] But this document fails to indicate just

---

[50] See, for example, B. Baba Kama 100a re Exod. 18:20 and Tos., s.v. "lifnim"; B. Sanhedrin 6b–7a re Zech. 8:9.
[51] www.knesset.gov.il/docs/heb/megilat.htm and www.science.co.il/Israel-Declaration-of-Independence.php

what an "historic right" means. Isn't the historic connection of the Jewish people to the land of Israel expressed in their claim on the nations of the world to let them fulfill the duty God has placed upon them to acquire and settle the land God has chosen for them? And in today's world, they can do that only by becoming a nation-state among the other nation-states of the world. This duty (*hovah*) is one that the Jews cannot abrogate, any more than they could repeal a commandment of the Torah, even when they could not fulfill this duty because of circumstances beyond their control.[52] Indeed, throughout much of Jewish history, when most Jews couldn't live in the land of Israel because of insurmountable physical, political, and economic obstacles, they still did not despair or lose hope (*ye'ush*) of resuming their independent communal life there. As the Zionist anthem *Hatikvah* puts it: "We still did not lose our hope."[53] Perhaps it could be said that the *historic right* of the Jewish people to the land of Israel is their right to return there to be fully the people God wants them to be, there especially, and which they have tried to be throughout their history, even when they were prevented from being there because of insurmountable political and economic factors.

Of course, this theological claim is primarily a claim to be made by Jews among themselves.[54] As was argued in the first

---

[52] B. Ketubot 110b, Tos., s.v. "hu omer."

[53] The phrase is taken from Ezek. 37:11.

[54] To designate this traditional Jewish claim on the land of Israel as "subjective," and our international claim as "objective," as does the historian Gideon Shimoni in his book, *The Zionist Ideology* (Hanover, NH: Brandeis University Press, 1995), pp. 348–59, makes the traditional claim a kind of special pleading, coming from idiosyncratic private motives. Nevertheless, when Jews invoke the traditional claim among themselves (and to those gentiles on their theological wavelength), their claim is based on revelation; and revelation is taken by them to be a higher, objective reality, whose Author has ultimate authority over them. Their claim is not a subjective preference or prejudice, therefore. It is dismissed as "subjective" only by those who think revelation is impossible, and who usually explain away the claim of those who do believe revelation is not only possible, but real, by subjective motives these people are unconscious of. However, the only impossibility is logical impossibility; yet there is a logic in what is represented as revelation. It clearly has meaning even if its truth cannot be proven, or disproven (M. Rosh Hashanah 2.6;

chapter, Jews need internal Jewish reasons for themselves for being Zionists before they can make external secular reasons for their Zionism to the nations of the world, reasons that seem to be genuine and not apologetic. These secular reasons can be made anywhere to anybody, but they must still come from somebody somewhere in the world. The authenticity of these external claims is suspect, though, if they come from anonymities who are nowhere or everywhere in their own minds. Nevertheless, contrary to the view of extreme secularists (who only argue *ad extra*) and extreme religious nationalists (who only argue *ad intra*), the two claims are not polar opposites. Instead, they can be coordinated rationally. So, Jews can claim that they are fulfilling the task assigned to them by God of acquiring and settling the land of Israel, and they are doing that by means of standards accepted internationally for the exercise of political sovereignty (*shilton* in Classical Hebrew) by a particular people in a particular country.[55]

Because Jews and Christians share the Hebrew Bible as divine revelation, the Jewish theological claim on the land of Israel is one that is theologically valid for them as well. Christians who are faithful to their own tradition, therefore, believe or should believe that God's covenant with the Jewish people and with the land of Israel as their inheritance is everlasting and forever valid. It has only been supplemented, not superseded or replaced, by Christianity.[56] (Whether, though, a similarly theological claim could be accepted by Muslims is questionable, however.) Nevertheless, Muslims might well resonate to arguments to be made in Chapter 7 that show how the Jewish tradition recognizes political equality between Jews and non-Jews

---

MT: Foundations of the Torah, 7.6). And, nobody can prove that something experienced by somebody else didn't actually occur, unless it can be shown that those who claim to have experienced an event in one place were actually somewhere else (M. Makkot 1.4).

[55] See David Novak, *Jewish Social Ethics* (New York: Oxford University Press, 1992), 199–201.

[56] See Maimonides, *Responsa* 1, no. 149, ed. Y. Blau (Jerusalem: Miqitsei Nirdamim, 1957), pp. 284–85; also, David Novak, *Jewish-Christian Dialogue* (New York: Oxford University Press, 1989), 64–72.

in the land of Israel, and especially between Jewish monotheists and non-Jewish monotheists.

The claim that God chose the land of Israel for the people Israel is also contrary to the claim that Jews have a natural right (as distinct from an historic right) to the land of Israel, even though Israel's Declaration of Independence speaks of the Jews' "natural right" (*zekhut tiv`it*) to the land. Yet the fact is, the Jews (or Israelites) are not the aboriginal people in the land. Like Abraham, they come from somewhere else to the land at God's explicit command. "The Lord said to Abram: 'Go, get yourself out of your land, and from your birthplace [*u-mi-moladetekha*], and from your patrimony, to the land I will show you" (Genesis 12:1). So, when Abraham deals with the aboriginal people of Canaan, he acknowledges: "I am only a transient resident [*ger ve-toshav*] among you" (Genesis 23:4).[57] From this it follows that just as the special covenantal status of the people Israel is not a natural fact, neither is the connection of the people to the land a natural fact. And, as we have already seen, every fact in the world, whether natural or historic, is taken by the Jewish people to be either the result of a divine choice or the result of a human choice. That is because neither historic facts nor natural facts themselves explain why they exist rather than not exist. Nothing is "just there." Everything has been "put there" by someone or other. That is why the land does not *belong* to the Jews – or to anybody else – for nothing in creation *belongs* to any creature. Everything and everybody belong to God alone.[58] As such, God assigns the land of Israel to the people Israel like an innkeeper assigns the room he or she wants a guest to inhabit during his or her brief sojourn there.[59] Therefore, their place in the world, their "somewhere," is to be in the land of Israel. The Jews are not meant to be anywhere (like nomads) or nowhere (like "rootless cosmopolitans").

---

[57] See Rashi's comment thereon. Cf. MR: Genesis 58.6 re Gen. 12:7, ed. Theodor-Albeck, p. 624.
[58] I Chron. 29:14–15.
[59] Rashi's comment on Gen. 1:1. See *Yalqut Shimoni*: Bo, no. 187.

God Chooses the Land of Israel

That the Jewish connection to the land of Israel is not a natural fact makes one think of why God chose *a* land for the Jewish people, but not why God chose *this* land for them. Ordinarily, it would seem that the only reason for the choice of a particular land would have to be because of its natural or geographic properties, that is, that it has more useful resources for the people than any other land has. However, what would these natural resources be, and how could we show that they are unique to this land? Therefore, just as we cannot know what inherent genetic characteristics the Jewish people have that would make them naturally superior to the other peoples of the world, so we cannot know what inherent geographic properties make the land of Israel superior to the other lands of the world.[60]

To presume, that the Jews are naturally superior and that the land is naturally superior suggests a type of racism that the Jewish tradition largely rejects. For, if the Jews are naturally or biologically unique, then how could the tradition encourage them to accept converts from non-Jewish stock?[61] If the land of Israel is naturally or geographically unique, then how could the tradition permit Jews to live anywhere else? Thus we can assume that God's specific reasons for both the election of *this* people Israel and *this* land of Israel do exist in the mind of God (who is not to be believed to be a capricious God), but they are unknown and unknowable to humans, at least while we are still in *this* world. "My plans [*mahshavotai*] are not your plans." (Isaiah 55:8). Hence the connection of the people Israel to the land of Israel is best thought of as being a fact of divine election. The Jewish connection to the land of Israel is not the result of the choice of the Jews. Their choice is only to either confirm or deny that connection, that is, to be or not to be a Zionist in the

---

[60] Cf. Judah Halevi, *Kuzari*, 2.10–23; 4.17, who sees the land of Israel having unique physical qualities to make it the site for the relationship between God and the people Israel, and which he seems to think are scientifically demonstrable. Aside from the theological problem with this view, it didn't stand up to the standards of natural science, even those of the early twelfth century when Halevi wrote *Kuzari*.

[61] M. Yedayim 4.4 and B. Berakhot 28a re Isa. 10:13.

deepest sense. This human choice is subsequent to God's choice to elect whomever God elects.[62] Perhaps the specific reasons for God's election of the people and of the land will be revealed in the "end-time" (*ahareet ha-yamim*), when other secrets will also be revealed to those whom God elects to be alive then.

That living in the land of Israel is God's choice for us, not our choice for ourselves, comes out in the following rabbinic ruling:

> Somebody who dwells in an inn in the land of Israel or who rents a house outside the land: for the first thirty days they are exempt from affixing a *mezuzah* [to the doorpost]; thereafter they are obligated [*hayyav*] to do so. But somebody who rents a house in the land of Israel must affix a *mezuzah* immediately [*l'altar*], because of the [duty] of settling in [*yishuv*] the land of Israel.[63]

The reason for this legal distinction, it seems to me, is that where a Jew dwells in the Diaspora is that person's choice, a choice that one needs to have a certain amount of time to deliberate whether where he or she has first settled down is actually the place he or she would really like to live in, or whether it is only a very temporary arrangement. But, because a Jew is obeying a commandment (what kind of commandment will be discussed in the next chapter) to dwell in the land has already been made for him or her by God. As such, in that case, we are not given the time for deliberation about our choice, as the choice is not ours to begin with. The decision has already been made for us at Sinai.[64] *That we should live in the land has been decided for us before we came to the land, indeed, before we were born. Our only legitimate decision is* how *we shall live in the land; whether we shall stay or leave the land is not our legitimate decision to make.*

The third option vis-à-vis the land that God could have chosen would be to designate the Jewish people to be an essentially world-conquering people (*Herrenvolk*), whose raison d'être is to extend its political domain throughout the entire world, thereby making *our* God *the* God over all humankind. Some

---

[62] Exod. 33:19.
[63] B. Menahot 44a. See Y. Shekalim 3.3/47c.
[64] Nedarim 8a.

have seen this to be the desideratum of restoring humankind the unity that was lost after the downfall of the Tower of Babel. However, wouldn't such a project turn Israel's dependence on God's redemption of us (and the rest of the world along with us) into Israel's presumptive redemption of the world and of God too along with the world? Wouldn't this compromise God's transcendence of the world by clearly implying that redemption (*ge'ulah*) is basically a matter of human initiation and projection, rather than properly asserting "dominion [*ha-melukhah*] is the Lord's" (Obadiah 1:21)?

By limiting the full national existence of the people Israel to the land of Israel, Jews are best able to live their specific covenantal relationship with God. In the land of Israel, that relationship is truly centered. Jews can thus overcome the sundering of their communal existence from their national existence, which would be the case were they to be an essentially "stateless" community in the world. And Jews thus overcome the imperialist temptation to regard the redemption of the whole world to be *their own* project, of which they could brag "my strength and the might of my hand have accomplished for me this success" (Deuteronomy 8:17).

Just as God's concern is not confined to the people Israel alone, God's relationship with them is *special*; yet it is not a *symbiosis*. So too, the relationship of the people Israel with the land of Israel is special, not exclusive. That means (as we shall see in the next chapter) the Jewish people are centered in the land of Israel; they are not confined there, however. Though inferior to Jewish life in the land of Israel, Jewish life outside Israel, in the Diaspora (*golah*) has Jewish legitimacy. Moreover (as we shall see in Chapter 7), we can acknowledge in good faith that the land of Israel is not confined to Jews. As such, Jews can recognize the right of non-Jews to live in the land of Israel: either as individual citizens in a Jewish state there, or *even* having a state of their own within the boundaries of the entire land of Israel. That is because, even though the land of Israel has been given to the Jews to govern, inhabit, and primarily develop, nonetheless they may not regard that land to be their own possession to do with as they please, to act in their *own* perceived self-interest. "You too are resident-aliens [*gerim ve-toshavim*] with Me" (Leviticus 25:23). An old rabbinic text has God saying to the people Israel in the land: "Don't make yourselves the chief factor [*iqqar*] ... whatever is yours is Mine."[65] All this presupposes that "the earth is the Lord's and all that fills it; the world [*tevel*] and all who inhabit it" (Psalms 24:1). Even God's elect people should not assume they are like God in this respect. They can only use what God has permitted them to use in this world, and in the way God has commanded them to use it.[66]

The Jews are not God's vicarious landlords. Like the first humans in the Garden of Eden, they are only placed in the land "to work it and to guard it" (Genesis 2:15). As King David is reported to have said at the time when he was at the height of his power and that of the Israelite nation, when he was already preparing to build the First Temple in Jerusalem his capitol city: "To You O' Lord is the greatness, the power and the glory, triumph and majesty ... But who am I and who are my people? ... for everything is from You, and from Your hand we give back to You. For we are but sojourners [*gerim*] before You, transient residents [*toshavim*] like all our ancestors, our days like a shadow, with no hope for anything more [*v'ein miqveh*]" (I Chronicles 29:11, 14–15). In other words, because we are mortal creatures, how could we be anything but transients, even in the land God has given us to develop and protect? Therefore, the difference between native-born Jews and "sojourners" is one of degree rather than one of kind.

The universal life of the Jewish people is not confined to the land of Israel. This is contrary, of course, to the notion of *shelilat ha-golah* or the "the [necessary] disappearance of Diaspora Jewry," which is still the view of many Zionists. To be sure, Jews living outside the land of Israel are still very much part of the covenant. This comes out in the Talmud's treatment of the words of David, who complains to King Saul about being alienated

---

[65] *Sifra*: Behar, ed. Weiss, pp. 108a–b.
[66] Y. Berakhot 6.1/9c.

God Chooses the Land of Israel

from the land of Israel by "accursed men before the Lord, who have now banished me from being connected to the Lord's portion [*be-nahalat adonai*] saying: 'Go worship other gods' [*elohim aherim*]!" (I Samuel 26:19).[67] Now it seems that David actually agreed with them that being outside the land of Israel automatically makes an Israelite an idolater *ipso facto* and, therefore, outside the covenant. David's complaint, then, is not with what they have said, as he seems to think it is true. David's complaint is with what they have done to him, that is, making him into a de facto idolater by banishing him from the land of Israel and its monarch. But, as is clear from the context of this discussion in the Babylonian Talmud (itself conducted in Babylonia), the editors of the discussion did not want to alienate the very Diaspora Jews they were living among and themselves conversing with. So, at first it is stated (in the name of an earlier source): "Whoever dwells in the land of Israel resembles [*domeh*] one for whom there is God [*she-yesh lo eloah*]; and whoever dwells outside the land [of Israel] resembles one for whom there is no God [*she'ein lo eloah*]."[68] The proof text brought here is David's complaint quoted earlier.

However, is there no legitimate covenantal life whatsoever except within the boundaries of the land of Israel? If so, that not only disenfranchises the Jews in the Diaspora, but it also seems to reduce the Creator God who chooses Israel (among His other choices) into some sort of tribal deity confined to a particular territory like the people themselves are confined there. Moreover, in an earlier rabbinic text it is asked: "How could you possibly think that David was an idolater [*oved avodah zarah hayah*]?!"[69] Because of these politically and theologically problematic implications, I think, the Talmud qualifies the earlier text by saying: "It means to say that whoever dwells outside, it is as if [*k'ilu*] he were an idolater."[70] As some of the commentators

---

[67] B. Ketubot 110b.
[68] Ibid.
[69] Cf. T. Avodah Zarah 4.6, ed. Zuckermandl, p. 466.
[70] B. Ketubot 110b. See *Sifra*: Behar re Lev. 25:38, ed. Weiss, p. 109c.

point out, even though God rules the whole universe, with the exception of the land of Israel that rule is indirect; it is mediated by certain lesser cosmic powers.[71] Only the land of Israel is ruled directly by God. Therefore, to leave the land of Israel, where you are living in the land God directly rules, to go live in any other land that is only indirectly ruled by God, it is *as if* you are going from (as the Talmud would put it) "a higher level of sanctity (*qedushah hamurah*) to a lower level of sanctity (*qedushah qalah*)."[72]

To be sure, the optimal life of the Jewish people can only be lived in the land of Israel, and now, even more so, in the Jewish state therein. Yet that only makes the difference between Israeli Jewry and Diaspora Jewry a difference of degree, not a difference of kind. (This point is discussed at length in the next chapter dealing with the question of *what* is the exact positive commandment to live in the land of Israel, and upon *whom* that commandment devolves.) Thus the land of Israel exists for the sake of the people Israel; the people Israel do not exist for the sake of the land of Israel. The "sanctity" (*qedushah*) of the land of Israel means it is the site of certain commandments that can be kept only there.[73] Nevertheless, it can be bracketed as it were if the enforcement of that sanctity impedes even the economic needs of the Jewish people. Thus we find in the Talmud: "Many towns were conquered by those who came up [to the land of Israel] from out of Egypt, but they were not reconquered by those who came up out of Babylonia. That is because the earlier sanctity [*qedushah ri'shonah*] was only temporary and not for the future."[74] And why was this the case? "It is because they left certain places alone [i.e., they didn't reclaim them] in order that the poor could be supported through them during the Sabbatical Year." In other words, Jewish authorities at the time of the return

---

[71] Solomon ibn Adret, *Responsa: Rashba* 1, no. 134.
[72] B. Yevamot 22a.
[73] M. Kiddushin 1.9.
[74] B. Hagigah 3b. See MT: Heave Offerings, 1.5–9.

of the Jews to the land of Israel from Babylonia could determine that a certain area usually considered to be within the boundaries of the land of Israel could by fiat be considered outside the land. As such, these areas became exempt from the obligation that they lie fallow during the Sabbatical Year, *if* the needs of the poor seem to require this fiat. On the other hand, the reason the rabbis decreed that leaving the land of Israel puts one in a state of pollution (*t'umah*) seems to be to have discouraged Jewish emigration from the land of Israel, which would no doubt be detrimental to the vibrant political and economic interests of the Jewish people in the land of Israel.[75]

Finally, when the Romans were about to destroy Jerusalem with the Temple in 70 C.E., the Talmud reports that the head of the Sanhedrin, Rabban Yohanan ben Zakkai, defying the orders of the Zealots who still controlled the city, was smuggled out of Jerusalem so he could negotiate directly with the Roman general, Vespasian. Being a man of great political prudence who understood what the true needs of the Jewish people were at that time and place and what was possible in a situation of realpolitik, he only asked for what he knew he could get, which was "Yavneh and her sages."[76] Like the aforementioned rabbinic ruling, this decision was not a permanent concession of the land of Israel or of Jerusalem to foreigners. Instead, it is the best historical example of how Jewish leadership did not adopt a "do or die" attitude to the land of Israel, that is, the needs of the people Israel took precedence in these cases.

In the same way, the State of Israel is for the sake of the people Israel in the land of Israel; the people Israel in the land of Israel is not for the sake of the State of Israel. And, most importantly, the people, then the land, then the state all exist for the sake of God; indeed the Jewish people's relation to all these entities are

---

[75] B. Shabbat 14b. See Louis Ginzberg, "The Significance of the Halachah for Jewish History," trans. A. Hetzberg, *On Jewish Law and Lore* (Philadelphia: Jewish Publication Society of America, 1955), 78–80.

[76] B. Gittin 56a-b.

to be responses to the God who has chosen the people, chosen the land for them, and whose commandment to settle the land and inhabit it gives the state its true warrant.[77]

The question that arises from what has been said in this chapter is: What would the political character be of a Jewish state that looked to the Torah for its warrant? Could such a Jewishly warranted Jewish state (*medinah yehudit*) be considered "democratic"? That is important to ask, as democracy in one way or another is for most modern Jews the *sine qua non* of any polity, even a Jewish polity, that could claim their support in good faith. That question leads us into the next chapter.

---

[77] See Joseph B. Soloveitchik, *Five Sermons* [Heb.], trans. D. Telzger (Jerusalem: Makhon Tel Orot, 1974), 89.

6

Can the State of Israel Be Both Jewish and Democratic?

Jewish Religion and Secular Law

Although the State of Israel does not yet have a formal constitution, it does have certain "basic laws" (*huqqei he-yesod*) that function very much like a constitution insofar as they determine how subsequent legislation is to be interpreted. These basic laws define the very character of the state to be governed according to them. They very much function like dogmas function in a religious tradition; and, in fact, their secularist proponents are usually quite dogmatic in their affirmation of them, often insisting they are beyond dispute.

The first of these basic laws, formulated in 1992, is about "liberty and dignity." It speaks of "the values of the State of Israel as a *Jewish and democratic state*."[1] Commenting on this basic law, the former President of Israel's Supreme Court, Aharon Barak, changes the syntax of the original statement, saying: "We are a democracy, and our values are the values of every democracy. But we are also [*gam*] a Jewish state, and therefore our values are the values of a Jewish state."[2]

---

[1] www.jewishlibrary.org/source/isdf/text/barak.html
[2] Ibid. In a lecture, "The State of Israel as a Jewish and Democratic State" [Heb.], published in *Iyunei Mishpat* 6 (2000), 9–14, Barak elaborates on the relation

Now these two values could be separated and each one could be seen to stand alone, that is, a Jewish state need not be democratic, and a democratic state need not be Jewish. Indeed, these two values might be antithetical, that is, an authentic Jewish state could not be democratic ipso facto, and an authentic democracy could not be Jewish ipso facto. So, it would seem in order to correlate these two separate "values" cogently, one must decide which value is primary and which value is secondary. Now Barak's syntax clearly indicates that he (and much of the Israeli secularist establishment along with him) takes democracy to be primary for the State of Israel and its "Jewishness" to be secondary. The Jewishness of the state, for him, is because of 'its Jewish heritage [*moreshet yisra'el*], symbols, holidays, language and other indicators."[3] And, even when it comes to Jewish law (*halakhah*), that aspect of the Jewish tradition that could play a significant normative role in Israeli legislation, tellingly Barak will accept only those aspects of *halakhah* that are "more easily integrated with the values of Israel as a democratic state."[4] However, we can certainly question whether the Jewish tradition itself could play such a decidedly secondary role in a polity that is still considered to be essentially Jewish. But, as I hope to show in this chapter, it is possible for a Jewish view of statehood to incorporate most democratic values (I prefer the term "principles") without violence to them in a way I do not think it is possible for the kind of secularist view of democracy proposed by most Jewish secularists like Barak to incorporate Judaism, without doing violence to Judaism.

In Chapter 3, we have already seen how Herzl's notion of a "Jewish state" (*der Judenstaat*) is really only a state whose citizens happen to be Jews. As such, it is only *a* state *of* Jews (*medinat yehudim*). (And it is safe to assume that Herzl envisioned this Jewish state to be at least as democratic in fact as

---

of democracy and Judaism, using Israel's Declaration of Independence as his basic text.
[3] http://en.wikipedia.org/wiki/A_Jewish_and_Democratic_State
[4] Ibid.

was the Austrian-Hungarian imperial state of which he was a citizen.) Those who have basically followed Herzl's political Zionism have usually relegated the Jewishness of the State of Israel to the status of some sort of cultural ornament, what in the Talmud is called "ancestral custom" (*minhag avoteihem*), which is done with willful ignorance of the original meaning of that term.[5] Of course, this lip service paid to the Jewish tradition is unacceptable to Jews who regard their Jewishness to be rooted in the Jewish religious tradition, which for them is a "present living authority" (*torat hayyim*), not a dead relic from the past. No religious Jew could in good faith agree to a secularist constitution of the Jewish state of Israel (which at present it does not have and is unlikely to have in the foreseeable future) that saw the prime authority of the state to be the will of a group of human beings. A truly *Jewish* state needs to be even more than a state *of* the Jews *by* the Jews *for* the Jews.[6]

The secularist concession to the Jewish religious tradition or Judaism can hardly be taken very seriously by the very people who have enunciated it, as it is one that cannot be argued for in any cogent way. Like the cultural Zionists also discussed in Chapter 3, those who would make the Jewish tradition, which is inextricably religious, into some sort of cultural ornament of a basically secular political reality, these secularists don't truly understand what "culture" is. That is because every historical culture is rooted in a divine revelation that has spawned a tradition that refuses to remain primarily in the past, but that makes real claims on its transmitting community here and now and into the future. Hence secularists can't argue cogently for a "culture" when they don't clearly understand what a culture really is and how it actually functions in history. Moreover, every culture has a system of law; but secularists like Barak do not think Israel's basic laws need grounding in the Jewish tradition and its law.

---

[5] B. Hullin 13b. Cf. B. Betsah 5b.
[6] See E. Shochetman, "Rabbi Isaac Herzog's Theory of Torah and State," trans. D. B. Sinclair, *The Halakhic Thought of R. Isaac Herzog*, Jewish Law Association Studies 4 (Atlanta, GA: Scholars Press, 1991), 113–25.

I suspect that the secularists' concession to the historical value of the Jewish tradition or culture is because they understand it to be a political necessity designed to accommodate those Jews who have the most cogent Jewish reasons to be in the land of Israel, to acquire it, and to settle it. In today's world of realpolitik, that means Jews have to have a Jewish state of their own in the land of Israel and not just be an association of like-minded individuals living in somebody else's society, even if that non-Jewish society is in the land of Israel. To adequately settle the land of Israel as the national Jewish homeland, Jews must be the self-conscious majority there, indeed, the overwhelming majority. As a minority there, Jews would be at the mercy of a non-Jewish majority, which, we know quite well, has shown itself to be hostile to their very presence in the land of Israel under any circumstances.

To want Israel to be a democratic state, one must accept majority rule to be an indispensable component of any democratic state. A democracy without majority rule is no democracy at all. And to remain a majority it needs to be an identifiable community with a definite historical identity. That historical identity could only come from the Jewish religious tradition. After all, the only cogent way a person can become a real part of the Jewish people is to do so by criteria set forth in traditional Jewish law (*halakhah*), that is, by being born to a Jewish mother, or by converting (*giyyur*) under the auspices of a Jewish religious tribunal (*bet din*) supervising traditionally mandated procedures.[7]

(In the next chapter, we shall see how being a Jewish majority does not mean the denial of the civil rights of a non-Jewish minority.) Nevertheless, that type of concession to the Jewish tradition must be more than a sop to religious citizens of Israel and religious supporters of Israel in the Diaspora. When it is such a sop, it is still an affront to Jews who regard the Jewish religion, that is, the Torah, to be what makes Jews Jewish and defines them as such, both as individuals and as a people. And that includes Jews who themselves are not fully observant of the

---

[7] B. Kiddushin 68b; B. Yevamot 47a–b.

commandments of the Torah, but who still define their Jewish identity in religious, not secular terms nonetheless.

However, what do we mean by a "religious state"? If it is a state whose law is *halakhah*, the question arises of whether such a legal system could be operative in a state in which the majority of its Jewish citizens do not recognize its full authority. As a famous text in the Talmud put it, quite dramatically, even God could only impose the Torah on the Jewish people; God could not force them to truly accept it, however.[8] And until the Jewish people did accept the Torah willingly, it could be said that the Torah had little effect on their lives, especially their national life. Little wonder, then, that government enforcement of a number of traditional Jewish laws, especially those laws dealing with matters of personal and familial identity, is taken to be quite undemocratic. In fact, the secular state's enforcement of religion has caused the chasm between religious and nonreligious Jews to widen considerably. It has caused chasms among various different groups of religious Jews to widen as well. As the ancient rabbis well knew, it is politically disastrous to make rules (*gezerot*) that are unacceptable to the vast majority of the people who would have to live by them.[9] Thus when the prominent Israeli rabbi, Judah Leib Maimon (d. 1962), who became the first "Minister of Religions" (*sar ha-datot*) of the State of Israel, suggested that the *Sanhedrin* as the national religious-legislative-judicial body of the Jewish people be reinstituted, his suggestion met with considerable skepticism as to its political feasibility in a society where the majority were not committed to *halakhah*, and even those who were committed to *halakhah* were deeply divided among themselves.[10] Indeed, there have been fears that such a radical move would lead to radical legal changes that would undermine the authority of *halakhah* itself (authority already considerably weakened in modernity by Jewish movements such as Reform Judaism and

---

[8] B. Shabbat 88a–b re Exod. 20:17 and Prov. 11:3, and Rashi's comment, s.v. "de-saginan" thereon.
[9] B. Avodah Zarah 35a, 36a.
[10] Rabbi Maimon's book was entitled *The Renewal of the Sanhedrin in Our Renewed State* [Heb.] (Jerusalem: Mosad Harav Kook, 1951).

secular Zionism). Also, there was the realization that the type of rabbinical consensus needed for the reinstitution of the Sanhedrin was very much lacking now and in the foreseeable future. Finally, even if a vast majority of the Jews wanted an *halakhic* state, there is the question of how the law, much of which in the area of societal relations was formulated under stateless conditions, could be applied in a modern nation-state like the State of Israel.[11] (Think of those Muslims who want the states in which they are the overwhelming majority to be governed according to *shari`ah* law and the political havoc that has wreaked.)

The problem for religious Jews, though, goes much deeper than the political and even the legal questions we have just seen. For, even if a good case can be made that in the Jewish tradition law is prior to politics, the philosophical question of why *halakhah* is authoritative *for Jews* needs much reflection by those who live according to its norms, so as to be able to work out an answer that tries to be convincing. As we saw in the first chapter concerning one's commitment to Zionism, one has to know the reasons for that commitment on his or her own part before that person can reasonably try to (minimally) argue effectively against those who deny the validity of that commitment; and (maximally) to effectively persuade others to join them in that commitment. Nevertheless, the examination of the theological roots of *halakhah*, which comprise the ultimate reason for one's commitment to it, might not lead religious Jews to conclude that their first task as religious Jews is to fight for an *halakhic* state, or even to fight for as much religious control of state institutions as is the current political reality in the State of Israel. The current state of affairs, where an oligarchy of rabbis imposes its power on a majority of indifferent or hostile citizens, gaining that power from a secular state, is probably doing the cause of Jewish religion in the State of Israel more harm than good by alienating more Jews from Judaism than attracting them to it.

---

[11] See Yeshayahu Leibowitz, *Judaism, Human Values, and the Jewish State*, trans. E. Goldman and Y. Navon (Cambridge, MA: Harvard University Press, 1992), 158–73.

The Problem with Current Israeli Secularism

The problem of the secularist proponents of a democratic Jewish state (even for those who might be privately religious) is that, like their secularist counterparts in other places in the West, they have a very myopic view of democracy. Their problem is not only with the specific norms of Jewish law, which they cannot accept as being what should govern a secular state. If that were their only problem, it could be shown that there is enough precedent in the Jewish tradition for the assertion that these specific *halakhic* norms need not be what must govern a civil society of Jews in many areas of interhuman relations.[12] Their problem with Judaism, though, runs much deeper than that (and their religious opponents who think the problem of the secularists is basically a legal problem are equally myopic). The fundamental problem of the Jewish secularists is with the central Jewish doctrine that all law comes from God (*torah min ha-shamayim*).[13] So, even in those areas of interhuman relations where it can be argued from the Jewish tradition that more general norms can govern, these more general norms (though not uniquely Jewish) are still to be considered to be in violation of the Torah's fundamentally divine authority. That is because these more general norms are not considered to be man-made laws that attempt to supplant God-made law. These norms too are considered God-made law.

This God-made law is considered to have been operative from the time of the creation of humankind to whom they apply, that is, before the revelation of the more specific norms of the Mosaic Torah.[14] That is why the Jewish tradition considers these more general moral norms to still be binding on all humankind. In fact, the more specific norms of the Mosaic

---

[12] See, for example, B. Baba Kama 84b; Maimonides, *Commentary on the Mishnah*: Baba Kama 8.1, ed. Kafih, p. 25.

[13] M. Sanhedrin 10.1, and Maimonides, *Commentary on the Mishnah* thereon, Principle 8, ed. Kafih, pp. 143–44.

[14] MT: Kings, 9.1. See David Novak, *The Image of the Non-Jew in Judaism*, 2nd ed., edited by M. LaGrone (Oxford: Littman Library, 2011), 154–56.

Torah build upon these more general norms, and with very few exceptions they do not contradict these general norms.[15] The difference, then, between the more specific norms the Torah prescribes, which might be inoperable under present political conditions, and the more general norms the Torah reiterates, is one of degree rather than one of kind. Therefore, the type of secularity that could be valid in an overall Jewish society is not secularist or atheistic. Even though there are areas of Jewish law that are not "religious" in the sense that they do not pertain to the God–human relationship, and are more rationally evident to all humans, nonetheless the source of all law is God's will.[16] As we have seen in Chapter 4, it is the same divine will that creates an orderly universe, and an orderly, intelligible human world, which is even more intelligible because it is populated by intelligent beings who can discover the beginnings of divine law by the exercise of their moral reason.

This traditionally acceptable secularity is quite different from the de facto atheism that claims that even if there might be God, that metaphysical assertion has no political significance, that is, it is irrelevant to a polity whether there is God or not. For, even the admission that "there might be God" seems to imply that the authority of this heretofore absent God could also be brought into political significance by those of this God's adherents who are impatient with their religious relationship with this God being totally separated from their secular politics. Recognizing a God perhaps lurking behind this mere agnosticism (which can still accept the possibility there is God), the more honest secularists, whether in Israel or elsewhere, are usually openly atheistic, regarding the Creator God proclaimed by Judaism, Christianity, and Islam to be their real enemy, an enemy whom (like Nietzsche) they feel they have to kill to prevent his return to the real world.[17]

---

[15] B. Sanhedrin 59a.
[16] B. Hagigah 3b re Eccl. 12:11; Exod. 20:1; MT: Kings, 8.11. See David Novak, "Law: Religious or Secular?" *In Defense of Religious Liberty* (Wilmington, DE: ISI Books, 2009), 141–82.
[17] *Thus Spake Zarathustra*, sec. 2, trans. T. Common, in *The Philosophy of Nietzsche* (New York: Modern Library, 1954), pp. 5–6.

Principled Agreement

Clearly, atheistic secularism is an ideology that religious Jews can make no common cause with, for it requires them to give up much too much.[18] It requires them to keep their most basic commitments "in the closet." Religion and secularism, at this level of stark contrast, are incompatible at the deepest metaphysical level. Therefore, it seems that the best way to work out a common basis for those who want a democratic Israel to still be cogently "Jewish" and those who want a Jewish Israel to be cogently "democratic" has to be a reasoned commonality. That requires compromise on both sides.

The deeper compromise between religious Zionists and secular Zionists will have to be more than agreement for the sake of agreement; it will have to be principled and not just provisional agreement. The compromise will have to be worked out through philosophical discourse to be like a real peace rather than merely like the temporary truces one usually sees in politics, both in Israel and the Diaspora.

This philosophical discourse is what some philosophers today call "public reason."[19] Both sides need to rethink their positions so that the present cultural/philosophical divide might be narrowed rather than widened. That will require religious thinkers to develop a Zionist philosophy that is not "theocratic" in the contemporary sense of that term, that is, where it is insisted that revelation-based law is the only warrant for a Jewish state, even to be imposed upon an unwilling majority by a rabbinical oligarchy. And that will require secular thinkers to develop a Zionist philosophy that can basically accept divine sovereignty (*malkhut shamayim*) as the state's warrant, yet without requiring secular Jews to personally accept revealed law as normative in their own personal lives or that Jewish religious practices must

---

[18] MT: Foundations of the Torah, 1.1.
[19] See, for example, Jürgen Habermas, *Moral Consciousness and Communicative Action*, trans. C. Lenhardt and S. W. Nicholsen (Cambridge, MA: MIT Press, 1993), 199–204; Amartya Sen, *The Idea of Justice* (London: Penguin Books, 2009), 31–51.

be enforced in public. Only this kind of rethinking might lead to a principled agreement that can rationally correlate Judaism and democracy through Zionism. Anything less than that kind of deep philosophical coming-together will simply exacerbate rather than alleviate the deep *Kulturkampf* that divides Israeli Jews, and that has severe repercussions among Jews in the Diaspora too.

Whose Democracy?

The problem I see with almost all the secularist proponents of a democratic Israel is that they have adopted what could be called the French approach to democracy. Coming out of the implicit atheism of the French Revolution and its attempt to do away with all religion (the two main targets being the Catholic Church and the semi-autonomous Jewish communities or *qehillot*), the French program of *laïcité* or "secularization" is one that actually goes deepest by refusing to recognize any divine authority over the state at all, not even mentioning the name of God.[20] (That also goes much deeper than merely outlawing certain public displays of religion, as has been done in France and in Québec recently.) And this dogmatic secularism, which only stops short of outlawing religion altogether (as has been done in various antidemocratic "revolutionary" regimes, both left and right), has its proponents in North America, especially in Canada and the United States. However, whereas in France there is no historical precedent for arguing against this dogmatic secularism, against this public atheism, the situation in North America is quite different. I can only suggest that Israeli secularists recognize that the French kind of secularity is not the only kind of secularity at hand in the modern world. Indeed, much can be learned from less radical North American secularity.

Although the preamble to the 1788 Constitution of the United States seems to base its political authority on the consent of

---

[20] See Michel Vovelle, *La révolution contre l'église* (Paris: Editions Complexe, 1988).

"We the people of the United States of America," in fact, many students of American history have taken the 1776 *Declaration of Independence* to be the true preamble to the Constitution. There the basis of political authority is explicitly stated to be God. The people's natural rights come from "Nature's God," that is, the people are "endowed by their Creator with certain unalienable rights."[21] It is because these rights come from God that they are "unalienable," that is, no human government has the right to take them away, because they are ontologically prior to the establishment of any human state and its government. In fact, the purpose of any human state and its government is to enforce these natural rights, like the right to life and the right to liberty, which means the right to act in one's own self-interest unencumbered (i.e., as long as that does not impinge on the rights of others or the common good), plus the right to develop one's own strengths (called there "the pursuit of happiness"). Certainly, Thomas Jefferson, the author of the Declaration, did not consider himself or any other human person to be the author of these natural rights. (Even now calling them "human rights" only means that humans are the subjects of these rights; they are about us humans, even though we humans are not their author.)

Also implied here in this use of theological language (which was certainly not lost on the many biblically literate readers of the Declaration) is that just as God has promised Noah in the first covenant (*brit*) that the natural order will not be overturned by God changing His mind, so God will not remove or "alienate" the rights built into nature manifest as human political nature. "I shall never again [*od*] curse [*le-qallel*] the soil because of man [that is, because of human misconduct] ... Never again [*od*] will all the earthly times cease" (Genesis 8:21–22). And, just as the earth would be cursed if God were to break His covenantal promise to overturn its natural order, so would humankind be cursed (literally, "made light of," i.e., made insignificant) if God were to take away our rights. Thus it could be said that these natural rights are unalienable by both

---

[21] See Novak, *In Defense of Religious Liberty*, 29–56.

God and other humans. They are unalienable by democratic human governments who, in the social contract, have pledged to protect and enhance these rights. And they are unalienable by God who, in the covenant, has also pledged to protect these rights and enhance them.[22] Indeed, the promise of a human government, like that which was being established in the United States, to protect and enhance these natural rights is believable only if it imitates the divine promise to do so. After all, what would prevent a subsequent regime change (like those that have taken place in a number of European countries during the past two centuries) from revoking or "alienating" the rights granted by a previous regime? It seems that the only thing to prevent that from happening, at least in principle, is if natural rights come from the Creator of nature (i.e., the universe, as we saw in the previous chapter), whose regime cannot be changed by any creature, and who has promised not to change it Himself. So, if God promises not to take back the rights He has given humankind, then all the more so no human government can take back rights it hasn't given its human citizens, but that they already had in hand when they came to negotiate the social contract. But, without this recognition of God as the "unalienating" Giver of human rights, how could one argue against a government that doesn't recognize and thereby implicitly denies this ontological principle by taking away rights it considers its prerogative to give or take away with impunity? To cogently challenge a government, one needs a point of reference beyond the government's power to do as it pleases.

All of this, needless to say, is the subject of fierce debate in the United States today. American secularists argue that the theological language of the Declaration is not to be taken literally; that it is only a sop to a religious majority who couldn't accept anything less in the founding document of their new state. But, of course, once part of the Declaration is presumed to not really mean what

---

[22] On the irrevocability of a divinely made covenant, see Isa. 54:9–10; B. Berakhot 32a re Exod. 32:13.

it says, what prevents anybody from doing the same to other parts of the Declaration with which they do not agree? Wouldn't that shift the authority in the document from the author's stated intent to the intent of its readers by using the document any way they see fit? Furthermore, inasmuch as the vast majority of Americans still consider themselves to be God-believers, it seems rather undemocratic to disregard their beliefs in favor of the beliefs of a secularist minority who regard themselves to be elite, even though the assertion of a divine source of law and rights does not and ought not entail any suppression of the rights of that minority to eschew theistic belief altogether if they so choose. In other words, a public commitment to God-given rights does not entail public enforcement of God-given duties on individual citizens.

In Canada, there needn't be any debate as to what is the preamble of the *Charter of Rights and Freedoms*, nor what it explicitly states, for the very first words of the Charter are: "Whereas Canada is founded on principles that recognize the supremacy of God and the rule of law." Now the fact that this is the preamble to a charter of "rights and freedoms" can be interpreted to mean that the purpose of affirming the "supremacy of God and the rule of law" is to give ontological backing to these rights and freedoms – and to the duties they surely entail. The coupling of "the supremacy of God" with "the rule of law" can be interpreted to be two phrases in apposition, expressing but one meaning. That is, the political meaning of the supremacy of God manifests itself in the rule of law, a law neither made nor to be repealed by its human subjects, that is, because of its divine origin. Thus the law itself is not a human invention, even though its numerous specifications are the work of human hands. And, of course, Canadian secularists in their attempt to trivialize words in their state's founding document that seem to mean exactly what they say undermine its actual authority the same way liberal Jews undermine the actual authority of the Torah when they deny that the Torah is divine revelation (however much the text itself seems to have been put together by humans).

Divinely Sanctioned Secularity

Now if Americans and Canadians regard the assertion of divine law to be essential for their own political self-definition, how much more so is that the case with the Jewish people who assert that God "has chosen us from among all peoples by giving us the Torah"? Moreover, both Americans and Canadians can locate their affirmation of divine law to be the foundation of their respective polities in the same source: English Common Law, which is regarded by its great interpreters as founded in God-made law. Now that God-made law is not the specific law revealed to and accepted by a particular historic community (*lex divina*); instead, it is the law the Creator has enabled all rational persons to discover through ongoing political discourse. Thus, when representing the foundations of the Common Law in 1765, William Blackstone, who had great influence on the American founders (and even more so on Canadians who remained within the British Empire), wrote: "The eternal, immutable laws of good and evil ... which he [God] has enabled human reason to discover ... [are] the foundation of what we call ethics or natural law."[23]

This law is secular in the sense of being discoverable by humans per se, irrespective of their specific historic traditions; and it is secular in the sense that it does not legislate for the realm of the God-human relationship. The substance of the God-human relationship, however, is determined by the respective revelations of the various faith communities to whom these revelations have been addressed; and their interpretation and administration is left to the traditional authorities in each of these faith communities. That is why Jews are bound to live under the secular law of whatever jurisdiction they find themselves, providing, of course, that this secular law is a specific and systematic manifestation of what the Jewish tradition recognizes and accepts to be universally valid standards of justice.[24] However, Jews are not bound,

---

[23] *Commentaries on the Laws of England* 1 (Chicago: University of Chicago Press, 1979), 40–41.
[24] See David Novak, *The Jewish Social Contract* (Princeton, NJ: Princeton University Press, 2005), 91–123.

Divinely Sanctioned Secularity

indeed they are forbidden to be bound, by the specifically religious law (for example, Canon Law) or anti-religious law of any other people in the world.

The question is, whether the Jewish people have any such preamble (formal or informal) like that of the Americans and that of the Canadians, and upon which a non-secularist and non-theocratic (in the current connotation of that controversial term) secular state could be based?

Now one could say that the 14 May 1948 (5 Iyyar 5708) *megillat ha`atsma'ut* or *Declaration of Independence of the State of Israel* (first called in Hebrew *hakhrazah al haqamat medinat yisrael*, i.e., "Announcement of the Establishment of the State of Israel") is the preamble to the constitution of the State of Israel yet to be written.[25] And, in fact, it does have that kind of canonical status in some decisions of the Supreme Court of Israel. Truth be told, though, it is a philosophically flawed statement, even though I fully appreciate the political pressures that didn't allow for the luxury of working out a principled agreement at the time. The statement itself had to be written and ratified hurriedly by the leadership of the prematurely born state. So, at least at the time, this document was politically effective by putting the State of Israel on the international map. Nobody should underestimate that accomplishment, any more than one shouldn't underestimate Herzl's political accomplishment despite his philosophical deficiencies. The question, though, is whether these philosophical weaknesses need be continued. So, despite its great historical value, this document is unconvincing. As such, it could only be the basis of a constitution that would be one no religiously serious Jew could possibly accept in good faith. (It is also clear that Israel could only have such a constitution, only if it were written and adopted by the people under circumstances that are far less pressing than those of 1948, or even of today.)

The Declaration of 1948 speaks of the "right [*zekhut*] of the Jewish people to national rebirth [*le-tequmah l'umit*] in its own

---

[25] For the text of the Declaration, see www.knesset.gov.il/docs/heb/megilat.htm, and www.science.co.il/Israel-Declaration-of-Independence

country." Now, if a "right" is a justified claim of one party on another party, then to *whom* is that claim being made, and *what* justifies it? Well, the Declaration makes that claim upon the international community, specifically upon the United Nations for recognition of Jewish national sovereignty in the land of Israel. The claim is justified by reference to the Balfour Declaration of 1917 that recognized this right, and that was subsequently ratified by the League of Nations. The fact that Israel's declared independence was quickly recognized by the United States and the Soviet Union (the two most powerful nation-states at the time), soon followed by the United Nations, was politically sufficient. It seemed to be good enough for the non-Jewish world. But on what integrally Jewish grounds, over and above realpolitik, was this recognition of the right of the Jewish people to a land of their own made? It is "the historic connection [*qesher historiyyi*] and Eretz-Israel." Moreover, the Declaration says that it is the "natural right [*zekhuto ha-tiv`it*] of the Jewish people to be masters of their own fate, like all the others nations, in their own sovereign state [*be-medinato ha-ribbonit*]." Thus it is a right that is "our natural and historic right" (*zekhutenu ha-tiv`it ve-ha-historit*).

However, how does an "historic connection" to a land give a particular people the right to establish themselves there politically? Does "history" grant or endow rights? In fact, natural rights are cogent only when the "nature" upon which they are based is considered to be the freely chosen creation of God (as we saw in Chapter 4), which means that we humans are entitled to make claims upon one another (and even upon God himself in petitionary prayer) based upon our nature as the image of God. Likewise, historic rights are cogent only when the "history" upon which they are based is considered to be the freely chosen creation of God. And, whereas God's choices in nature are discovered through our general experience of being naturally oriented to God and to each other, God's choices in history are revealed through one's particular experience of being part of a community commanded by God in the Torah. (Whereas there is the general experience of human nature, there is only the particular experience of your particular history; hence we can speak of one human nature, but only of many human histories.) In other words, for either nature or history to have normative force, in the sense of granting rights, there must be recognition of the God who has chosen to act one way in nature or the human world, and quite another way in the history of the Jewish people (even though natural divine action and historic divine action should not be seen to be at loggerheads).

Without that explicit God-affirmation, talk of "rights," whether "historic" or "natural," is rather empty rhetoric. Thus when the Declaration does speak of someone declaring or actually uttering Jews' right to the land of Israel (and all rights have to be spoken into existence), it is Theodor Herzl, not God, who "proclaimed [*ve-hikhriz*] the right [*zekhut*] of the Jewish people to national rebirth in its own country." Here again, none of this is untrue; it is only insufficient for Jews to understand why they are claiming their statehood the land of Israel from the nations-of-the-world if they don't have better reasons for making this claim than by vague references to "history." That is because recognition from the nations-of-the-world is hardly "irrevocable" (*einah nitenet le-hafqa`ah*) as the Declaration puts it. Only God's promise that "there is hope for your future," and that "your children will return to their own precincts" (Jeremiah 31:16), like all of God's promises, is irrevocable because God has also unconditionally promised not to revoke them. And, as we shall see shortly, that return to the land of Israel is more an ongoing task than it is an outright gift.

Of course, the Declaration is not totally devoid of any reference to God. It closes with the words "placing our trust in the Almighty" (*mi-tokh bitahon be-tsur yisrael*). However, there is a big philosophical problem with that assertion. Even though the official English translation of the Hebrew text says "the Almighty," the Hebrew text itself is rather vague, literally referring to "the rock of Israel." Now, even though this is a term taken from the traditional liturgy, there are other theological terms that are far less vague.²⁶ In fact, years ago, a very secularist relative of mine in Israel told me that in his opinion, "rock of Israel" means a "strong army" (*tsav'a hazaq*). Now, even though God is certainly "the Rock of Israel," meaning God is the people Israel's source of strength, it would seem that it would be more truthful to express to the nations-of-the-world (*ummot ha`olam*) their reliance upon the Creator of the universe (*bor'e olam*), for only the Creator of the universe could choose a particular people for a special covenantal relationship, plus assign to them a particular land to settle.²⁷ Conversely, the *gods* of the other ancient peoples do not choose them; their gods, like them, are only part of a common geographic landscape. In other words, these gods are "domestic" or "ethnic" (as we saw in the critique of the secularist ideology of Ahad ha`Am in Chapter 3). Thus the Lord God of Israel is not so much "of Israel" as God is "for Israel," that is, God is Israel's Protector – and more. (Indeed, if God were only Israel's Protector, he could be taken to be but Israel's "helper," that is, Israel's servant.) In the Jewish tradition, God is much more than the Jews' Protector; God is the source of the Torah, through which God governs His people, and according to which God judges His people. Yet, the Declaration only dimly alludes to divine commandment and judgment when it speaks of "freedom, justice, and peace as envisaged [*l'or hezyonam*] by the prophets of Israel." I assume that the author of the Declaration knew (and many of his biblically literate readers surely knew) that the vision of the prophets of Israel is to be affirmed by the people Israel now by obeying the commandments of God that are to be, as Maimonides taught, the full constitution of the promised messianic state in the future, a state whose realization in the future cannot be predicted by humans.²⁸ Thus the only political authority the "prophets of Israel" had was when they were "the prophets of the Lord" (*nevi'ei adonai*), uttering (in the

---

²⁶ In fact, though, when the word "rock" (*tsur*) is used in Scripture metaphorically rather than literally, it always refers to God (see, e.g., I Sam. 2:2; cf. the pun on B. Berakhot 10a).
²⁷ Rashi on Gen. 1:1.
²⁸ MT: Kings, 11.1–4.

case of Moses) or reiterating (in the case of all the other Jewish prophets) the commandments of God's Torah.[29]

I can well understand the political reasons that impelled the religious signers of the Israeli Declaration of Independence to agree to a basically secularist statement. Their agreement was made under great duress. For an urgent realpolitik end, they had to basically accept a document written by a secularist for the non-Jewish world and for a clearly secularist Jewish majority, certainly in the land of Israel.

However, can't we now look upon this document as itself a "cultural ornament," that is, a relic that played its politically necessary role in the past, but that has no authority in the present and no authority for the future? Therefore, we need to look elsewhere for a model of Jewish secularity that could be acceptable to both religious and secular Jews.

Authentic Jewish Secularity

The questions now are: Does the Jewish tradition have a secular law (or at least an idea of secular law) that is neither atheistic, which would be antithetical to the Torah, nor specifically religious, which would require a complete *halakhic* polity to interpret it, administer it, and even enforce it? Can we find in the Jewish tradition an affirmation of a secular realm that is based neither on dogmatic secularism nor on the particular revelation of the Torah (i.e., Jewish religion) to the Jewish people, claiming both the people collectively and each and every Jew individually? In other words, can we find in the Jewish tradition grounds for asserting a theistically based polity, which is presupposed by, yet not identical with, the optimal theocratic polity the Torah seems to be intending for Israel? Furthermore, could this Jewish secularity be the basis of a truly democratic polity in Israel? And, could this democratic secularity guarantee to secular Jews that it has good reason to eschew any coercion of religious belief and

---

[29] Cf. Isa. 29:13–14.

religious practice? Only then will the assertion of a "democratic and Jewish" Israel not be an oxymoron.

We can now look at the tradition. Thus Maimonides, basing himself on earlier rabbinic sources, states: "Regarding six matter was the first human person [*adam ha-ri'shon*] commanded: [the prohibitions of] idolatry, blasphemy, murder [*shefikhut damim*], sexual licence [*gilluy arayot*], and robbery, plus [the positive commandment] to establish a system of applying justice and rectifying injustice [*dinim*]."[30] He then continues: "Even though all of them are [known through] the tradition [*qabbalah*] we have in hand from Moses our master, and reason is inclined to them [*ve-ha-da`at noteh lahen*], nevertheless, it is evident from the words of the Torah in general [*mi-khlal*] that they [i.e., humankind] have been so commanded [*nitstavu*]." Now I have dealt with all of this quite extensively in my earlier work; but let me draw a few basic points here.[31]

The actual commandments themselves are prescribed for all humans, but it is from traditional Jewish sources that gentiles living under Jewish governance learn of them.[32] As for gentiles who are not living under Jewish governance, these norms are known to be requirements of rational-political human nature. In other words, living according to these basic norms is the way God wants all human persons to live as the image of God in the world. Arguably to be sure, this can be seen as the Jewish version of natural law, that is, moral law that applies to every human being, and that is knowable to every rational human person. They are also known in the Jewish tradition as the "Noahide commandments," as all humankind after the Flood are considered to be the descendants of Noah.

Even though these norms are not explicitly prescribed in the Mosaic Torah (unlike the commandments prescribed there for Jews), they are implied there, nonetheless. And what is most

---

[30] MT: Kings, 9.1.
[31] *The Image of the Non-Jew in Judaism*; and *Natural Law in Judaism* (Cambridge: Cambridge University Press, 1998).
[32] B. Avodah Zarah 64b.

important to understand here is that these norms are assumed to be commanded by God to all humankind. So, for example, when Joseph is tempted to commit adultery with Potiphar's wife, he refuses, ultimately justifying his refusal by saying: "But I would be sinning against God [*ve-hata'ti l'elohim*]!" (Genesis 39:9). Therefore, we could say that the Jewish tradition in its most universal application is confirming what human reason discovers to the intelligent, morally earnest way of life, commanded by God for the world. To be sure, there are those who live this way only because it is accepted tradition; and there are those who live this way only because it seems to be reasonable in a pragmatic way.[33] And there are those who live this way only because it is commanded by God in revealed scriptures. Yet, as Maimonides emphasizes, the most astute humans realize that what they were doing is because of the rational commandment of God, which would hardly be universal if no particular tradition taught it.[34] Therefore, each one of these three levels of moral understanding reinforces the others, and no one of them contradicts the others.

Finally, the last commandment is the commandment to a society to set up a legal system that enforces the other five norms prescribed to individuals, norms that are themselves pre-political. This is the first business of government. It is the beginning of the politicization of that particular society: it is becoming a real polity. Now these pre-political norms are prescribed to protect individual rights. Thus murder is prohibited because every innocent human being created in the image of God has the right not to be killed. Thus sexual license is prohibited because every human being created in the image of God has the right not to be sexually violated. Thus robbery is prohibited because every human being created in the image of God has the right not to have his or her property misappropriated. The purpose of the establishment of the polity, then, is to systematically protect the rights of human beings. Being created in the image of God means that every human being is the object of special divine concern; thus

---

[33] MT: Kings, 8.11.
[34] Ibid. See Novak, *The Image of the Non-Jew in Judaism*, 153–75.

every other human being is obliged to imitate that divine concern, at least by not violating the object of that concern. (When somebody actually expresses that concern positively, that person is truly imitating the God in whose image he or she is created.[35])

In the Talmud it is assumed that a public affirmation of these basic laws is what is required of any non-Jew who wanted to obtain the status of a resident-alien (*ger toshav*) in Jewish polity, especially in a completely Jewish polity in the land of Israel.[36] (There will be more about the status of non-Jews in a Jewish polity in the next chapter.) Such a resident-alien actually had what might be called "associate citizenship," that is, he or she had full civil rights and duties, but without having the strictly religious rights and duties that are only prescribed to those fully Jewish, either by virtue of their birth or by virtue of full conversion (*giyyur*). Nevertheless, any such candidate for what in Canada would be called "landed immigrant" status did not have to personally affirm in public the kingship of God (*ol malkhut shamayim*) or God-made law (*ol shel mitsvot*), something that is required of a full convert (*ger tsedeq*).[37] All that person had to do is accept as a political obligation the basic moral norms cited previously, which their free acceptance implies they accept it to be a reasonable obligation, not the arbitrary decrees of an oppressive majority. Moreover, that would-be resident-alien only had to renounce idolatry, which even a non-believer in God could do in good faith. In other words, that person could, if asked, say something like this: "I don't know (which is what "agnostic" means) whether God exists or not. But, if the name God means *that which nothing greater can be thought*, then certainly the gods worshiped by the people you Jews call *idolaters* does not fit even this minimal definition; hence I renounce them as frauds."[38]

---

[35] B. Shabbat 133b re Exod. 15:2 (the view of Abba Saul).
[36] B. Avodah Zarah 64b.
[37] MT: Forbidden Intercourse, 14.2.
[38] This definition of the name "God" was most famously made by the eleventh-century Christian theologian, Anselm of Canterbury, in his *Proslogion*. Because this work is basically his exegesis of the scriptural verse, "The fool says in his heart there is no God [*ein elohim*]" (Ps. 53:2), Jews

However, if would-be resident-aliens were to ask the Jewish court they are petitioning for acceptance into the Jewish polity about the basis of the court's affirmation and enforcement of this law, the learned members of the court would have to say something like this: "We did not invent this law to impose on you. In fact, this was the only law we ourselves had before being the recipients of the higher and more complex law God revealed to us at Mount Sinai. We only affirm God's law for all humankind, and require acceptance of it by those non-Jews who choose to live under our political control. We are only affirming and enforcing what any just, decent human polity ought to affirm and enforce whenever and wherever it can." However, no non-Jew living under the political control of Jews may be forced to accept Judaism and Jewish praxis.[39] Furthermore, even though we need to be sure that the members of a Jewish court themselves need affirm the divine foundation of the law and practice its commandments in good faith they are commanded to enforce, that affirmation is not required of those who are the subjects of that law. Finally, just as when, under great duress, Jews cannot observe much of Jewish law, they are still obliged to observe the three cardinal Noahide prohibitions of idolatry, murder, and sexual license, so when a Jewish polity cannot enforce much of Jewish law because it lacks enough of an overwhelming majority consensus among its Jewish citizens, it might be said that it ought to fall back on the basic Noahide laws that still bind all humankind, Jews included.[40] These laws guarantee basic human rights.[41] As such, their public affirmation by a Jewish polity is the best foundation of a state that is both Jewish and democratic.

---

can certainly acknowledge it in good faith. So, those using the name "God," whether they actually believe it has a real referent or not, are not using it correctly if that name refers to anything less than the Absolute.

[39] MT: Kings, 8.10.
[40] B. Sanhedrin 74a; see ibid. 57a.
[41] Even though Jewish normative discourse seems to emphasize duties (*hovot*) rather than rights (*zekhuyot* or *reshuyot*), these duties presuppose the rights/claims to which they are the appropriate responses. See David Novak, *Covenantal Rights* (Princeton, NJ: Princeton University Press, 2000), 3–24.

The Israeli Declaration of Independence expresses that concern with human rights, albeit in secular terms, when speaking of the survivors of the Holocaust whose human rights had been most outrageously violated. There it speaks of the survivors, especially in rebuilding the land of Israel, who "never ceased to assert their right [*li-tbo`a zekhutam*] to a life of dignity [*kavod*]." The Declaration only lacked, however, an explicit assertion of who the source and who the guarantor of that human dignity truly is. That is why we have to go back earlier in Jewish history to find a more adequate expression of what is needed to justify a state where both the Jewish and the democratic components are sufficiently coordinated.

This suggestion of Jewish secularity is not just a matter of theological speculation. In fact, it has a real historical precedent. In thirteenth- and fourteenth century Christian Spain, the Jewish community had considerable political and legal autonomy, up to the point of even having the right to execute criminals guilty of capital crimes.[42] However, the gentile government insisted that the Jewish courts adjudicate civil and criminal cases according to more universal criteria of justice. Thus some of the more specific norms of traditional Jewish civil law (*dinei mamanot*) and criminal law (*dinei nefashot*) had to be bracketed. Nevertheless, it seems that the rabbinical authorities (who were the Jewish jurists) were willing to accept this compromised juridical position. Had they insisted on applying all the specific norms of traditional Jewish law (*halakhah*), they would not have been able to have as much juridical autonomy as they did have by accepting of what could be called "Jewishly administered secularity."[43] That secularity, though specifically departing from a number of Jewish penal procedures, was actually a fallback to the normative preconditions of traditional Jewish law found in Noahide law, which in my opinion is the Jewish version of natural law. It seems that the Jewish jurists had to conform their juridical practices to what the

---

[42] See Novak, *The Jewish Social Contract*, 124–56.
[43] See B. Sanhedrin 23a; Solomon ibn Adret, *Responsa: Rashba*, 2, no. 290.

gentile authorities considered to be justified in any decent society (what in later Roman law is called *ius gentium*).

The Commandment to Acquire and Settle the Land

Even though as we have seen so far, why the public affirmation of God's law provides a polity with the best reason to protect and enhance the natural rights of its citizens (without, however, requiring its citizens to publicly profess God), it does not explain what actually makes any such polity Jewish. Moreover, it does not explain why *this* particular people should establish its polity in *this* land of Israel. (It will be recalled from Chapter 3 that Herzl's Political Zionism couldn't answer either of these questions.)

As for the first question, it is not good enough to say that the Jewish tradition provides a model that is philosophically cogent as a kind of manifestation of universal justice in a particular history. For that would make this secular democratic precedent nothing more than the type of "cultural ornament," the recognition of which (as we saw earlier in this chapter) basically marginalizes the Jewish tradition, making it only a nostalgic relic. No; what is needed here is the affirmation of God's general law for all humankind as the necessary preparation for the acceptance of the more specific law of God. That more specific law is revealed to the particular people God has chosen for the intimate covenantal relationship between God and *this* people. The revealed law or Torah supplies the thick content of the covenantal relationship. Furthermore, the more general natural law is not superseded by the more specific revealed law; rather, the more specific law builds upon the more general law, saying more but not less than the more general law. Thus the more general law functions as a minimal criterion, below which the specific law must not go.[44]

---

[44] See Aharon Lichtenstein, "Does Jewish Tradition Recognize an Ethic Independent of Halakha?" In *Modern Jewish Ethics*, ed. M. Fox (Columbus, OH: Ohio State University Press, 1975), 62–85.

Theologically, this means that because God has elected the people Israel does not mean God is no longer concerned with the rest of humankind and the moral law that still pertains to all humankind, from which the people Israel are expected to build upon, not tear down.[45] (As we shall see in the next chapter, this has special political significance for how the Jewish people are to treat those non-Jewish representatives of humankind – "Adam's children" – over whom Jews have political power.)

The covenantal relationship between God and humans is fully adequate to human nature only (as we saw in the previous chapter) when it is a relationship between God and a *people*. That is the only way the covenant can be between God and fully human persons, who are both related to God individually and related to one another collectively, that is, politically. This is the correlation of our religious nature with our political nature. Moreover, the people have to already be constituted, minimally, as a political community before they are ready to be chosen by God for something more. In other words, before God could choose a people there has to be an intact people who are ready to be chosen. The covenant is not creation from nothing. Indeed, in human experience we are related to one another before we are related to God. So, when the election of the people Israel begins with Abraham, despite Abraham's individual relationship with God, he is already the head of a clan, who are the people in nascent form.

Furthermore, the land where this people is to be centered is chosen for them by God. That prevents the people from choosing a land for themselves autonomously, which would make their geographic presence something apart from the covenant God has chosen them for. That would enable them to look upon themselves as the permanent owners of the land rather than being God's "sojourners and tenants" (*gerim ve-toshavim*) there (Leviticus 25:23). Unlike those who consider themselves to be the owners of a land, thus believing themselves to have the right to make the rules for settling that land by themselves for themselves, the people Israel must say as King David is reported to

---

[45] B. Sanhedrin 58b–59a.

have said to God: "I am but a sojourner (*ger anokhi*) in the land; do not hide from me your commandments" (Psalms 119:19). Moreover, choosing a land for themselves to be the base of an imperial project to conquer the world would be something that would make their worldly presence even further removed from the covenant with God that is envisioned to be fully consummated when God, not the people Israel acting as God's successors, "becomes the King of the whole world" (Zechariah 14:9).

The Torah teaches that the land of Israel is God's gift to His people Israel. Nevertheless, even though God "gives [*natan*] the earth to humankind" (Psalms 115:16), that gift still must be obtained by humans actively populating the earth and all that this entails as their moral imperative. "Be fruitful and increase, filling the earth" (Genesis 1:28) is an imperative, not just a blessing.[46] So too, the Jewish people are commanded acquire the land. What God actually gives them is the ability to do so. "You shall acquire [*ve-horashtem*] the land and settle it [*vi-shavtem bah*], because I give you the land to acquire it" (Numbers 33:53). The question now is: What does this commandment actually command, and who is so commanded? And, what does this commandment intend, that is, what is the reason (*ta`am*) of this commandment?

The most influential opinion as to the status of the commandment to permanently settle, that is, take possession of, the land is expressed by Nahmanides (d. 1270), basing himself on the verse quoted above, as follows:

> We are commanded to acquire the land ... and not to leave it in the hand of others [*zulateinu*] from the nations or to be desolate ... and this commandment is repeated in many other places ... this direction [*hora'ah*] is a commandment [*mitsvah*] ... and I say that it the commandment the sages even exaggerate is [that which commands] dwelling [*dirat*] in the land of Israel ... All of this pertains to this positive commandment [*me-mitsvat aseh*] that we are commanded to take possession of the land and settle it. As such, it is a positive commandment that is perpetually binding [*le-dorot*], one which every individual Jew is obligated by [*mithayyev*], even

---

[46] M. Yevamot 6.6. Cf. B. Ketubot 5a.

in times of exile [*galut*] ... they [the sages] even say that settling in or dwelling in the land of Israel is the equal [*shequlah ke-neged*] of all [the other] commandments.⁴⁷

From this statement of the commandment to acquire the land and settle it, the following four points emerge: (1) It is obvious this is a Torah commandment, the point having been made several times in the Torah. (2) The importance of this commandment is emphasized by the sages, who determined the relative status of the commandments of the Torah, even elevating it to the highest status they could. It is not simply an isolated decree; hence it is especially important to understand its reason (*ta`amah shel mitsvah*). (3) This commandment is considered to be a positive commandment for perpetuity, like all such commandments directly revealed by God in the Torah. (4) This commandment obliges every individual Jew wherever and whenever he or she happens to be found.

Nahmanides' statement of the status of this commandment is made in his extensive notations on Maimonides' *Sefer ha-Mitsvot* or *Book of the Commandments*, and in shorter version in his own comments on Numbers 33:53 in his *Commentary on the Torah*. Now in his *Sefer ha-Mitsvot*, Maimonides painstakingly enumerates what he considers to be the 613 (a number mentioned in the Talmud in a rather general way) specific norms commanded in the Mosaic Torah (the Pentateuch) as precepts that are perpetually binding on the Jewish people. These precepts are to be distinguished from various ad hoc (*le-sha`ah*) orders that were given when the Jews were in Egypt or in the Wilderness or even in the land of Israel before the revelation of the Torah at Mount Sinai.⁴⁸ In his addenda to these notations, Nahmanides criticizes Maimonides for not having enumerated among the 613 commandments some commandments that Nahmanides thinks are clearly mandated in the Mosaic Torah,

---

⁴⁷ *Maimonides' Book of Commandments with Nahmanides' Critiques* [Heb.], no. 4, ed. C. B. Chavel (Jerusalem: Mosad Harav Kook, 1981), pp. 244–46.
⁴⁸ B. Sanhedrin 23b–24a re Deut. 33:4; Maimonides, *Commentary on the Mishnah*: Hullin 7.6; idem., *Sefer ha-Mitsvot*, intro., no. 3.

The Commandment to Acquire and Settle the Land 181

and that ought to be included therefore. For Nahmanides, probably the most blatant omission in Maimonides' list is the positive commandment to acquire and settle the land of Israel, which, like most of the positive commandments, devolves on each and every individual Jew. Having been mentioned more than once in the Torah (Nahmanides cites some other verses to that effect) should have made its revelatory status (*min ha-torah*) obvious.[49]

It is clear from Maimonides' legal writings that he did not ignore the special status of the land of Israel in the Jewish normative system, plus the special merit of the Jews who live there.[50] Later commentators, though, attempt to answer Nahmanides' critique of Maimonides, speculating in various ways. The most plausible answer, for me anyway, is that of the sixteenth century commentator Isaac de Leon, who argues that Maimonides could have thought the scriptural commandment cited earlier, that is, "you shall acquire the land and settle it" (Numbers 33:53) applied only to the initial conquest of the land at the time of Joshua until the time of King David (only to apply again in the messianic age).[51] Or, perhaps this verse is not prescribing an actual commandment, but it is only predicting how the first Israelis would dispossess the Canaanites to permanently settle the land. In other words, the verse should be translated as "you *will* acquire the land and settle it" rather than as "you *shall* acquire the land and settle it."[52] But if this verse does prescribe

---

[49] For a full representation and discussion of the many subsequent authors who deal with this whole question, see Yaakov Zisberg, *Naḥalat Ya`akov: Explications of the Commandment to Settle the Land of Israel* [Heb.], 2 vols. (Etsiyon, Israel: Merkaz Shapira, 2005).
[50] MT: Marriage, 13.19–20; Kings, 5.12.
[51] *Megillat Esther* on the *Book of Commandments* re Nahmanides' critique, pos. no. 4.
[52] This is Rashi's view in his *Commentary on the Torah* thereon, a view with which Nahmanides explicitly disagrees in his *Commentary on the Torah*. Furthermore, in his critique of Maimonides' silence in the *Book of the Commandments*, Nahmanides says that this verse is neither a "promise" (*yi'ud*) or a "blessing" (*berakhah*). For a defense of Rashi's reading of the verse, contra that of Nahmanides, see Hayyim ibn Attar, *Or Ha-Hayyim* on Num. 33:53.

an actual commandment, perhaps it is the type of general commandment that Maimonides did not include among the 613 specific commandments of the Written Torah.[53]

Maimonides' omission might indicate that the sanctity of the land of Israel (*qedushat ha'arets*) is because certain commandments of the Torah can be observed only there. If so, then the imperative to acquire and settle the land is only a preparation for the observance of these other commandments (*hekhsher mitsvah*), whereas the observance of these other commandments is the true object of this preparation.[54] As such, this "commandment" is a means to another end, just like (for example) building a *sukkah* is not an end in itself but is, rather, the means to this end, which is the obligation of each Jew to "dwell in a *sukkah*" (Leviticus 23:42).[55]

Nevertheless, dwelling in the land of Israel seems to be an end in itself in Jewish tradition, though it should lead to the observance of those other commandments that are dependent upon dwelling there (*teluyah b'arets*).[56] However, if the commanded dwelling in the land is an end in itself, then even somebody who does not intend to observe these other commandments dependent on dwelling in the land, even that person will still have kept a complete commandment of the Torah. However, if that person didn't intend to observe this commandment or any other commandment as a commandment of God, either because he or she doesn't believe in a God who commands, or doesn't believe in any God at all, it is arguable whether that person has actually observed the commandment to dwell in the land.[57]

No doubt, the greater role the land of Israel plays in Nahmanides' theology is why it plays a more important role

---

[53] *Book of the Commandments*: Introduction, no. 4, ed. Chavel, pp. 63–66.
[54] B. Yevamot 6a and Rashi, s.v. "ela"; and Tos., s.v. "she-ken." Note *Sifre*: Devarim, no. 67 re Deut. 12:10; *Tosefta*: Sanhedrin 4.5; B. Sanhedrin 20b. In these texts, "entering the land" is not called a *mitsvah*, whereas appointing a king, destroying the Amalekites, and building the Temple are called *mitsvot*.
[55] B. Sukkah 46a; B. Menahot 42a.
[56] M. Kiddushin 1.9.
[57] Joseph Karo, *Shulhan Arukh*: Orah Hayyim, 60.4.

in his writings than it does in the writings of Maimonides.[58] (Like all great and comprehensive Jewish thinkers, law and theology are constantly integrated in the thought of both Maimonides and Nahmanides.) That might also explain why Nahmanides says every Jew is "obligated" (*mithayyev*) rather than just "commanded" (*metsuveh*) to dwell in the land of Israel. Here Nahmanides might be employing a distinction made by Maimonides between an "obligation" (*hovah*) and a "commandment" (*mitsvah*).[59] In the case of a *mitsvah*, like placing a *mezuzah* on the doorpost of one's house, one is *commanded* to do so only *if* that person wants to dwell in a house rather than in a tent; yet there is no prior obligation to dwell in a house (even though most people want to dwell in a house and do so). One could, after all, choose to dwell in a tent, and thus be exempt from the commandment to affix a *mezuzah* to the doorpost of the house one doesn't live in. Thus a person could avoid the commandment altogether with impunity, unlike the evasion of an obligation that is considered to be an unavoidable transgression therefore. That dwelling in the land of Israel seems to be more than a means to another end probably explains why the preponderance of subsequent Jewish thinkers preferred Nahmanides' designation of the importance per se of this commandment to Maimonides' seeming denigration of it.[60]

Throughout Jewish history there have been individual Jews who have upheld this positive commandment and moved to the land of Israel. They often suffered great hardships in doing so. In fact, that is why most Jews regarded themselves as being exempt from keeping this commandment, as there are no positive commandments (and only three negative commandments) for which Jews are required to risk definite danger to their lives to keep them.[61] As a medieval commentator on the Talmud put it

---

[58] See David Novak, *The Theology of Nahmanides Systematically Presented* (Atlanta, GA: Scholars Press, 1992), 89–97.
[59] MT: Benedictions, 11.2.
[60] Zisberg, *Nahalat Ya`akov*, 67.
[61] B. Sanhedrin 74a.

when dealing with the seeming imperative to settle in the land of Israel: "It doesn't apply at the present time because of the dangers of travel [*sakkanat derakhim*]."[62] In other words, individual and in effect stateless travelers with no government of their own to protect them would be the helpless prey of bandits, pirates, and hostile governments on the way to the land of Israel.[63] Thus the individualist interpretation of the commandment might also explain why so few Jews actually did settle in the land of Israel until the beginnings of the Zionist movement in the late nineteenth century. Without an organized political structure in place, though, it is very difficult for individuals who are unwilling to become part of the existing regime in a country, especially because of profound religious differences, to survive, let alone develop as a community, there.

The most extreme individualist interpretation of the commandment to acquire and settle the land of Israel comes from those who take to be normative a statement in the Talmud that speaks of three oaths God imposed upon the Jewish people, presumably sometime after the aborted rebellion against Roman imperial rule over the land of Israel and the Jews there, in the second century C.E.[64] The first oath was that the Jews "should not scale the wall [of Jerusalem]." The second oath was that the Jews "would not rebel against the nations-of-the-world." The sixteenth-century Talmud commentator Samuel Edels (Maharsha) notes: "Certainly, it is permissible [*reshut*] for any Jew to go up to the land of Israel, but not collectively [*be-yahad*] with force ... As for not rebelling, that refers to other matters while they [the Jews] are in exile [*be-galut*]."[65] Now this

---

[62] B. Ketubot 110b, Tos., s.v. "hu omer."
[63] Yet even without a government, individual Jews and Jewish communities were to be ready to ransom Jews captured by pirates (*pidyon shevuyyim*). See M. Gittin 4.6; B. Kiddushin 21a-b and Rashi, s.v. "v'afilu Rabbi Joshua"; B. Baba Batra 8a-b; MT: Gifts for the Poor, 8.10 and Slaves, 2.7. Nevertheless, as Jews learned from their experience of political impotence in the 1930s and 1940s, mass rescue of endangered Jews requires the coordinated operations of the government of a Jewish state.
[64] B. Ketubot 111a re Song of Songs 2:7.
[65] *Hiddushei Aggadot* on B. Ketubot 111a.

interpretation is consistent with the continuation of the Talmud text, where it is also stated that the Jews took an oath "not to force the end (*she-lo yidahqu et ha-qets*)," that is, not to attempt to bring about messianic redemption by a humanly conducted campaign of political and military conquest.[66] It would seem, though, that a less eschatological political program by Jews to regain and resettle the land of Israel might not violate the oath after all. However, a non-eschatological political program for acquiring and settling the land of Israel was too remote a possibility to even be considered prior to the end of the nineteenth century.

Anti-Zionist traditionalists have used this text to argue against the legitimacy of the collective enterprise of the Jewish state with its exercise of political, military, and economic power.[67] Nevertheless, several traditionalist Zionists have counter-argued against the normative evocation of this text on two grounds.[68] One, no post-Talmudic authority has given it any normative weight at all. Two, the above commentator, Samuel Edels,

---

[66] B. Ketubot 111a, following the variant reading in Rashi, s.v. "she-lo yirhaqu et ha-qets. See *The Babylonian Talmud with Variant* Readings: Kethuboth 2, ed. M. Hershler and J. Hutner (Jerusalem: Institute for the Complete Israeli Talmud, 1977), p. 538. Also, in parallel text where the account of the oath is related (MR: Song of Songs 2.18), one of the reasons for the oath having been sworn is because of what happened at the time of Bar Kokhba, the messianic pretender whose revolution was crushed by the Romans in 135 C.E. Clearly, the author of this statement, Rabbi Helbo, agreed with earlier rabbis who harshly criticized Rabbi Akivah for his support of what were considered the messianic pretensions Bar Kokhba's attempt to "force the end," and whose rebellion caused the Jewish people great suffering. See Y. Taanit 4.5/68d and MR: Lamentations 2.2, ed. Buber, p. 51a re Num. 24:17. Maimonides takes the support shown for Bar Kokhba (whom he calls by his original name "Bar Kozba") to indicate how an ordinary person, having no supernatural powers, can still be taken to be the Messiah (MT: Kings, 11.3). Nevertheless, Maimonides accepts the view of Rabbi Akivah's critics that Bar Kokhba was not the Messiah, not having fulfilled the natural qualifications for anybody claiming to be or who is claimed to be the Messiah by others.

[67] See, for example, Joel Teitelbaum, *On Redemption and Its Counterfeit Substitution* [Heb.] (Brooklyn, NY: Jerusalem Book Store, 1989), 194.

[68] See Isaac Halevi Herzog, *Complete Writings* 1 [Heb.], 5, n. 3; also, Zisberg, *Nahalat Ya`akov*, 1:118–19; 2:780.

mentioned as an exception to this "prohibition" the right exercised by Nehemiah to rebuild the Second Temple in Jerusalem through the exercise of the political power he was entitled to exercise by his monarch: the Persian king. In other words, he had the permission of the most powerful of the nations of the world at that time. And, in 1948, when the State of Israel came into existence, it was quickly recognized by the two most powerful nations of the world: the United States and the Soviet Union, plus being accepted as a member state by the United Nations, the closest thing possible to the nations of the world functioning together in concert.

A Communal Obligation

As we have just seen, the main reason why so few Jews did settle in the land of Israel until the rise of the Zionist movement is because of the danger, the danger individual Jews need not expose themselves to uphold a positive commandment that devolves on individual Jews. However, if the commandment to acquire land in Israel and settle there is considered to be a communal obligation (*hovat tsibbur*), then exposure to danger and even death by individual Jews could be required of those who are participating in this communal obligation. So, for example, one person is not required to risk his or her life to save somebody else's life.[69] Yet in wartime one person is required to risk danger and even death not only to protect the lives of his or her fellows, but also to protect the liberty of the community: the body politic.[70] Now, a communal obligation like this can be exercised only by a politically operative community, which in the world today means by a nation-state. As a political movement that led to a viable nation-state in the land of Israel, Zionism has enabled the Jewish people to become such a politically operative community.

---

[69] B. Baba Metsia 62a re Lev. 25:36.
[70] B. Sotah 44b. See Novak, *Covenantal Rights*, 179–86.

A Communal Obligation

Even if one thinks the words "you shall acquire the land and settle it" (Numbers 33:53) to be a commandment having perpetual binding force, it is arguable whether it really devolves on each and every individual Jew.[71] In fact, if you look at the context in which this commandment was given, and in the context in which it was actually applied, it seems to be more of a communal obligation to be upheld by certain individual members of the community rather than a commandment each and every Jew is simply to take upon him- or herself to observe. Thus the section of the Torah in which this commandment is found begins with the words: "The Lord spoke to Moses on the plains of Moab at the Jordan near Jericho saying: Speaking to the children of Israel you shall say to them, that you are crossing the Jordan into the land of Canaan" (Numbers 33:50–51). A communal act is being commanded here; it is not something each individual Jew is to do for him- or herself. As a political act, that kind of individualism would surely lead to virtual anarchy (such as happened in the American "Wild West" when individual settlers were turned loose to claim land for themselves, but without a definite political structure already in place).[72]

---

[71] Settling the land of Israel can be seen to be the necessary precondition of the *mitsvah* to build the Temple. Maimonides (*Book of* Commandments, pos. no. 20; MT: The Temple, 1.1) bases this *mitsvah* on the scriptural mandate: "They shall make for Me a sanctuary" (Exod. 25:8). The author of *Sefer ha-Hinukh* (no. 95) writes: "This is one of the commandments that does not devolve on an individual [*yahid*], but on the community [*ha-tsibur*] collectively." Indeed, the building of the original Sanctuary (*miqdash*) only called for individual volunteers to fulfill this communal *mitzvah* (Exod. 25:2 and *Targum Jonathan* thereon; also, M. M. Kasher, *Torah Shlemah* thereon, n. 24). Usually, the plural "you" designates each and every member of the community as the subject of the commandment, but some times the plural "you" designates the community collectively (see B. Menahot 65a–b). This too could be the meaning of the plural "you" in Num 33:53.

[72] Though agreeing with Nahmanides that this commandment devolves on each and every Jew, Yaakov Zisberg, in *Nahalat Ya`akov* (2:527), still admits the plausibility of treating this commandment as a communal obligation only (*mitsvah tsibburit*). For Zisberg's teacher Tzvi Yehudah Kook (d. 1982), the commandment devolves on both the community and each and every Jew (ibid., 1:42–42; 2:481).

Indeed, the need for centralized political leadership, which the people Israel didn't have since the time of Joshua, who did apportion the land as a communal act, is expressed by Scripture in these words: "In those days with no king in Israel, every man did what was right [*yashar*] in his own eyes" (Judges 21:25).[73] Furthermore, when the tribes of Reuben and Gad want to settle a territory they have conquered outside what was to be the land of Israel, Moses tells them they may do so only if they first join with the rest of the people Israel in the conquest of the land. The leaders of the two tribes accept Moses' conditions, saying: "We ourselves will cross over [the Jordan] in the vanguard [*halutsim*] before the Lord, into the land of Canaan" (Numbers 32:32). Only after they have fully participated in the conquest of the land God has commanded all Israel to acquire and settle, because this is the land God has chosen for them, will these two tribes also be permitted to go back and settle the land they chose for themselves. In other words, even tribal individualism is trumped by the commandment given to the whole people. In addition, it is clear that like all that of the other tribes, the obligation of the tribes of Reuben and Gad is fulfilled by select individuals, not by each and every member of the tribe. And, it might well have been that these "vanguard troops" were volunteers. In fact, the actual allotment of the various parts of the land was a communal act, as we shall see shortly.

To be sure, any individual who chose to leave the land of Israel to settle elsewhere is considered in subsequent Jewish tradition to be (as we have seen in this chapter) "as if he had no God."[74] And, as the rabbinics scholar Louis Ginzberg (d. 1953) argued, the ancient rabbinic decree (*gezerah*) that deemed land outside of the land of Israel to be "impure" (*tum'at erets ha`ammim*) was probably made to discourage Jews from descending from a higher level of sanctity to a lower level by emigrating from the land of Israel.[75] Because one is to avoid impurity whenever

---

[73] B. Baba Kama 80b–82a.
[74] B. Ketubot 110b.
[75] *On Jewish Law and Lore* (Philadelphia: Jewish Publication Society of America, 1955), 78–80 re B. Shabbat 14a. See *Talmudic Encyclopedia*, 2:196–99, s.v. "erets ha`amim."

possible, it would seem that any Jew who chose to leave the land of Israel after already having lived there would be regarded as somehow or other tainted. Many Jews, especially Israelis who have remained in Israel, feel those Jews who have left Israel for the Diaspora, the so-called *yordim* or "those who have gone down from Israel," to be similarly tainted. In fact, many of these *yordim* feel the same way about themselves.[76] Nevertheless, at least following Maimonides, it doesn't seem that there would be a similar taint of those Jews who, for whatever reason, choose to remain living in the Diaspora rather than becoming *olim* or those who "go up" to Israel.[77] At most it could be said about them is that their sisters and brothers living in the land of Israel are living a fuller Jewish life there.

This has considerable theological import. For, if you designate all those Jews who willingly live in the Diaspora to be "living in sin," then you have in effect confined God's covenant with the Jewish people to but one place on earth. The practical effect of this judgement could be twofold. On the one hand, this could send a message to the Jews in the Diaspora that God still claims them, even though they are not where they are supposed to be, and that God's most immediate claim on them is to prepare to come up (*aliyah*) to the land of Israel by removing obstacles to that ascent. This is a religious version of the secularist idea of "the nullification of the Diaspora" (*shelilat ha-golah*), that is, that that Jewish life in the Diaspora has no validity, once living

---

[76] From later rabbinic sources we learn of an actual rabbinic prohibition of leaving the land of Israel and thereby becoming tainted (*tam'e*) at least by rabbinic, but not by scripturally based, criteria (B. Avodah Zarah 13a; Nahmanides, *Torat ha'Adam*: Concerning Priests, ed. Chavel, pp. 138–39 re B. Berakhot 19b). Though Maimonides extended this prohibition to include any Jew who leaves the land of Israel (as he himself did), he didn't state that those who violated this prohibition are tainted (MT: Kings, 5.9). Moreover, most post-Talmudic halakhists are quite lenient in permitting any Jew to leave the land of Israel. See B. Avodah Zarah 13a and Tos., s.v. "li-lmod" re *She'iltot d-Rav Ahai Gaon*: Emor, no. 103, ed. Kenig, pp. 87b–88a; Jacob ben Asher, *Tur*: Yoreh De`ah, 372 and Joseph Karo, *Bet Yosef*, s.v. "af-al-pi"; idem., *Shulhan Arukh*: Orah Hayyim, 531.4 and Abraham Gumbiner, *Magen Avraham* thereon.

[77] MT: Kings, 5.7.

in the land of Israel is possible for most Jews; indeed, the only validity of the Diaspora is to be, in effect, a holding area for eventual immigration to Israel. On the other hand, though, if that preparation for immigration to Israel requires the strong sense of Jewish identity afforded by religious practice, then couldn't one draw the opposite (secularist) conclusion, that is, that religious practice is but the means to the political end of Israeli residence and citizenship, a means that is no longer needed once its end has been achieved? In other words, while leaving the Diaspora for Israel can be seen as rising from a lower level of religious sanctity to a higher one, that is, a Jew can start being religious in the Diaspora and become more religious when settled in Israel, it can just as easily become an excuse for leaving Jewish religious practice behind in the Diaspora because it is an essentially transient diasporic (*galuti*) institution: a temporary substitute for statehood when there was no Jewish state. As such, this *nullification of the Diaspora* surely could be for many Jews, in effect, the nullification of the covenant itself. For the theological message that comes from any delegitimization of Jewish life in the Diaspora is that the covenant cannot be lived there for its own sake. But if that is the case, why do Jews have to affirm the God who created the whole universe (and the whole world therein), and affirm the God who gave the Torah to his people in the Sinai Desert, outside the land of Israel?[78] Doesn't this in effect diminish God's cosmic status (and *beyond* as we saw in the previous chapter) to that of a tribal deity, even to that of a local deity?

So, just as God's choice to create does not mean that God is no longer interested in His own life (which is totally hidden from creaturely view), and just as God's special creation of humankind (and our world) doesn't mean God is no longer interested in the rest of the universe, and just as God's covenantal election of the people Israel does not mean God is no longer interested in the rest of humankind, so doesn't God's choice of the land of Israel for his covenanted people still mean that God has not lost interest in the rest of his people who are not living in the land of

---

[78] *Mekhilta*: Yitro, re Exod. 19:2, ed Horovitz-Rabin, p. 205; also, ibid., p. 222.

Israel? In other words, whereas the universe has no independence beyond its dependence on God, God does transcend His causal relation to the universe. And, whereas humankind has no independence beyond its being the object of God's special concern, God is still interested in more of creation than just humankind alone. And, whereas the Jewish people have no independence beyond their being the elect of God, God is still interested in the rest of humankind. And, whereas God is especially concerned with his people Israel in the land of Israel, that does not mean that God is not also concerned with his people wherever they happen to be found in the world.

The special status of the people Israel dwelling in the land of Israel is that God can claim more of their lives in this land than anywhere else. But even God's claim upon his people wherever they might be living does not make those covenantal claims an ultimately dispensable means to a separate permanent end. As the Talmud notes, you should not call somebody "wicked" (*rash`a*) just because that person hasn't done what is best (*mitsvah min ha-muvhar*).[79] In our case, what is certainly best for any Jew is to live permanently in the land of Israel, especially in the land of Israel within the boundaries of the State of Israel. Anything else is second best, that is, if a Jew can live a life faithful to the covenant between God and the people Israel, which means in a viable Jewish community where both communal and individual commandments can be kept consistently.

Human Volition

Heretofore, we have been discussing God' choices, culminating in God's choice of the land of Israel wherein the people Israel is to be centered. In all of these choices, God alone is *autonomous* insofar as God's choices are not responses to any prior claims. God alone has absolute freedom of will, which is the prerogative of the Creator to initiate everything. Conversely, there is no creaturely autonomy at any level. Nevertheless, as

[79] B. Nazir 23a re Hos. 14:10.

we move from the first choice to the second, then from the second choice to the third, and then from the third choice to the fourth, the role of creaturely volition increases. Thus regarding God's first choice, that is, God's choice to create the universe, there is no role for creaturely choice: the universe has nothing to say about being created or not, and the universe has nothing to say about how it is to respond to the fact of its being created by God. There is no creaturely choice here at all, let alone any creaturely volition.

Regarding God's second choice, though, that is, God's choice to create humankind and its world in God's image, we humans have no say in our creation as human *beings*, yet we do have a say in our creation as human *persons*. That "say" is our freedom of choice (*behirah hofshit*). We can either respond to God's concern for our personhood by obeying God's commandments, or we can reject God's concern for us by attempting to "be like God" (Genesis 3:5), that is, to be God's equal, having God's same autonomy. That means we would be subject to no one else's commandment but our own, thus justifying our disobedience of the commandment of the one true challenge to our autonomy, which is God's unqualified sovereignty. Yet we humans have more than just freedom of choice between the two options of obedience or disobedience; we have a good deal of volition in deciding for ourselves *how* we can cooperate with God in the ongoing development of our personhood, especially our personhood as political beings. This is especially evident in the variety of human institutions we voluntarily construct to administer social justice, which is rooted in God's cosmic justice (*mishpat*), but that are left to human political authorities (however the people authorize them) to propose policies as to how that justice is best to be administered for their own society at any particular point in its history.[80]

The difference between our freedom of choice and our volitional freedom is that God judges our moral choices: somehow punishing our wrong choices with bad consequences or

---

[80] See Novak, *The Jewish Social Contract*, 70–90.

rewarding our right choices with good consequences. But in those areas of politics left to our voluntary discretion, as long as our voluntary proposals there do not directly reject God's law, there are no truly right or wrong choices, only wise or unwise choices. Moreover, these voluntary choices, not being moral in the strict sense, should not be seen to be subject to ultimate divine judgment. That is, they are made with impunity – unless of course, the motivation of those making these political choices was either good or evil, though that is something known to God alone, and thus something we humans should not pretend to know and publicly praise or condemn.

Regarding God's third choice, that is, God's choice of the people Israel for the covenantal relationship, here again the fact of the Jewish people being chosen is not their choice. The Jews are chosen by God whether they like it or not. Yet they do have the choice to either respond to that fact or reject it by either developing their covenantal status through observance of the positive and negative commandments of the Torah that express it, or by rejecting that status through disobedience of these commandments. And, each of these choices has its consequences. But Jews have more than just the freedom of choice to obey or disobey the explicit commandments of God; they also have considerable communal volition through the public reasoning that goes on continually as a traditional process in deciding *how* these commandments are to be kept. Then there is also the volitional authority of the sages (*hakhamim*) to make humanly devised enactments (*taqqanot*) that are not derived from specific Torah commandments, but rather are made because of what the sages infer to be the overall purposes or ends the Torah implicitly intends, that is, the proposed answer to the ultimate question: *why* the Torah itself?[81] Moreover, because these enactments are not the result of strictly moral choice, and because they do not directly contradict Torah law, they are not subject to divine judgment of right or wrong acts. They too are made with impunity. (Judgment of the motivation of those making

---

[81] MT: Rebels, 1.1–3.

these enactments, as we saw regarding the second divine choice, is God's alone, as we can't praise or condemn what we can't possibly know but only imagine.) Finally, the range of volition in the God–Israel relationship is greater than in the God–human relationship, as it covers not only what pertains to inter-human political matters (*bein adam le-havero*), but also to what pertains to divine–human matters (*bein adam le-maqom*) considered to be more strictly religious.

The volitional freedom of the law-abiding Jewish community (*keneset yisrael*) is most evident in the power the community has in determining how the Jewish people is to acquire and settle the land of Israel. The power of the community to distribute and redistribute property is one of the main powers any government needs to have to govern effectively. This is seen by one opinion in the Talmud to be based on the power of the leaders of Israel to determine just how the land of Israel was to be apportioned at the time of the conquest of the land under Joshua's leadership. "These are the portions allotted [*ha-nahalot*] by Eleazar the [high] priest, Joshua son of Nun, and the chief ancestors, to the tribes of Israel" (Joshua 19:51).[82] Here the emphasis is on the term "chief ancestors" (*rash'ei ha'avot*; literally "head fathers"), that is, "just as fathers [*avot*] may allot to their sons whatever they want [*mah she-yirtsu*], so may tribal chiefs [*r'ashim*] allot to the people [*ha`am*] whatever they want." Thus the political structure had to be in place before any individual Jew could acquire a portion in the land of Israel and settle it. In another place in the Talmud, it is stated that "Israel was commanded [to uphold] three commandments upon entering the land: to appoint themselves [*le-ha`amid lahem*] a king; to destroy the Amalekites; and build themselves the Temple."[83] And, even though the first formally appointed king of Israel was Saul, the fact is that Joshua was de facto king, whose first acts were to conquer the land so that the individual tribes and their individual families could acquire it and settle it.

[82] B. Yevamot 89b.
[83] B. Sanhedrin 20b.

Furthermore, Joshua's royal powers came from the people themselves. In other words, the people themselves had considerable power to choose just how they were to be governed, especially in the land of Israel. As such, no specific type of government was chosen for them by God. This brought the volitional power of the people to a level of semi-autonomy. So, even though it is God who tells Joshua: "You shall allot [*tanhil*] the land to this people, as I promised to their ancestors to give it to them [their descendants]" (Joshua 1:6), nevertheless it was the people themselves who gave Joshua his governmental powers. "They answered Joshua saying: all that you have commanded us, we shall do ... and whoever rebels [*yamreh*] against what you have said, and who doesn't listen to your words, to all you have commanded him, he shall be put to death" (Joshua 1:18). And, the only limit on that governmental power was that it didn't attempt to override any commandment of the Torah.[84] Yet, as the Spanish statesman and theologian Isaac Abravanel (d. 1506) pointed out, the people didn't necessarily have to have a monarchy as their form of government.[85] (He actually preferred a republican form of government, and argued for its preferability should the Jews ever regain their sovereignty.)

All this is because the state is devised by the people to serve the needs of the people, not vice versa. Thus, even how far or near the sanctity of the land of Israel's (*qedushat ha'arets*) extends may be determined by the sages in a way that best suits the political, economic, and even religious, needs of the people. All the more so, any Jewish state, even in the land of Israel, which itself has no sanctity (*qedushah*), is there solely to fulfill the needs of the people. Because the Jewish people have a definite need to acquire and settle the land God has given them to acquire and settle, and because that can be done in today's world of realpolitik only by having a sovereign state with the political, economic,

---

[84] B. Sanhedrin 49a re Josh. 1:18; MT: Kings, 3.9; Abravanel's comment on Josh. 1:18.
[85] See his *Commentary on the Torah*: Deut. 17:14–17; Novak, *The Jewish Social Contract*, 150–56.

and military power necessary for its survival in the world, the State of Israel has a justified claim on the support of the entire Jewish people. That claim extends to the citizens of the State of Israel, and indeed to the entire Jewish people, to even risk life, limb, and property for the survival of the Jewish state. However, as we shall see in Chapter 8, it is a great theological error to invest the humanly devised State of Israel with the sanctity of the land of Israel, and even more so, with the sanctity of the people Israel. Human choices are both necessary and desirable, but only when they are subordinate to God's choices. In our case, these divine choices are God's choice to endow or entitle humans with unalienable rights; God's choice to elect the people Israel for the covenantal relationship; and God's choice of the land of Israel for the people Israel. The people's human choice of what kind of state they want for themselves in the land of Israel is legitimate only when it does not trump these three divine choices and what they have established in the world. It is very important to keep these priorities in mind.

But what about non-Jews? What role could they play *in* an authentically Jewish state? What role could they play in relation *to* such a state? These two questions lead us from this chapter directly into the next one.

7

What Could Be the Status of Non-Jews in a Jewish State?

Rethinking the Status of Non-Jews

It has only been since the establishment of the State of Israel in 1948 that the question of the status of non-Jews in a Jewish polity could be anything more than a purely theoretical question. Before that time, it could only be the subject of theological speculation that had no practical political implications for the present. From the time of the final Roman takeover of the Hasmonean kingdom in 137 B.C.E. until 1948, no group of non-Jews lived under the control of a Jewish polity, because there was no such Jewish polity. During those two millennia, as a people the Jews were stateless. And for most of that time, individual Jews were stateless too, not being full citizens of any of the non-Jewish states in which they lived. In other words, Jews were always being ruled by non-Jews, they never ruled the latter. Nevertheless, this speculation did have some normative significance, for it was concerned with the question: What *would be* the status of non-Jews in the future Jewish polity in the land of Israel that Jews *hope* will actually return to the world? (Questions about the messianic or eschatological significance of the restoration of the Jewish people to the land of Israel will be discussed in the next chapter.) That theological speculation did engage in historical reflection too insofar as it looked for a model of the *restoration* of what was thought to have been the political reality at a time when Jews had had enough political independence to actually rule over non-Jews living among them. As such, this historical reflection has been more than an antiquarian enterprise, and it has now been helped by employing some of the methods of modern historical research.

On the other hand, *individual* gentiles did live under the rule of *individual* Jewish masters as their slaves, at least until the mid-nineteenth century in certain places, though slavery has, happily, been abolished in every society in which Jews live today.[1] In fact, already in Talmudic times, there was some questioning of its necessity.[2] Certainly for Jews, slave-owning should be part of their irretrievable past, at least for those Jews for whom democratic ideas about human rights have some Jewish value.[3] Furthermore, in the rabbinic sources slaves are considered to

---

[1] Writing in the late nineteenth century, after slavery had been abolished in all "civilized" countries, the influential Russian halakhist Yehiel Michal Epstein (d. 1908) stated: "Know that the laws of slavery do not apply in our times, because it is the law of the realm [*dina de-malkhuta*, B. Baba Batra 54b] in all states [*be-khol ha-medinot*] that nobody can purchase a slave and that nobody can be anybody else's slave" (*Arokh Ha-Shulhan*: Orah Hayyim, 304.1). This legal and political fact is by no means bemoaned by Epstein.

[2] B. Berakhot 47b re Lev. 25:46; B. Baba Metsia 60b re M. Avot 1.5. See David Novak, "The Transformation of Slavery in Jewish Law," *Law and Theology in Judaism* 2 (New York: KTAV, 1976), 87–97.

[3] In 1861, when slavery as a moral issue was being hotly debated throughout the United States (though having been abolished in all the European countries), a leading New York rabbi, Morris Raphall (d. 1868), argued publicly that slavery was not contrary to biblical teaching (a point made much of by southern Christian slaveholders), although he urged American slaveholders to adopt the more humane institution of slavery found in the Bible (where slaves are considered "persons," not mere "chattel"). His remarks were published and widely distributed, and they became a topic of much controversy in the American Jewish community. Yet even Raphall insisted he himself did not advocate slavery as a desideratum for Jews or for anybody else. See Bertram W. Korn, *American Jewry and the Civil War* (New York: Atheneum, 1970), 15–31. I mention this to show that even when slavery was a real option (for Jews too), even traditionalists like Raphall were already distancing ancient Jewish slaveholding from modern slaveholding. Moreover, it could be that Raphall's position on slavery was a reaction to the abolitionist statements of some Reform rabbis, whose political radicalism seemed to function in tandem with their religious radicalism, which he vigorously opposed.

be quasi-Jews, even being subject to the usual requirements for conversion, that is, circumcision and immersion (*tevillah*).[4] Thus they were considered to be more Jewish than non-Jewish.[5] That is why the institution of slavery offers no real precedent for understanding what the status of unambiguous gentiles in a modern Jewish state could be. (I have to mention all this, though, because there are some antidemocratic elements among the Jewish people who seem to think of non-Jews as if they are or should, in effect, be treated like slaves.)

Since 1948, however, the status of non-Jews in a Jewish polity is now a practical political question, yet it is a question that needs more than a political answer. So, for example, Israel's Declaration of Independence speaks of "equal rights for all citizens, regardless of religion, race, or gender."[6] But, when more than forty years later it was officially stated that Israel is "a Jewish and democratic state," the president of Israel's Supreme Court, Aharon Barak, though emphasizing "democratic" far more than "Jewish," still had to allow some Jewishness to the State of Israel (as we saw in the previous chapter). His two main Jewish emphases were that Hebrew be the official language of the state, and "the right of every Jew to immigrate to the State of Israel [i.e., *hoq ha-shevut* or "the law of return"], where the Jews will constitute a majority."[7] Nevertheless, how in a true democracy can one people be so privileged? Aren't all the citizens of a democracy, their ethnicity notwithstanding, supposed to be equal across the board? So, indeed (as we also saw in the previous chapter), both "Jewish" and "democratic" have to be rethought so the two elements of Israeli statehood might be correlated.

That rethinking must be theological if it is to be rooted in the Jewish tradition. But it cannot invoke legal precedent, that is, case law (*ma`aseh she-hayah*), because there are no such precedents. Even when the Talmud does discuss the possibility of

---

[4] B. Yevamot 46a; MT: Forbidden Intercourse, 13.11.
[5] B. Hagigah 4a re Deut. 24:1 and Lev. 19:20.
[6] www.knesset.gov.il/docs/heb/megilat.htm and www.science.co.il/Israel-Declaration-of-Independence
[7] www.jewishvirtuallibrary.org/source/isdf/text/barak.html

Jews having political power over gentiles, the discussions are not about any present political situation. Instead, the discussions are about what happened in the past when Jews did have such power, or they are about a future of which Jews are assured they will have such power, in fact, far greater power than they ever had in the past.[8] The theological discussion now, which does deal with the political reality of Jewish political power over gentiles, must be one that employs theological principles that do have legal significance, even though actual legal rulings should not be simply deduced from such principles.[9] That makes the task of the location and interpretation of primary sources, plus philosophically astute reconceptualization of the issues they deal with, be of more contemporary significance than similar efforts were in the past. As such, the effort here is more than mere academic speculation.

The Resident-Alien

The question of the status of non-Jews in a Jewish polity, that is, their rights and duties there, involves three distinct questions. One, there is the question of the status of non-Jews in a Jewish polity who want to remain gentiles, that is, who do not want to fully convert to Judaism (*gerei tsedeq*) and thus cease to be non-Jews altogether. Two, there is the question of the status of non-Jews who are not yet ready to fully convert to Judaism, but who also do not want to be considered as gentiles either. Three, there is the question of the status of non-Jews who want their own state in the land of Israel, and whether or not that non-Jewish state could be recognized by the Jewish state in good faith. All three questions can be dealt with when we look at the rabbinic concept of the *ger toshav*, sometimes called the "resident-alien," especially as thought through by two of the greatest medieval Jewish theologians: Maimonides (d. 1204) and Nahmanides

---

[8] See, for example, B. Baba Kama 97b.
[9] Y. Peah 2.6/17a. See *Talmudic Encyclopedia* 1 [Heb.], s.v. "aggadah," p. 62.

(d. 1270).¹⁰ But we need to first look at the biblical institution of the *ger*, the "sojourner," which is the basis of the rabbinic concept of the *ger toshav*.

The rabbis contrast the *ger toshav* with the *ger tsedeq*: the "righteous proselyte," that is, the gentile who becomes fully Jewish. This contrast is made between a status the rabbis had experience in dealing with, that is, that of the *ger tsedeq*, and a status they either had a tradition about what it actually was or they imagined what they thought it could have been in the far away past, and what it could be in the future. So, when the Torah uses the term *ger*, it is almost always assumed by the rabbis that it means a full proselyte, because they were mostly concerned with scriptural norms that could the basis of their current legal rulings.¹¹ In fact, it seems that in the days before the destruction of the First Temple, there were no proselytes, that is, gentiles who could become full members of the Jewish people through the event of conversion (*giyyur*). The reason for this absence of proselytism at that time is that in order to be considered a full member of the people Israel (who had a polity then), a person had to be a male member of a particular tribe, who had an ancestral portion (*ahuzah*) in the part of the land of Israel apportioned to his tribe. Anyone who did not have this kind of patrimony could only be a *ger*, which older English translations of Scripture call a "sojourner."¹² A gentile woman it seems, at least in the days of the First Temple, could become a full member of the people by simply marrying a Jewish man, it being assumed that by so doing she would take upon herself the specific religious obligations of Jewish women.¹³ Thus the two paradigmatic proselytes for the rabbis, who lived before the destruction of the First Temple, that

---

¹⁰ Parts of this chapter have been reworked from an earlier essay in David Novak, "Non-Jews in a Jewish Polity: Subject or Sovereign?," *Jewish Social Ethics* (New York: Oxford University Press, 1992), 187–205.
¹¹ See, for example, M. Baba Metsia 4.10 re Exod. 22:20.
¹² See David Novak, *The Image of the Non-Jew in Judaism*, 2nd ed., edited by M. LaGrone (Oxford: Littman Library, 2011), 19–23.
¹³ Y. Kiddushin 3.12/64d; B. Yevamot 45b. Cf. MT: Forbidden Intercourse, 13.9 and Vidal of Tolosa, *Magid Mishneh* thereon.

is, Jethro (the father-in-law of Moses) and Ruth (the ancestress of King David), are really not paradigms at all for later proselytes. Ruth, after all, is a woman who becomes a Jew by virtue of her marriage (even though the rabbis assume she went through a formal conversion procedure).[14] And as for Jethro, the rabbis had to admit that the reason he refused to accompany the people Israel into the land of Israel is because he didn't want to be a second-class landless resident-alien (*ger toshav*) there (when he had first class, aristocratic status in his native Midian).[15]

Theologically speaking, the difference between a *ger* as a sojourner or resident-alien is essentially a difference of degree, not of kind. Because true ownership of the earth and all its lands belongs to God alone insofar as "the earth is the Lord's, the world and all who dwell therein" (Psalms 24:1), even persons fully and unambiguously Jewish are still "sojourners and transient tenants [*gerim ve-toshavim*] with Me" (Leviticus 25:23). Even when King David prepares his son Solomon to ascend the throne after him, which was very much a national occasion, in a publicly uttered prayer he is still recorded as saying: "We are sojourners [*gerim*] before you, transient tenants [*ve-toshavim*] like all our ancestors" (II Chronicles 29:15). And the reason for calling the people Israel "sojourners and transient tenants" is the two last enigmatic words in this verse (*ein miqveh*), literally "without hope," but that could be translated "without future prospects in this world."[16] That is, unlike God, no humans can truly own anything or any place in this world, because we are all mortal creatures: here today and gone tomorrow.[17] Thus King David states thereafter, "everything is yours" (29:16). Accordingly, full Jews only have a longer lease on our landed "property" even in the land of Israel than do resident-aliens. We are all sojourners in

---

[14] B. Yevamot 47b; MR: Ruth 2.23–24 re Ruth 1:16.
[15] *Sifrei*: Numbers, no. 78 re Num. 10:29, ed. Horovitz, p. 75. Cf. *Mekhilta de-Rabbi Ishmael*: Yitro re Exod. 18:27, ed. Horovitz-Rabin, p. 200, where it is assumed that Jethro became and *ger tsedeq*, who then returned to his native native Midian to proselytize his fellow Midianites on behalf of Judaism.
[16] See comments of Rashi and David Kimhi (Radaq) thereon.
[17] Psalms 49:7–13.

The Resident-Alien

God's world.[18] All this notwithstanding, though, there are important differences between full Jews and resident-aliens.

Although there are times when a *ger* is included by the Torah in some religious ceremonies, for the most part it seems that a *ger* only enjoyed equal civil rights and was only obligated to perform equal civil duties.[19] Thus the Torah states as a general principle: "There shall be one civil law [*mishpat ehad*] for both the sojourner [*ka-ger*] and the native-born [*ka-ezrah*], for I am the Lord your God" (Leviticus 24:23).[20] This is the point that is emphasized by central text in the Talmud dealing with the institution of the *ger toshav*.

> Who is a *ger toshav*? Anybody who in the presence of three ordained rabbis [*haverim*] takes it upon himself not to engage in idolatry [*avodah zarah*]; which is the view of Rabbi Meir. But the sages say he is anybody who accepts upon himself as obligatory the seven Noahide commandments. Others say that these men haven't reached the status of the *ger toshav* yet. So, who is a *ger toshav*? He is the *ger* who eats nonkosher meat [*neveilot*], but who accepts upon himself as obligatory all the commandments stated in the Torah, except the prohibition of eating nonkosher meat.[21]

All later discussions of the *ger toshav* endorse the view of the sages, who regard the *ger toshav* to be the person who publicly accepts the Noahide commandments.[22] Now the difference

---

[18] Psalms 119:19.
[19] See B. Keritot 9a.
[20] See Simon Federbush, *The Nature of the State in Israel* [Heb.], 2nd rev. ed. (Jerusalem: Mosad haRav Kook, 1973), 20–23.
[21] B. Avodah Zarah 64b. With the exception of a prohibition of a *ger toshav* doing work directly for a Jew on the Sabbath (B. Keritot 9a and Tos., s.v. "l'eil" thereon; Jacob ben Asher, *Tur*: Orah Hayyim, 304 and Joseph Karo, *Bet Yosef* re Solomon ibn Adret, *Hiddushei Ha-Rashba* on B. Yevamot 48b and Tos., s.v. "zeh ger toshav" thereon), it is assumed by all the medieval codes and commentaries that a *ger toshav* is only to observe the seven Noahide commandments. See MT: Kings, 10.9; also, Akiva Eger, *Responsa*, no. 121, citing B. Sanhedrin 58b re Gen. 8:21.
[22] MT: Kings, 8.10. The other opinions are minority opinions not to be followed in practice (*halakhah le-ma'aseh*), even though they are to be remembered for situations where they can be casuistically invoked. See B. Berakhot 9a; M. Eduyot 1.5.and comment of Ra'avad thereon. Nevertheless, an important twentieth-century halakhist, Israel Meir Kagan (Hafets Hayyim, d. 1932),

between a *ger toshav* and a full Jew (albeit only in theory) was considerable, as there are many more commandments that the Jewish community could enforce among its fully Jewish members than the mere seven Noahide commandments to be enforced among its gentile members. However (as we saw in the previous chapter), if an Israeli state that is both Jewish and democratic can only enforce basic natural law norms (which for us are expressed in the Noahide commandments), then the public gap between Jewish and non-Jewish citizens will be much less than it would be in the fully Jewish state envisioned by the rabbis.

In our attempt to find a source in the tradition for determining the status of non-Jews in the Jewish state, the problem with employing the rabbinic idea of the *ger toshav* is that in one place the Talmud says that as a real social institution the institution of the *ger toshav* operated only when the Jubilee year (*yovel*) operated, which was in the days of the First Temple when all twelve tribes of Israel were actually living in their allotted locations in the land of Israel.[23] The main feature of the Jubilee was that "you shall return, every man, to his ancestral portion [*ahuzato*] ... to his family [*mishpahto*]" (Leviticus 25:10). As such, it would seem that as a real social institution the *ger toshav* is either anachronistic or messianic. That is, the *ger toshav* is either part of the irretrievable past or the unattainable (i.e., by human effort) future. Nevertheless, Maimonides, in his main discussion of the Noahide laws and to whom they apply, doesn't mention this stipulation. He only mentions it when discussing the Jubilee year.[24] Thus he writes: "And so did Moses our master command, from

---

argues, largely basing himself on the view of the "others" cited earlier, that a *ger toshav* has the right to obligate himself for more (specifically Jewish) commandments, even though an ordinary *ger toshav* (whom he calls *stam ger toshav*) only has the duty to observe the seven Noahide commandments (*Bi'ur Halakhah* on Joseph Karo, *Shulhan Arukh*: Orah Hayyim, 304.3). This is an important perecedent for developing a category of a gentile who is more than an ordinary *ger toshav*, but still less than a full convert (*ger tsedeq*) or even explicitly committed to becoming a *ger tsedeq*.

[23] B. Arakhin 29a re Deut. 15:6 and 23:17; B. Gittin 45a.
[24] MT: Sabbatical Year and Jubilee 10.9; Forbidden Intercourse, 14.8; Circumcision, 1.6.

divine revelation [*mi-pi ha-gevurah*], to force all the inhabitants of the world to accept all the commandments Noah was commanded ... and whoever does accept them is called a *ger toshav* wherever [*be-khol maqom*]."[25] Though this sounds like Jews are expected to go out and conquer the world for the sake of enforcing Noahide law), its meaning is probably less grandiose. It probably means that any human person who comes to live under Jewish political rule (i.e., in a Jewish state) must accept Noahide law or the severe consequences of his non-acceptance of it.

The acceptance of Noahide law by the *ger toshav* implies that acceptance entitles him to equal civil rights like Jews and obligates him for equal civil duties like those expected of Jews. In fact, not only does Maimonides not stipulate that this institution could operate only when the Jubilee year operates, but he doesn't even stipulate that the Jewish polity enforcing Noahide law need be in the land of Israel. That seems to be why, when in another place Maimonides does state that "a *ger toshav* is not accepted except when the Jubilee operates [*noheg*]," the commentator closest to his views, Joseph Karo (d. 1575), explains: "His [Maimonides'] reasoning is that even though a *ger toshav* is not accepted except when the Jubilee operates, if he does accept the seven commandments, then why prevent him from living in the land. We need not be concerned that they will cause others to sin [having renounced idolatry] ... [so] he only meant that there is now no need for a court to [formally] accept them."[26] Accordingly, Karo has saved Maimonides' teaching about the *ger toshav*, making it a powerful precedent for consistently and justly dealing with non-Jews in the Jewish state today. The essence of the status of the *ger toshav* is the acceptance of the universal moral standards legislated in the Noahide laws; everything else is secondary and conditional.

In fact, the Mishnah mentions that when the Jews returned to the land of Israel from the Babylonian Exile (around seventy years after the destruction of the First temple in 586 B.C.E.),

---

[25] MT: Kings, 8.10. See MT: Idolatry, 7.1.
[26] MT: Idolatry, 10.6, and Joseph Karo, *Kesef Mishneh* thereon.

there were ten different kinds of people who did return. One of them was the Gibeonites (*netinim*), who had long been attached to the people Israel since the time of the first conquest of the land of Israel led by Joshua.[27] Obviously, some of them went into Babylonian exile with the Jews and then returned to the land of Israel with them.[28] In another context in the Talmud, one rabbi bemoans the fact that the rights of these not-fully-Jewish sojourners (*gerim*) had once been seriously violated by the Jews, a violation that could have brought disrepute (*hillul ha-shem*) to the entire Jewish people and their religion.[29] It would seem that there would be no concern with the rights of the Gibeonites had they not accepted upon themselves the duties of Noahide law or something like it. That would be what entitled them to become permanent residents (*toshavim*) in the land of Israel.

What is remarkable about the rabbinic discussion of the rights and duties of the *ger toshav*, whether they be individuals or a group, is that they were conducted in the land of Israel when the same rabbis were living under capricious, often brutal, Roman imperial rule in the Roman province of Palestine. Nevertheless, despite suffering great injustice at the hands of the dominant "others," they were still advocating for "others" they hoped would, someday, be living under Jewish rule as they had in the pre-exilic past. In other words, we would not treat non-Jews living in our polity like the stateless people we are, who are so badly treated by the Roman conquerors.

The moral point of this rabbinic speculation about the *ger toshav* is rooted in Scripture. "You shall not oppress the resident-alien [*ger*], knowing as you do the life [*nefesh*] of a resident-alien, because you were resident-aliens [*gerim*] in the land of Egypt" (Exodus 23:9). Indeed, this might be a scriptural support for the famous maxim of Hillel the Elder: "What is hateful [*sanei*] to you, do not do to a fellow human being [*le-haverakh*]."[30] This should be contrasted with the way the

---

[27] M. Kiddushin 4.1.
[28] Ezra 2:43; 8:20.
[29] B. Yevamot 79a re II Sam. 21:10.
[30] B. Shabbat 31a.

rabbis see Samson's cry when he destroys the temple of the Philistines (and himself along with them): "Let me [*nafshi*] die with the Philistines" (Judges 16:30). Instead of being taken to be a noble act of martyrdom, it is taken to be the mean-spirited rationalization of someone who wants others to suffer as he or she has suffered.[31] Or, as the Anglo-American poet, W. H. Auden, put it: "Those to whom evil is done, do evil in return."[32] Therefore, the proper Jewish response to suffering at the hands of more powerful others is to extend justice to weaker others over whom Jews might have power. But, of course, in order for gentiles to receive full justice from Jews, they must become at least like a *ger toshav* by demonstrating they accept the basic moral norms the Jewish community regards to be binding on all humankind. Indeed, Jews are required to enforce and protect the rights these norms command dutiful responses, that is, when Jews do have power over non-Jews living among them. This is like the peace Jews are to promote between themselves and non-Jews dependent on their charity.[33]

If the institution of the *ger toshav* were to be revived in the State of Israel, this gentile citizen of the state would have to affirm what the state itself has to affirm in order to be a state worthy of the moral allegiance of any rational person. Moreover, just as Jewish citizens of the state ought to acknowledge that the raison d'être of this Jewish state is to uphold the communal commandment to acquire the land of Israel and settle it (of which the establishment of a modern nation-state is the best means thereto), even if some individual citizens do not regard themselves to be personally bound by the commandments of the Torah, so too gentile citizens of the state ought to acknowledge the raison d'être of the *Jewish* state they have chosen to live in, even if they themselves do not regard themselves to be bound by the specifically Jewish commandments of the Torah. And, of

---

[31] B. Yevamot 118a and 120a.
[32] "September 1, 1939" in *Seven Centuries of Verse*, 2nd ed., edited by A. J. M. Smith (New York: Charles Scribner's Sons, 1957), 686.
[33] B. Gittin 61a; also, MT: Kings, 10.12 and note of Karo, *Kesef Mishneh* thereon.

course, if they begin to personally identify with this Jewish communal commandment, then it would seem they are on the road to full conversion to Judaism, and full membership in the Jewish people as well as full citizenship in the State of Israel.

The Equalization of Civil Rights

There is a great moral difficulty facing any revival of the institution of the *ger toshav* in a religiously constituted Jewish polity, for the fact is that in *halakhah* as it stands now, gentiles do not have equal civil rights with Jews. First, their property does not have the same legal protection as Jewish property does. Second, gentiles may not serve as either witnesses or judges in cases before a Jewish court involving them, whether they be litigants in a civil trial or whether they be either victims or those indicted in a criminal trial. But, because no Jewish religious court (*bet din*) today has criminal jurisdiction (even in the State of Israel), we need only look at the civil disability suffered by non-Jews in a Jewish religious court. Nevertheless, there are halakhically valid solutions to these two moral difficulties. One is more specifically legal and thus more conservative; the other is more generally political and thus more radical. The first solution can be done within the *halakhic* court system as it functions here and now; the second solution requires a full reconstitution of the *halakhic* court system in a future time.

As for the legal vulnerability on non-Jewish property, there is this famous (some would say infamous) ruling in the Mishnah: "When an ox of a Jew gored an ox of a gentile, the Jew is not at all liable [*patur*]; but when an ox of a gentile gored an ox of a Jew, the gentile is liable [*hayyav*] to pay full damages."[34]

---

[34] M. Baba Kama 4.3; also, T. Baba Kama 4.2-3, and my late revered teacher, Saul Lieberman, *Tosefta Kifshuta: Neziqin* (New York: Jewish Theological Seminary of America, 1988), 38–39. Note Mekhilta: Mishpatim re Exod. 21:35, ed. Horovitz-Rabin, p. 290; similarly, Sifre: Devarim, no. 278 re Deut. 24:4), ed. Finkelstein, p. 296. In these tannaitic texts, the source *of* this ruling is seen to be scriptural, but no reason is given there *for* it. See also, Novak, *The Image of the Non-Jew in Judaism*, 41–45.

The Equalization of Civil Rights

This ruling seems to have been embarrassing to the editors of both the Palestinian and Babylonian Talmuds, who had to deal with it nonetheless, which explains the necessity of justifying it or explaining it away subsequently.[35] Thus Maimonides, following the Palestinian Talmud, suggested that the reason for this ruling against gentile ox owners is that it is a penalty (*qenas*), incurred by gentiles because non-Jewish law does not obligate its subjects to pay for damages their animals inflict on the animals of others.[36] This explanation probably has some historical validity, because we know that in Roman Palestine (where the Palestinian Talmud was produced), which was a conquered territory administered by usually corrupt Roman imperial officials, there was no systematic system of law enforced there (unlike *ius civile* in Rome, or *ius gentium* in the old established Roman provinces).[37] Moreover, it seems the property rights of Jews were discriminated against in these non-Jewish courts. Finally, it is most unlikely that this ruling was ever put into practice, inasmuch as we have no record of non-Jews in Roman Palestine being subject to the rulings of Jewish legal authorities who, certainly, had no civil jurisdiction over gentiles (and probably very little even over their fellow Jews). Hence this ruling might well have been a hypothetical quid pro quo. In other words, it is likely saying: "If we had the power to do to you as you do to us, we would do that." Nevertheless, it is morally problematic to deny a civil right (i.e., the right to restitution of property for damages suffered due to the behavior of the property of others) to a foreigner just because the law of the polity of that foreigner doesn't enforce the civil right of property owners to restitution for similar damages.[38]

---

[35] B. Baba Kama 38a; Y. Baba Kama 4.3/4b.
[36] MT; Monetary Damages, 8.5. Cf. his *Commentary on the Mishnah*: Neziqin re Baba Kama 4.3, ed. Kafih, p. 16.
[37] See David Novak, *The Jewish Social Contract* (Princeton, NJ: Princeton University Press, 2005), 103–14.
[38] For the notion of legally sanctioned quid pro quo, see B. Baba Batra 48b. For the moral suggestion that this not be done, however, see MT: Renting, 7.7 re B. Baba Metsia 101b.

However, if property owners do have the right to restitution for damages in non-Jewish systems of law, irrespective of who injures whom and who is injured by whom, wouldn't Jewish law look morally inferior to these non-Jewish systems of law? In other words, isn't the moral respectability of Jewish law besmirched by letting the ruling of an ox of a Jew goring an ox of a gentile be applied literally? To leave the law as is would constitute what is called *hillul ha-shem*, literally, "profanation of the divine name," that is, making God's law for the Jews seeming to be unjust in comparison to non-Jewish law.[39] This point was fully explicated and developed by the fourteenth-century Provençal jurist and theologian Menahem Meiri. He argued that this law no longer applies to contemporary Christians and Muslims, whose law is essentially just and does not condone, let alone encourage, irresponsibility for damages done by one's property. Moreover, Meiri asserts that their systems of law are "divinely revealed law" (*darkhei ha-datot*).[40] That means that their law is like Jewish law, having the same moral status because it has been revealed by the same just God whom Jews, Christians, and Muslims generally revere as the Source of all morally compelling law, and not only as the Source of one's own revealed law. It would seem, then, that the attempt of the Palestinian Talmud and Maimonides to deal with this problem is more conservative, and that Meiri's attempt to deal with it is more radical.

When comes to the problem of dealing with the fact that a gentile may not serve as either a witness or a judge in a case before a Jewish court, there is also a more conservative way and a more radical way to deal with the problem.[41]

A more conservative approach to this problem of the civil disenfranchisement of non-Jews in a religiously constituted Jewish polity would be to rely on the rabbinic opinion mentioned

---

[39] B. Baba Kama 113a-b; also, *Sifre*: Devarim, no. 16 re Deut. 1:16, ed. Finkelstein, pp. 26–27.
[40] *Bet ha-Behirah*: Baba Kama 113b, ed. Schlesinger, p. 330. See Novak, *The Image of the Non-Jew in Judaism*, 195-99.
[41] The sources of this restriction are: M. Baba Kama 1.3; B. Baba Kama 15a re Exod. 21:1; M. Shevuot 1.4.

The Equalization of Civil Rights

in the Talmud that in a civil case between a Jew and a non-Jew, the litigants have the option of taking their case to either a Jewish or a non-Jewish court.[42] Now even if a gentile is confident that he or she will receive a just verdict in a Jewish court, wouldn't that gentile be more likely to opt for a court where he or she could also (in other circumstances) be a witness or a judge? And, how could the Jewish litigant object to that option if he or she could also have the same privilege in that non-Jewish court? When that is the situation, however, it would then seem that the choice of which court to submit the case to would have to be dependent on the two parties deciding which court procedures, of the Jewish or the non-Jewish court, are more attractive. In fact, there is *halakhic* support for Jews being allowed to go to a non-Jewish court when it is the only court able to effect justice.[43]

Nevertheless, that choice of courts could be avoided altogether if both litigants agreed to some sort of binding mediation. Jewish law allows and even encourages would-be litigants in a civil case to avail themselves of this option. This allows them to work out some sort of compromise by settling the matter among themselves. Thus the two parties themselves become their own judges. (It is unlikely that witnesses would be required here, as the two parties wouldn't submit themselves to this kind of extra-legal procedure unless they were not disputing facts but trying to find a practical solution to their dispute). Moreover, although a number of legal specifics are not required in this kind of interpersonal mediation, basic principles of justice must prevail nonetheless.[44]

A more radical solution to the problem of this double standard in Jewish law would be to interpret the scriptural commandment, "there shall be one civil law [*mishpat ehad*] for the

---

[42] B. Baba Kama 113a. Furthermore, according to Rabbi Akiva (whom the law is to follow, even when another colleague like Rabbi Ishmael in this text, disagrees with his opinion; see B. Eruvin 46b), this is to be done without any deception (*iqafin*) of the gentile that would besmirch the moral sanctity of God's Torah.

[43] Mt: Sanhedrin, 26.7 (cf. MT: Personal Injury and Damage, 8.9); M. Gittin 9.8. See, also, Novak, *The Jewish Social Contract*, 114–20.

[44] B. Sanhedrin 6b re II Sam. 18:15.

sojourner [*ka-ger*] and the native-born" (Leviticus 24:22), specifically. This would mean that not only are non-Jews to have equal civil rights as subjects of the law, that is, as litigants, but that they are to have equal civil rights as witnesses and judges who administer the law as well. Now the impediment to this equalization is the scriptural verse, "when two men [*anashim*] having a legal dispute [*riv*] stand before the Lord, before the priests and the judges who are [functioning] at that time" (Deuteronomy 19:17). This verse is interpreted by the rabbis to mean "men" literally, and that it doesn't refer to the litigants (*ba`alei dinin*), but to the witnesses and, *a fortiori*, to the judges. "Men" in this situation is interpreted to exclude women who, it is argued, are not subject to all the commandments (*shayyakh be-mitsvot*) and, therefore, may not be full participants in the system of adjudication of the commandments.[45] So, non-Jews, who have even fewer commandments to perform than do women, are to be similarly excluded a fortiori. All this notwithstanding, a re-established Sanhedrin could reinterpret "men" to mean what is usual, but not necessary. That is, it was usually men who were involved in legal and political or public matters (which is a point mentioned en passant in the Talmud), and are thus men are assumed to be the only persons capable of adjudicating public disputes *ipso facto*.[46] So, in a political situation, when both and non-Jews would be full participants in public matters, it would be the prerogative of the fully reestablished Sanhedrin to reinterpret the Torah's commandment concerning witnesses and judges in civil trials. In other words "men" (*anashim*) could now mean "persons."[47] Maimonides, most forcefully, emphasizes this radical prerogative of the Sanhedrin.[48] And, in fact, the full restoration of the Sanhedrin is probably needed to fully restore the institution of the *ger toshav* in a polity that accepted its full authority.

---

[45] B. Baba Kama 15a.
[46] B. Shevuot 30a re Ps. 45:14. See Tos., s.v. "kol bat melekh penimah" thereon.
[47] See, for example, *Sifra*: Aharei-Mot, chapter 13, and B. Sanhedrin 57b, re Lev. 18:6.
[48] MT: Rebels, 1.2 and Joseph Karo, *Kesef Mishneh* thereon re B. Rosh Hashanah 25b (à la Deut. 17:9).

Potential Jews

Moreover, it is also Maimonides who emphasizes that a *ger toshav* has rights over and beyond those of an ordinary gentile in a Jewish polity, thus suggesting civil equality among Jewish and non-Jewish citizens of a religiously constituted Jewish polity.

Potential Jews

This leads us into the second kind of *ger toshav*. "Rabbah bar bar Hannah quoting Rabbi Yohanan said that any *ger toshav* who had not been circumcised with twelve months [of his becoming a *ger toshav*] is considered to be like a gentile heretic [*meen*]."[49] Some have interpreted a "gentile heretic" to be a gentile who is an idolater.[50] If so, that would imply that this person's life is not to be saved from mortal danger because he is now like any other idolater, but unlike a *ger toshav*, whose life is to be saved (and even supported).[51] However, some have interpreted Maimonides' paraphrase of this passage to read that "it is as if he were from [*min*] the nations."[52] Now this could mean that such a person returns to the status of an ordinary *Noahide*, who is not necessarily an idolater. This seems to be borne out by the fact that Maimonides does not mention any penalty for a *ger toshav* who decides not to go through with full conversion to Judaism by refusing to be circumcised, even when as Maimonides put it, he originally committed himself (*ha-meqabbel alav*) to be circumcised within twelve months of his becoming a *ger toshav*. It would seem, then, that these twelve months are a trial period during which this would-be convert is preparing him- or herself for conversion, but minus the pressures of a conversion that he or she is committed to begin ab initio as a process and is required to conclude as an event (i.e., through immersion and/or circumcision). Once he or she has been fully converted, though, there is no going back to the status of being a *ger toshav*.[53]

---

[49] B. Avodah Zarah 65a.
[50] B. Hullin 13b and Tos., s.v. "shehitat meen." Cf. Y. Shabbat 16.1/15c.
[51] B. Avodah Zarah 26a–b. See Meiri, *Bet ha-Behirah* thereon, ed. Sofer, pp. 59–61.
[52] MT: Kings, 8.10 and Abraham di Boten, *Lehem Mishneh* thereon.
[53] B. Yevamot 47b; MT: Kings, 8.10.

The revival of this kind of *ger toshav* might help Israel deal with a large number of people living there who, though legally non-Jews, want to be full members of Israeli/Jewish society nonetheless. Often they are married to Jews (their weddings have taken place outside of Israel or before they immigrated to Israel), or they are involved in long-term "relationships" with Jews. Some rabbis in Israel have attempted to resolve this problem by quickly performing conversion ceremonies for many of these people. Nevertheless, the legal (i.e., *halakhic*) validity of these conversions is questionable because it is obvious that the vast majority of these people did not convert for truly religious reasons, but that their motivation was much more pragmatic, that is, to gain full Jewish citizenship in Israel with all its privileges.[54] As such, their acceptance of the authority of all the commandments of the Torah, plus their commitment to try to consistently practice them, is considered by many other rabbis to be fraudulent. And, even if conversion without sincere acceptance of the obligation to live a religiously Jewish life is valid post factum, this isn't something to be permitted let alone encouraged ab initio.[55] However, by making conversion a process, which a gentile in this kind of limbo can enter into when he or she feels ready and can back out of at any time with impunity, this gentile is thus not to be pressured into a full conversion, for which he or she is not ready (and might never be ready for). In fact, there is precedence for developing a category of gentiles who are more than an ordinary *ger toshav*, but still not fully Jewish, and who are not explicitly committed to full conversion. (This is probably the closest a religious system like *halakhah* could come to recognizing a quasi-secular concept of citizenship.[56])

There are three kinds of such "potential Jews." One, there are men whose legal status is that of a gentile, but who are parties to what are domestic unions (often under official non-Jewish

---

[54] Cf. B. Yevamot 24b.
[55] MT: Forbidden Intercourse, 13.16–17.
[56] See Hermann Cohen, *Religion of Reason Out of the Sources of Judaism*, trans. S. Kaplan (New York: Frederick Ungar, 1972), 121–27.

auspices) with Jewish women. If or when they do convert fully, their domestic union could be quickly elevated to that of a full Jewish marriage (*qiddushin*), because these men are only initiating a new relationship de jure. In fact, though, they are only legally restructuring a de facto marital relationship already in place.[57] Two, there are women whose legal status is that of a gentile, and who are parties to what are domestic unions with Jewish men (also, often under official non-Jewish auspices), who on their conversion could also have these unions be just as quickly elevated to full Jewish marriage, because they too are not leaving a totally gentile social identity. Though their children are legally gentiles, they could be converted along with them for the very same reason.[58] Finally, there are couples, neither of whom has the legal status of Jews, but who have long given up any identifiable gentile identity because they have long lived among Jews. In their case, their having been such "potential Jews" should be taken as sufficient preparation for their conversion, the conversion of their children, and the immediate elevation of their marital relationship to that of a full Jewish marriage de jure.

Non-Jewish Autonomy

This leads us to the third kind of *ger toshav*. These are non-Jews whose nation has been conquered by Jews. What is now their relationship with their Jewish conquerors? And, we should always be aware when looking at the following sources that they only apply to a Jewish state in the land of Israel.

---

[57] They would, however, have to wait three months from the time of his conversion (and refrain from sexual intercourse with his former "partner" during that time) so as to ensure that there would be an identifiable distinction between children he sired as a gentile (even those children who were converted along with him) and children he sired as a Jew, as the former would not be considered siblings of the latter were a levirate situation to arise in their family (B. Yevamot 42a and 97b; MT: Levirate Marriage, 1.8). This applies to the second and third kind of potential Jew as well.

[58] B. Kiddushin 68b re Deut. 7:11. B. Yevamot 62a; MT: Marriage, 15.6; Jacob ben Asher, *Tur*: Even Ha`Ezer, 1 and Joseph Karo, *Bet Yosef*, s.v. "hayu" thereon.

Even though Scripture mandates that in the case of the Israelite conquest of Canaan, "you shall not let any of them [i.e., any Canaanite] live" (Deuteronomy 20:16) because peace was not to be offered to any of the Canaanite nations, it is clear from the book of Joshua that several Canaanite nations did make peace with the invading Israelites.[59] Because of that, their people were left alone. But the question is: How could the Israelites have avoided the mandate not to make peace with any of the Canaanite nations and thereby spare the lives of any Canaanite? Is there any way to avoid this mandate with impunity? The following Talmudic passage seems to address this question. Like all such rabbinic discussions of Jewish power over gentiles, as we have seen, this one too is theoretical (though the practical implications are more real for contemporary Jews than they were for our rabbinic forbearers).

> Before entering the land, Joshua sent three proclamations [*prostigiyot*] to the land of Israel: Whoever wants to leave, let them leave; whoever wants to make peace, let them make peace; whoever wants to make war, let them make war ... the Gibeonites made peace: [as it is written] "the inhabitants of Gibeon made peace with Israel" (Joshua 10:1).

Thirty-one kings made war with Israel and fell.[60]

The Gibeonites are the biblical paradigm for the *ger toshav* the rabbis speculated about.

The question now is: What were the conditions that enabled the Canaanite nations to negotiate peace with their Israelite conquerors? When we look to an early rabbinic comment, we find this condition stipulated: "If they repented [*asu teshuvah*], they are not to be killed."[61] But what is that "repentance" for? It would seem that it is for their violation of those matters about which they had already been commanded. Thus in Leviticus a moral reason is given for why the Canaanites *ought* to be

---

[59] Josh. 11:19 16:10.
[60] Y. Sheviit 6.1/36c; MT: Kings, 6.1-4.
[61] *Sifrei*: Deuteronomy, no. 202, ed. Finkelstein, p. 238.

expelled by the Israelites. "You [Israelites] shall not do all these abominations [ha-to`evot] ... which the people there before you in the land did ... so that the land not vomit you out because of your defilement of it as it vomited out the nation who was there before you" (Leviticus 18:26–28). Now these "abominations" are primarily violations of the three cardinal transgressions: the prohibitions of idolatry (especially with its attendant practices of deviant sex and bloodshed), deviant sexual practices (such as incest), and bloodshed (such as human sacrifice). The prohibition of these practices comprises the core of Noahide morality. Their violation justifies Israeli conquest of the land; but it also requires the Israelis to allow the gentiles in the land of Israel to repent. By so doing, it enables them to survive under Israelite rule. (We shall shortly see that this moral commitment enables the gentiles in the land of Israel, even collectively, to do more than just survive.)

Maimonides makes this connection of moral commitment to Noahide law and political negotiation explicit. His basic discussion of the *ger toshav* (as we have seen) comes in the context of his discussion of what is to be done with gentiles conquered by Jews. Thus when discussing the status of a gentile woman captured in war (*yefat to'ar*), he says: "If she doesn't want to convert [*le-hitgayyer*], we given her twelve months [to decide]. If she still doesn't want [to convert] but accepts the seven commandments commanded to the Noahides, she is to be set free, and she becomes like any other resident-alien [*ha-gerim ha-toshavim*]."[62] In other words, this vulnerable woman has definite rights to be protected by the Jewish polity because she has accepted the minimal duties incumbent upon anybody choosing to live among the Jewish people. This then leads him to generalize, saying that "any gentile who doesn't accept the commandments commanded to the Noahides is to be executed, that is, when they are under Jewish rule [*tahat yadeinu*]."[63] Furthermore, Maimonides extends this moral condition to gentile nations as collective

---

[62] MT: Kings, 8.9.
[63] Ibid., 8.10; also, MT: Circumcision, 1.6.

entities to whom the people Israel are required to offer them the opportunity to make peace one way of another.

> No war is to be waged against any human being [*adam*] in the world until peace is first offered them ... as it is written: "When you approach a city to wage war against it, you shall offer it peace [*le-shalom*]." (Deuteronomy 20:10) If they make peace, and accept the seven commandments commanded to the Noahides, no life is to be killed; they are to pay tribute [*le-mas*], as it is written: "They shall pay tribute and serve you." (Deuteronomy 20:11)[64]

So far, Maimonides has been basically paraphrasing some earlier rabbinic discussions of the practical implications of the "peace offering" mentioned above. In these sources what "tribute" (*mas*) actually means practically and what servitude" (*shi`bud*) means practically are not spelled out.[65] Maimonides, however, does spell it out:

> The servitude they are to accept is that they are to be humiliated [*nivzim*] and put down at the lowest [social] status. And they shall not be able to lift their head among Jews, but they shall being subjugated [*kvushim*]. They shall not be appointed [*ve-lo yitmanu*] to any office where they would have authority over Jews for any reason whatsoever. The tribute to be received from them is that they are to be ready for the service of the king with their bodies and with their property.[66]

Non-Jewish *communities*, for Maimonides anyway, seem to have the same status as do Jews and Christians who are subject to Muslim rule, i.e., they seem to have the status similar to that of *dhimmis*.[67] (This was a status Maimonides was well of aware of, for it was his own status as a Jew living under Muslim regimes, first in his native Spain and finally in Egypt.) These people are not like an individual *ger toshav* who is not to be treated this way, probably because he came to the Jewish community freely

---

[64] MT: Kings, 6.1.
[65] *Sifrei*: Deuteronomy, no. 200, ed. Finkelstein, p. 237.
[66] MT: Kings, 6.1.
[67] See Anver M. Emon, *Religious Pluralism and Islamic Law* (Oxford: Oxford University Press, 2012).

on his own, not as a member of a captured community whose members had to collectively take whatever their captors offered them. Nevertheless, despite the harshness of Maimonides' words about them, these people still have the right not to be arbitrarily mistreated or deceived by their Jewish rulers. So, immediately after the harsh words above, Maimonides writes: "It is forbidden to be deceitful in the covenant with them [*be-vritam*], to lie to them. That is because they made peace [with us] and accepted the seven [Noahide] commandments."[68] Furthermore, he does not mandate the enslavement of non-Jewish communities who have been conquered by a Jewish state, which would be the usual method of subjugation and humiliation.

Surely, humiliation and overt subjugation are inconsistent with the overall purpose of peace between Jews and non-Jews that enabled the Rabbis to see the commandment "you shall offer them peace terms [*le-shalom*]" (Deuteronomy 20:10) to extend even to the Canaanite nations, thus making the commandment "you shall not let any of them live" (Deuteronomy 20:16) contingent on whether the Canaanite nations accepted the peace offer of the Israelis. We should be aware of the fact that the rabbinic sources Maimonides drew upon do not specify "subjugation" to mean "humiliation" as does Maimonides. As such, *subjugation* could mean nothing more than that the non-Jewish group should formally recognize that their political autonomy is something they are morally indebted to the Jewish state for having granted them. As for "tribute," that could be nothing more than some kind of minimal (even symbolic) payment as their recognition of the political legitimacy of the Jewish state in the land of Israel.

Right and Might

Maimonides has attempted to work up into a coherent mandate regarding non-Jewish communities living under Jewish rule. He has thus attempted to synthesize two distinct criteria: one, the

---

[68] MT: Kings, 6.3. See B. Baba Kama 113a.

criterion of Noahide law that any gentile living under Jewish rule, whether individually or collectively, must accept; and two, the criterion of servitude and tribute that Jewish rulers must impose upon gentile collectives living under their rule. The question is whether subjugation is for the sake of the enforcement of Noahide law, or whether the acceptance of Noahide law is part of the whole process of subjugation. This, then, deals with the perennial question facing all political theory: Is power (in our case, subjugation) for the sake of enforcing right (in our case, Noahide law), or is enforcing what is right part of the exercise of political power?[69] In other words, does right justify might, or does might simply employ right? Both criteria are required by the rabbinic sources Maimonides draws upon, but which criterion takes precedence?

The answer to this question might be found when we look at Maimonides' discussion of war in general, that is, what is the overall purpose for which any war is to be fought, especially a war that has been initiated by Jewish authorities?

> And in all of these matters the king's law is law. In all of them his deeds should be for the sake of God, and his purpose [*magamato*] and thought are to be in order to elevate the status of the true religion [*dat ha'emet*] and to fill the world with what is right [*tsedeq*] … for the king is not made king except to implement justice [*la`asot mishpat*] and wage war.[70]

Now here, "the true religion" is not the imposition of Judaism on gentiles, because Maimonides rules against any such forced conversion, as we have seen.[71] Also, the "implementation of justice" is the enforcement of Noahide law. And, if the Jewish authorities are to enforce Noahide law only among gentiles, then it seems likely that they are required to employ its standards of justice in their own actions and policies. So, a careful reading of all of

---

[69] See Plato, *Republic*, 338C–340A.
[70] MT: Kings, 4.10.
[71] Instead, the Jews are "to proclaim [*le-farsem*] this true faith [*ha'emunah ha-z'ot ha`amitit*] in the world." *Book of Commandments*, pos. no. 9, ed. Heller, pp. 37–38.

Maimonides' statements on war and the subjugation of non-Jews captured in war (in his treatise on kingship and war) seems to indicate that the only justification for any war and, therefore, the only justification for any subjugation of non-Jews is a moral one. The political implications of this emphasis of moral primacy are considerable.

It will be recalled that when Maimonides indicated that servitude meant that no member of a conquered non-Jewish community could be appointed to an office where he would have authority over Jews. Moreover, these gentiles do not have full legal authority even when ruling themselves. Even when gentiles are allowed to adjudicate cases involving other gentiles, their specific authority comes from their Jewish rulers, whether these gentile litigants are lone individuals or members of a conquered gentile group.

> The Jewish court is obligated to appoint judges for these resident-aliens to judge them according to these standards of justice [*al-pi mishpatim elu*], so that human society [*ha`olam*] not be destroyed. If the Jewish sees fit to appoint judges from among them [it may do so]. But, if they see fit to appoint judges for them [i.e., the gentiles] from among Jews, they may appoint them.[72]

Even though non-Jewish residents in a Jewish state are to be subjects of their own law, that is, the law God has commanded to all humankind, the administration of that law is not essentially in the hands of its gentile subjects. Maimonides' biblical example of this is the story of how the two sons of Jacob, Simeon and Levi, were justified in executing the men of Shechem, because the men of Shechem did not react to their prince's rape of Jacob's daughter Dinah.[73] (It is important to note that Maimonides doesn't justify this action as proper vengeance for what the prince did to *their* sister, but because what the prince did was wrong to do to *any* woman.[74]) In other words, at least according to Maimonides, non-Jews do not have full political autonomy

---

[72] MT: Kings, 10.11.
[73] Ibid., 9.14.
[74] See MR: Genesis 80.6 re Gen. 34:7.

because they do not have full legal autonomy. (Let it be noted that in the Jewish tradition the law precedes the state, so that Jews can have authentic law even without a state to enforce it; but we can't have an authentic Jewish state without a prior law for that state to enforce.[75])

Nahmanides (d. 1270), who it could be said was Maimonides' most astute (and systematic) critic, takes issue with Maimonides' justification of the action of Simeon and Levi in executing justice in lieu of the (gentile) people of Shechem executing justice among themselves. But, as we shall now see, his objections are not only exegetical; they are also conceptual, that is, they question Maimonides' limitation of gentile legal autonomy altogether. So, after making his exegetical counterpoint, Nahmanides notes:

> In my opinion, the obligation of adjudication [*dinin*, i.e., the rectification of injustice] that was assigned to the Noahides through their seven commandments required that they place judges in every district. He [God] commanded them concerning such matters as stealing and cheating ... just like the obligation of adjudication [i.e., the administration of justice] for which Jews are commanded [*she-nitstavu*] ... the matter is not something that was turned over to Jacob and his sons to be done [by them].[76]

It would seem that Nahmanides view of the Shechem story is that it indicates that the imposition of Jewish political power over a group of non-Jews will inevitably invite political disaster, even when that imposition does have a certain moral justification. In fact, he approves of Jacob's condemnation of the action taken by his sons, Simeon and Levi, that is, "You have made trouble for me [*akhartem oti*], making me odious among the inhabitants of the land ... and I am few in numbers, and they will come together against me; I and my house will be destroyed" (Genesis 34:30). Thus Nahmanides seems to be implying that when Jews

---

[75] See Deut. 17:18–20, where the appointment of a Jewish king presupposes that there is already a law to which the king is beholden. Thus "the law makes the king" (*lex facit regem*), not that "the king makes the law" (*rex facit legem*). See Oliver O'Donovan, *The Desire of the Nations* (Cambridge: Cambridge University Press, 1996), 72, 232; Novak, *The Jewish Social Contract*, 124–56.

[76] *Commentary on the Torah*: Gen. 34:13, ed. Chavel, pp. 191–92.

do enforce a law among gentiles that ought to be enforced by gentiles themselves, political considerations of self-interest (i.e., imperialism) inevitably outweigh the moral zeal that was supposed to have been the essential reason for the enforcement of the law in the first place. (I think here of how the Romans often used the moral need to enforce Roman legal rule throughout the world as a pretext for their conquest of non-Roman peoples.) The assumption of the basic moral capacity of all human persons – in our case, of a non-Jewish group who have accepted Noahide law – implies that their legal-political autonomy is preferable to their basic subjugation to even authentic Jewish interpreters and administrators of Jewish law, whose authority comes from the Jewish community. Too often, seemingly noble moral reasons become, in fact, rationalizations of far baser political motives.

Nahmanides' view of the moral dangers of political subjugation enable us to look on the institution of the *ger toshav* as a hopeful way of dealing with the question of the legitimacy, for Jews, of a non-Jewish polity within the land of Israel. Now there might be very good realpolitik type reasons why the Jewish state cannot recognize the legitimacy of a non-Jewish (Palestinian) state at the present time. After all, it does not seem that the Palestinians are ready now to recognize that their autonomy could only come from it being conceded to them by the Jewish state already in full control of the land of Israel. And it does not seem that the Palestinians are now ready to even recognize the political legitimacy of the Jewish State of Israel. Nevertheless, it is still within the realm of human possibility that things could change. Surely, the Torah's teaching is that there is no human being (or human group) who cannot fundamentally change their orientation to others in the world.[77] (Look at how most Christians today have fundamentally changed their whole orientation vis-à-vis Jews and Judaism.) Therefore, even though this reflection on the political significance of the institution of the *ger toshav* seems to have no practical application now, it still might

[77] See MT: Repentance, 5.1–2.

have practical application in the as yet unpredictable future. This might be a case of where a practical opportunity can be more intelligently seized when there is a history of thinking about it already in place. Finally, in the case of the two earlier suggestions about reviving the institution of the *ger toshav*, that is, giving true Jewish status to non-Jewish citizens of the Jewish state, and giving a status to non-Jewish citizens of the Jewish state who no longer want to be gentiles while still not wanting to become fully Jewish, the practical implications are closer at hand.

It is hard for many Jews to contemplate what should be the presence of non-Jews in the land of Israel or as citizens of the State of Israel. That is because of the experience of the Holocaust. For many Jews, the message that emerges from that shattering experience is that the State of Israel represents the Jewish reaction to the abandonment of the Jews by the nations-of-the-world during the Holocaust. So, why should Jews be concerned with gentiles who have been so unconcerned with the Jews, if not continually hostile to the Jews? I can well understand that kind of feeling, but I don't sympathize with it. It seems to me that it distorts the true raison d'être of a Jewish state in the land of Israel. Nevertheless, Zionists can hardly ignore the significance of the Holocaust experience in dealing with the present and future of the State of Israel: the object of their great concern. That is why, in the following chapter, we shall examine good and bad interpretations of the relation of the Holocaust to the life of the State of Israel.

8

What Is the Connection Between the Holocaust and the State of Israel?

Historical and Political Sequences

To see a connection between the Holocaust and the reestablishment of the State of Israel is inevitable when looking at the historical facts. There is a virtual juxtaposition between January 1933, when Hitler and the Nazi regime came to power in Germany, and May 1948, when the independence of the State of Israel was declared. In the incredibly brief historical period of just fifteen and a half years, the Jewish people suffered their greatest calamity ever and celebrated perhaps their greatest victory ever. Nevertheless, we must avoid the logical fallacy of *post hoc ergo propter hoc*, which assumes that mere temporal juxtaposition automatically signifies some necessary causal connection between an earlier event and a later one that follows right after it. Instead, the burden of proof is on those who assert that there is a deeper nexus within this temporal proximity, one that essentially links these two epoch-making events in the history of the Jews and, perhaps, in the history of the world. This is especially important for Zionists to ponder, for it seems that the experience of the Holocaust is what made most of the Jews in the postwar world into Zionists.

In the secular and secularized world in which most contemporary Jews live and speak, the method most readily at hand for making an essential connection between historical events is political. In the case of the Holocaust and the reestablishment of the State of Israel, the connection is usually made by correlating political experience and political action. Many see the connection as a transition from passive Jewish impotence to active Jewish power. The Holocaust is the experience of Jewish impotence; the reestablishment of the State of Israel is the activation of Jewish power.

In terms of the experience of the Holocaust and the question of Jewish passivity, some quite recent scholarship has done much to dispel the impression that the six million Jewish victims of Nazi murder "went to the slaughter like lambs." Many Jews did not simply cooperate in their own destruction, but bravely resisted as best they could despite the nearly impossible odds against them.[1] Indeed, we need to learn much more about this resistance to properly honor the memory of those who can no longer speak of themselves and for themselves. Nevertheless, in terms of "suffering," both in the modern sense of enduring pain and in the earlier sense of being acted upon, for the Jewish people the Holocaust was far more what *happened to* Jews than what Jews *were able to do*. That is why attempts to fix any responsibility for the Holocaust on the Jews, whether by religious or secular thinkers, are regarded by most Jews (and by most fair-minded persons in general) as downright obscene.

It is not that everything done by every Jew at that time was right, but to fix our attention on what the Jews might have done to cooperate with their own destruction, either before or during the Holocaust, deflects full moral judgment away from the Nazi murderers themselves by, in effect, "blaming the victim." (Aside from proven Jewish collaborators and informers who can and should be brought to human justice, whatever other sins were committed by Jewish victims either before or during the Holocaust are beyond the range of our judging and are best left to the Judge of the whole world and everybody in it.[2]) However,

---

[1] See Ruby Rohrlich, *Resisting the Holocaust* (Oxford: Berg Publishers, 1998).
[2] M. Avot 1.6; 2.4.

the psychological fact that most Jews during the Holocaust did not accept what was being done to them does not dispel the political fact of their overwhelming weakness in relation to the power of the Nazis and their cohorts nonetheless. Thank God, the Allies defeated the Nazi regime on the battlefield. If they hadn't, all of the Jews here today would likely be dead, or would have never been born. Yet, as far as the Jews are concerned, those who did survive did not defeat the Nazis; they just managed somehow or other to escape. There is an enormous difference between being a refugee and being a victor. Later, we shall explore this point theologically.

Of course, at least two generations before the rise of Nazi genocide, the Zionists, who rightly deserve credit for being the most direct cause who brought the State of Israel into existence, advocated the idea of a Jewish state in the land of Israel as the solution to the so-called Jewish question (especially, what came to be known as *die Judenfrage in Europa*). National sovereignty was intended to transform the Jewish people from a state of passive victimhood to one of active political responsibility. The experience of radical Jewish vulnerability in the Holocaust became for many a necessary condition of the political claim of the Zionists on the Jewish people themselves, and on the world at large, for Jewish national sovereignty in the land of Israel. As a result of their our horrendous experience during the years 1933–1945, the Jews now had a powerful argument for a state of their own to protect them from anything else like the Holocaust ever again. There is no doubt that the experience of the Holocaust made Zionists out of almost all Jews, except for a fringe on the religious right and a fringe on the secularist left. Along these lines, I remember quite vividly standing in the main plaza in Auschwitz in 1992 and hearing Ehud Barak, then an Israeli general (and now Israel's defense minister), tell a group of Israeli high school students, in impassioned Hebrew (with simultaneous translation into Polish for the benefit of his Polish military hosts), that had there been an Israeli army in 1942–1945, the atrocities committed in that place would not have happened, there or anywhere else. Being pure supposition about the irretrievable past, though, the truth of Barak's boast cannot be ascertained. Yet, most Jews believe this would be true in the future were another Holocaust being planned, God forbid, anywhere else in the world. Apparently, enough of the political powers in the world (especially the United States and the Soviet Union) in 1947–1949 believed this too. Without the Holocaust, it is difficult to see how the Zionist claim for a sovereign Jewish state in the land of Israel would have been so internationally successful. In fact, it is quite significant in terms of political rhetoric that when any important world leader comes for an official visit to Israel, he or she is taken for a highly publicized visit to *Yad Vashem*, the official Holocaust memorial and museum in Jerusalem.

At the political level, this is as good an explanation as one could conceive to connect the Holocaust to the State of Israel. It has been the major political formulation of a raison d'être of a state still containing deep internal divisions. But, whether that is still sufficient as a raison d'être of the State of Israel when the memory of Jewish helplessness is receding further and further into the past is an issue that can be resolved only by Israeli Jews. Even when Jews are strongly Zionistic, Diaspora Jews can only be nonvoting advisors. The existence of the State of Israel as a political fact seems to be a stunning confirmation that despite horrendous Jewish suffering in the Holocaust, the Jewish people have survived and have taken hold of their own lives and future as never before. This has even developed into what can only be seen as a secular ritual these days, namely, highly organized tours for Jewish teenagers that begin with a trip to the sites of the death camps in Poland, then immediately followed by a direct flight to Israel. The very medium is the message. As we shall soon see, this political message quickly leads to theological interpretations.

Holocaust Theologies

What seems cogent at the political level becomes much more problematic at the theological level, as it is much harder to think theologically than politically. So, for that very reason, some Jews advocate that the theological reflection on an issue as difficult as the Holocaust or the State of Israel, let alone the connection of the two, be bracketed or even be eliminated altogether. Isn't theological reflection beside the point and thus a hopeless distraction from our real political needs here and now? Of course, that seems right if one conceives of "theology" as the type of "God-talk" that deals with God-as-God-is-in-Godself, which is the kind of God-talk Plato, Aristotle, and Plotinus engaged in, and in which they were followed of the great Jewish thinkers their metaphysics so heavily influenced. But if, as Spinoza so rightly recognized (however much those who have remained Jews might differ with his ultimate conclusions from that recognition, as we saw Chapter 2), Jewish thought always concerns a theologico-political realm, Jewish thinkers cannot escape the theological component of Jewish politics any more than they can escape the political component of Jewish theology. That is because the most comprehensive and coherent idea of Jewish identity is that the Jews are a people involved in an everlasting, irrevocable covenant with God. Jewish theology, then, is about a national or communal *relationship* between God and the Jewish people. Surely, without the Jewish past, of which the covenantal dimension is ubiquitous, can anyone think that a "Jewish" anything, much less a "Jewish state," would be historically cogent? Accordingly, Jewish political reflection has to become theological sooner or later.

The theological problem of connecting the Holocaust to the reestablishment of the State of Israel is that it is very hard to see how it was the same God who was involved in both events. That is the most serious challenge to Jewish monotheism presently imaginable. The historical juxtaposition of the two events raises two great theological questions. Regarding the Holocaust, we ask: *Where was God?* Regarding the reestablishment of the State of Israel, we ask: *How was God there?* Can the same God who seemed to have been so absent in the Holocaust suddenly become so present in the reestablishment of the State of Israel? Let us now look at the main theological explanations offered.

That intellectual coherence is not the same as intellectual satisfaction is shown by the theology of some Jews who propose what might well be the most explicit theology conceivable of the Holocaust and the State of Israel and their inner connection. We might call their thinking on the subject "pietistic," even though it is not shared by all *haredi* or "ultra-Orthodox" Jews. With chilling coherence, they argue that the Holocaust is God's punishment for the Jews having been seduced by the modern temptation to become part of the non-Jewish world, the worst example of that temptation being Zionism. Like all modern ideologies, for them, Zionism is a pseudo-messianism, albeit of a particularly Jewish sort. They see Zionism as the arrogant attempt to solve the cosmic problem of the Jewish people by human political means rather than waiting for the apocalyptic deliverance of the Jewish people (and with them the whole world) by God alone through His chosen Messiah.

The most articulate and influential proponent of this view was the leader (or "rebbe") of the Satmar Hasidim Joel Teitelbaum (d. 1979). In a treatise on redemption, originally written in the wake of Israel's 1956 incursion into the Egyptian-held Sinai peninsula (to open the Suez Canal which had been closed by the Egyptians), he charged that the Zionists now running the State of Israel were "the lowest of the low, who have caused awful calamities on the Jewish people."[3] He then becomes more specific, accusing "the Zionist movement of playing a leading role in the bloodshed [*shefikhut damim*] such as never happened to the Jewish people before … which was caused [*be-sibbat*] the polluted idea about the establishment of that state."[4] In other words, for Teitelbaum, the idea that seems to be the cause of the political success of the State of Israel is actually the cause of the Holocaust! Thus, contrary to the religious nationalists,

---

[3] *Concerning Redemption and Its Counterfeit Substitute* [Heb.], Introduction (Brooklyn, NY: Jerusalem Book Store, 1989), p. 11.
[4] Ibid., sec. 113, p. 171.

whom Teitelbaum condemns even more severely than their secularist counterparts, the Satmar Rebbe sees the Holocaust to be God's punishment for even entertaining the idea of a reestablished Jewish state in the land of Israel, plus setting up a political movement to make that idea a reality.

Truth be told, these pietists have a good deal of Jewish tradition behind their assertions. There is a whole strand of the tradition that assumes, in the words of the Talmud, that "when a person sees suffering [*yisurin*] come upon him, let him carefully examine his deeds."[5] (The big question, though, is which deeds cause which suffering.) Present suffering, especially Jewish suffering, is divine judgement for past sins. It is God's warning to us to repent before it is too late. Certainly, even the pietists, in their denunciation of the Jewish people, do not exonerate the Nazi murderers. Nevertheless, their primary intention is to tell us where God was during the Holocaust: God was there as the avenger of the sins of the Jewish people. (Where and when God will avenge all the sins committed against the Jewish people by their enemies seems to be of less interest to these pietists.)

Regarding the Holocaust as being ultimately a divine act, they want to justify the ways of God. In the case of the State of Israel, conversely, being a human act, the pietists want to condemn the ways of humans. Thus they seem to want to echo Moses when he said to the people, "The Rock, His work is perfect, for all his ways are just [*mishpat*], a faithful God with no wrong, just and upright [*tsaddiq ve-yashar*] is he. Is corruption His? No, it is the fault of his children, a generation crooked and twisted" (Deuteronomy 32:4–5). In other words, following this strict logic, because the Jews were punished for their sin of Zionism by God through the Holocaust, they should expect further punishment, perhaps even worse than the Holocaust, for their sin of supporting Zionism's historical fruit: the State of Israel.

Turning their argument on its head, the American Jewish thinker Richard Rubenstein has argued that if God is innocent then the Jews are guilty; but, if the Jews are innocent, then God is

---

[5] B. Berakhot 5a re Lam. 3:40.

guilty. However, because it seems religiously impossible to have a relationship with such a guilty God, Rubenstein concludes that because of Auschwitz no relationship with the covenantal God is possible ever again. Better to have no God or an indifferent God than a guilty one, for him.[6]

Now, if I understand him correctly, for Rubenstein, God has died, that is, the covenanting God presented in Scripture has died for him (and he correctly assumes for many other contemporary Jews as well). This God, then, is the most significant victim of the Holocaust. Because God wasn't there to save the Jews then, the Jews cannot and should not ever try to "resurrect" this God again, as it were. (I remember Richard Rubenstein being the most prominent Jewish advocate of "God is dead" theology, or "a-theology," in the late 1960s.) To bring this God back, so to speak, would mean that we could blame God for His not saving the victims of the Holocaust, especially the Jews whom this God has promised to save. Yet, even if we could bring this God back into Jewish life, anger at God for His seeming inaction during the Holocaust would still trump any attempt to attribute salvation to God, even the salvation many Jews think they have experienced in the establishment of the State of Israel and in the victories of the Six Day War in 1967. So, in order not to blame the Jewish victims of the Holocaust (as does Teitelbaum), Rubenstein denies the presence of a God who could be so angrily blamed by the Jews (which the Psalms and subsequent Jewish liturgy show God that Jews are allowed to do, short of blaspheming God's name, i.e., short of indicting God).[7] From this it follows, though, that there would be no reason to assume that Jews should praise God for what God has done for them, nor is there any reason for Jews to hope that God will reward them for what they have done for his covenant with the Jewish people. Removing anger, blaming,

---

[6] Richard Rubenstein, *After Auschwitz*, 2nd ed. (Baltimore, MD: Johns Hopkins University Press, 1992), 157–76.

[7] Blaspheming, that is, cursing God's name or presence (*qilelat ha-shem*), like any strong curse, means trying to kill or "pierce" or "stab" (*noqev*) God with your words (B. Sanhedrin 56a re Lev. 24:16). Obviously, like the practice of idolatry, this ends the relationship with God (MT: Idolatry, 2.6). See Job 2:9–10

praise, and reward from the God–Israel relationship, however, is to eviscerate it to the point of insignificance.

Conversely, in the pietistic approach, most forcefully articulated by Teitelbaun, we still see an essentially theological explanation for this dual problem. In this view, monotheism has been preserved: it is the same recognizable God who was both at the Holocaust and at the reestablishment of the State of Israel. At the time of the Holocaust, God was judge; since the time of the reestablishment of the State of Israel, God has been warning the Jews not to defy the words of the Talmud (as we saw in the previous chapter) that we "not rebel [*she-lo yimrodu*] against the nations of the world."[8] Thus, for the pietist, the Jewish task is to live under the political rule of the various nations of the world and not defy God's commandment by declaring Jewish national sovereignty before the arrival of the Messiah and his reign over all the earth. Thus the true meaning of the Holocaust should trump Zionism.

If one doesn't like this theology, that person can employ it as a *reductio ad absurdum* of all Jewish theology. That is, one can use it to dismiss Jewish theology altogether (which even Rubenstein did not do in his efforts to radically remake it) as not only irrelevant to the present situation of the Jewish people, but even more so, as an inevitably sadistic assault on still open wounds from the Holocaust plus the newfound strength in the State of Israel. But for the Jews to do that would be to lose their connection to classical Jewish theology as the most coherent explanation of Jewish historical-political identity and continuity. So let us look at another theological approach that seems to be the direct opposite of that of Teitelbaum and the pietists.

This counter-theological approach is usually termed "religio-nationalist" (*dati le'umi*), even though all religious Zionists do not accept it. In direct opposition to the pietistic approach, the religio-nationalists regard the reestablishment of the State of Israel to be the most important religious imperative of our time. For them, this imperative is not just the commandment

---

[8] B. Ketubot 111a.

to settle the land of Israel (*yishuv erets yisrael*) and make it habitable by Jews. Instead, the imperative to reestablish the Jewish state in the land of Israel is an imperative for Jews to actively help bring about the reign of the Messiah. In this view, the messianic reality is a process that begins with the reestablishment of the State of Israel and is to culminate in the full messianic reign in the land of Israel and beyond. This view has found liturgical expression in the prayer composed in 1948 for the new State of Israel, which asks God to bless the state as "the beginning of the growth of our redemption" (*ge'ulteinu*). (This prayer is recited in most Orthodox synagogues, except in those synagogues whose congregations are explicitly *haredi* anti-Zionist.) Thus the significance of the founding of the state is eschatological. It is the beginning of the end of history itself, that is, "the beginning of redemption" (*atehalta de-ge'ulah*).[9] At this final juncture of history Jews as Zionists in the land of Israel are called upon by God to play a unique and central role in this redemptive process.[10]

Now the use of this kabbalistic term in connection with Jewish resettlement of the land of Israel goes back to two what might be called "proto-Zionist" nineteenth-century Jewish thinkers, the Ashkenazic (in his case German) rabbi Zvi Hirsch Kalischer (d. 1874) and the Sephardic (in his case Croatian) rabbi Judah Alakalai (d. 1878).[11] Both thinkers made much of

---

[9] *Zohar*: Lekh-lekha, 1:77b and 88b, based on the kabbalistic teaching about how the divine–human relationship is "awakened from below" (*itar`uta de-letatta*), that is, by human initiative, to which God reacts by completing what this human initiative started.

[10] On the other hand, in his 1947 essay, "Two Peoples in Palestine," Martin Buber (d. 1965) used this term in a more universalistic way, calling "the beginning of redemption" to be "the harmonization of the world under the sovereignty of God," and "the renewal of a godly society." *A Land of Two Peoples*, ed. P. R. Mendes-Flohr (New York: Oxford University Press, 1983), 195–96. Even though Buber affirmed how the Jewish people needs to be centered in the land of Israel, early on and consistently thereafter he saw nationalism per se to be an impediment to that universal vision and task. See ibid., 52–53; also, Shlomo Avineri, *The Making of Modern Zionism* (New York: Basic Books, 1981), 218. Nevertheless, Buber is quite vague about what this vision and task actually involve.

[11] See Kalischer's Seeking Zion 1.1 [Heb.], ed. Y. Etsiyon (Jerusalem: Mosad Harav Kook, 1972), pp. 37–39; and Alkalai's essay "Hear O' Israel,"

a rabbinic passage (importantly, found in the "Israeli Talmud," better known as *Talmud Yerushalmi*) that teaches the redemption of the Jews (*ge'ulatan shel yisra'el*) will be a slow incremental process rather than a sudden apocalyptic event.[12] And, both Kalischer and Alkalai were impressed with the rise of nationalism in various parts of Europe, seeing the time to be now ripe for Jews to have their own nationalism for the sake of resettling the land of Israel.[13] Of course, the reality of an actual Jewish state in the land of Israel was beyond their imagination. But they were, nevertheless, precedents for the type of religious Zionism that looked to the reestablishment of the Jewish state in the land of Israel to be of messianic significance, which in the twentieth century became a political reality. Following their lead, Issac Jacob Reines (d. 1915), a Lithuanian rabbi who founded the religious Zionist movement called *Mizrahi*, cited several mediaeval theologians who had said that redemption will come about naturally (*be-derekh tiv`i*).[14]

Tzvi Yehudah Kook (d. 1982), an Israeli rabbi and yeshivah dean, who became the spiritual, intellectual (and politically

---

Writings of Rabbi Judah Alkalai 1 [Heb.], ed. Y. Raphael (Jerusalem: Mosad Harav Kook, 1974), p. 563. See also see Dov Schwartz, *Faith at the Crossroads: A Theological Portrait of Religious Zionism*, trans. B. Stein (Leiden: Brill, 2002), 162–67.

[12] Y. Berakhot 1.1/2c and Y. Yoma 3.2/40b re Micah 7:8.

[13] See Kalischer, *Seeking Zion*, p. 167; Alkalai, "Encourager of the Humble," *Writings* 1, p. 589. Here Alkalai rebukes those who advocate "redemption" for the Jewish people is "to make a colony in America," probably meaning the American (Sephardic) Jew, Mordecai Manuel Noah (d. 1851), who in 1825 tried but failed to found such a colony at Grand Island, New York. Also, in his 1891 essay, "Truth from the Land of Israel," Ahad Ha`Am worried about a widely held view among his contemporary Jews that the solution to "the Jewish problem" (i.e., the political problem the Jews have) is in America, whereto large numbers of his fellow East European Jews were emigrating, but only as individuals. *Complete Writings of Ahad Ha`Am* [Heb.] (Tel Aviv: Dvir, 1949), 23.

[14] Cited in a collection of his writings, *The Mizrahi Book* [Heb.], ed. J. L. Maimon (Jerusalem: Mosad Harav Kook, 1946), 18–19. However, some religious Zionist leaders were wary of any messianic speculation and cautioned at least public silence on the subject in their Zionist rhetoric. See Gideon Shimoni, *The Zionist Ideology* (Hanover, NH: Brandeis University Press, 1995), 150.

influential) leader of the religio-nationalists, called the State of Israel "a divine matter (*inyan elohi*)."[15] For him and his followers, "the state is wholly sacred [*qodesh*] ... a heavenly revelation."[16] Now many of these ideas were taught to him by his father, Abraham Isaac Kook (d. 1935), the first Ashkenazic Chief Rabbi of Israel (then "Palestine").[17] But, as the Israeli philosopher Aviezer Ravitzky has pointed out, Kook-fils carried these ideas of Kook-père "to the uttermost limit."[18]

One would think, though, that with this emphasis on the active role of Jews so newly enfranchised politically, the Holocaust would be an event to be forgotten as much as possible. After all, isn't the suffering of the Holocaust the very antithesis of what Jews are now being called upon to *do*? And, in fact, during much of the early period of the state, Zionist theory and teaching, both secular and religious, seemed to almost ignore the Holocaust. It has often been said that Zionists, and especially Israeli Zionists, were embarrassed by the Holocaust, for it seemed to be the epitome of the very Jewish political passivity that Zionism's project was supposed to get the Jews over once and for all actively. However, with the large number of Holocaust survivors both in Israel and in the Diaspora whose memories and questions simply would not go away, the Holocaust and its significance for

[15] Quoted in Aviezer Ravitzky, *Messianism, Zionism, and Radicalism in Israel* [Heb.] (Tel Aviv: Am Oved, 1993), 115, 183.
[16] Ibid., 189. Note Ravitzky's incisive comments on these and similar utterances of Kook and his followers throughout this book. It is now translated into English as *Messianism, Zionism, and Jewish Religious Radicalism*, trans. M. Swirsky and J. Chipman (Chicago: University of Chicago Press, 1996). See Haim Drukman, *Lords of the Land: The Settlers and the Land of Israel* [Heb.] (Or Yehudah: Kinneret, 2004), 283–84.
[17] Already in 1904, on the occasions of Theodor Herzl's death, Abraham Isaac Kook compared Herzl to "the Messiah son of Joseph (B. Sukkah 52a re Ps. 2:7–8), who is to provide the physical or material foundation for the more spiritual "Messiah son of David," who will complete the process of redemption. This essay is now published as *Mourning in Jerusalem* [Heb.], ed. E. Eliner (Jerusalem: Reuven Mas, 1987). The general point about the Messiah son of Joseph was made earlier by Alkalai (see his *Writings*, 518); however, it was Kook who first identified this Messiah with a real person in the present.
[18] Ibid., 171. See, also, Yehudah Mirsky, *Rav Kook* (New Haven, CT: Yale University Press, 2014).

Jewish life and thought too would not go away. Add to that the continuing genocidal threats of Israel's enemies, like Iran, and one sees why the present still suggests to many Jews certain terrifying repetitions of past threats having quickly turned into deadly realities.

Because what many wanted to be forgotten would not be forgotten, the religio-nationalists had to include the Holocaust in their theological-messianic vision. They did this by basically redrawing the boundaries of their view of the messianic reality as a process. Whereas in the past, the beginning of this eschatological process was located in 1948, a new beginning for it is now located in 1933 with the rise to power of the Nazi regime, which planned all along the total extermination of the Jewish people. But how is all of this a divine plan? The answer given by some religio-nationalists is that the Jewish people *had* to suffer the Holocaust *in order* to be worthy of the State of Israel. The Holocaust, then, becomes the necessary price to be paid for the State of Israel so that its Jewish citizens and supporters may be in the vanguard of the emerging messianic process in history leading toward history's true goal: the "End of Days" (*aharit ha-yamim*). Indeed, it could be said that in the pietistic view the dead of the Holocaust are a guilt offering (*qorban asham*) for the Jewish past, whereas in the religio-nationalist view the dead of the Holocaust are a burnt offering (*qorban olah*) for the Jewish future. Thus Kook saw the Holocaust as necessarily required to wrench the Jewish people from the depths of their infatuation with the exile (*galut*) toward the authentic Jewish reality of the State of Israel. In fact, he calls this "heavenly urgency performed through [*al yedei*] the destroyers (may their name and memory be blotted out!)."[19] Thus he continues, "from out of the cruel surgery ... the essence of our life is revealed: the revitalization of the people and the revitalization of the land [*tehiyyat ha'arets*]."

---

[19] Quoted in ibid., 176. See Dov Schwartz, *Religious Zionism: History and Ideology* [Heb.] (Jerusalem: Ministry of Defense, 2003), 132; also, Hannah Eshkoli-Wagman, *Between Rescue and Redemption* [Heb.] (Jerusalem: Yad Vashem, 2004), 212.

He sums up this historical nexus by saying: "The settlement of the land of Israel and the destruction [*hurban*] of the Diaspora go together."[20]

Messianic Theologies

In their messianic theology, the religio-nationalists often try to find precedence in the messianic theology of Maimonides, who asserted that the reign of the Messiah is brought about by a Jewish ruler powerful enough to gather the Jewish exiles back to the land of Israel, reestablish a Torah government there, and rebuild the Temple in Jerusalem.[21] Also, for Maimonides, this reestablishment of full Jewish sovereignty will have a political influence on the entire world.[22] This messianism, then, requires a maximum of Jewish political activity in the world, and it is to be centered in the land of Israel. It follows from this messianism that Jewish political subservience to any regime other than a Jewish one in the land of Israel, whether that subservience be from religious or secular motives, would be the greatest Jewish sin when Jewish political independence can be actually exercised in the world. So, it is not difficult to see why religio-nationalists are so fond of Maimonides' messianism. It seems to justify the Jewish seizure of political power as itself a messianic process. However, they seem to ignore the transcendent other-worldliness of Maimonides' doctrine of the world-beyond (*olam ha-ba*). Indeed, for him, it is the world-beyond, not the messianic reign, which the Torah prepares the Jews for.[23] For Maimonides, this is the true goal of all human life, and it is a goal that is clearly transpolitical. There is nothing supernatural about the messianic regime, yet that is what makes it quite secondary to the world-beyond. It is the object of a realistic hope, a desideratum

---

[20] *Paths of Israel* [Heb.] (Kiryat ha-yeshivah Bet-El: Me'avnei ha-Maqom, 2002), 70.
[21] MT: Melakhim, 11.1–12.5.
[22] Ibid., 11.4.
[23] MT: Repentance, 8.1-8. See B. Berakhot 34b re Isa. 64:3.

in this world, yet it is not even necessary for the ongoing covenantal existence of the Jewish people.

However repugnant the anti-political stance of pietistic anti-Zionism is, and however repugnant is its assertion that the Holocaust was God's punishment of the Jews for the sin of Zionist political activism, I think there is truth in Joel Teitelbaum's condemnation of the pseudo-messianism of the religio-nationalists. "It is evident throughout the words of our Sages of blessed memory that the future redemption will only be brought about by God Himself, not by means of flesh-and-blood agents."[24] For, if the redemption from Egypt, which only foreshows the future (and final) redemption, was brought about by God Himself (as the Torah teaches), then surely the future redemption will be a uniquely divine event.[25] Nevertheless, agreement with Teitelbaum on this theological point by no means entails agreement with his anti-Zionism or with his views on the Holocaust as divine punishment of the Jews. Only his theological point, which is clearly directed against the religio-nationalists, is still apt.

The reign of the Messiah is not the culmination of a discernible process within history leading to its end.[26] Instead, the coming of the Messiah is one event, and it will have no active preconditions on the part of any human being. There is no potential in the world for the coming of the Messiah. The Messiah is the object of Jewish

---

[24] *Concerning Redemption*, sec. 65, p. 113. As the Israeli historian-philosopher Gershom Scholem (d. 1982) noted: "The Bible and the apocalyptic writers know of no progress in history leading to the redemption. The redemption is not the product of immanent developments ... It is rather transcendence breaking in upon history ... from an outside source." *The Messianic Idea in Judaism*, trans. M. A. Meyer (New York: Schocken, 1971), 10.

[25] Thus the traditional Passover Haggadah (in any of its numerous additions) states about the redemption from Egypt, commenting on the scriptural words, "The Lord brought us out of Egypt" (Deut. 26:8): "It was not done by an angel, or by a fiery-angel [*seraph*], or by a human agent [*shaliah*], but by God Himself in His majesty." See Y. Sanhedrin 2.1/20a re Exod. 12:12. For the rabbinic assertion that the redemption from Egypt is ancillary to the final redemption, see T. Berakhot 1.10–11 and B. Berakhot 13a re Isa. 43:18.

[26] Yet Tzvi Yehudah Kook speaks of "the process [*tahalikh*] of redemption." *Paths of Israel*, 171.

hope, not the result of Jewish effort.[27] The Messiah is transcendent, coming into the world, but not coming from the world or from any worldly processes. Intending as it does a transcendent object, Jewish messianic hope functions as a limit on the pretensions of this-worldly projects. It reminds Jews of the dangers of identifying with any totalizing schemes in the world, which claim to be able to generate the end of history from within political resources at hand.[28]

At the theological level, the options seem to be the political messianism of the religio-nationalists, the anti-Zionist messianism of the pietists, both of which see the Holocaust as part of a divine cosmic plan into which each of them claims to have special insight, or a Zionism that doesn't make any political use of the Holocaust (positively or negatively). However, before a choice can be made from among these three options, a needed component should be added for the persuasive assertion of one theological position over the others. That necessary component is the practical implications of any theological position. The choice of one theological position over another might very well be, if not actually determined, then at least heavily conditioned by the fact that it implies a better practical position than the alternatives, or that the alternatives imply a worse practical position. This methodological point needs some explanation before I apply it.

Theory and Praxis

The relation between theology (*aggadah*) and law (*halakhah*) might well be clarified in the light of the Talmudic dialectic between the theoretical and the practical. All the questions discussed in the Talmud (and related rabbinic literature) should be

---

[27] B. Sanhedrin 97b–98a re Isa. 52:3 and Jer. 3:4 (an interpreted by Rabbi Joshua), Even Rabbi Eliezer, who thinks redemption is dependent on Jews repenting (*teshuvah*) and doing good deeds, still does not make this human action a discernible and predictable political process as does Kook.

[28] See David Novak, "Judaism, Zionism, and Messianism: Telling Them Apart," *First Things*, no. 10 (1991), 22–25.

seen as normative questions. Either they are questions of what one is to think or what one is to do. But thought and action are meant to be correlated. Every prescribed thought has some practical implication; every prescribed act has some theoretical implication. Thus in a dispute evidently about what is to be done, the editors of the Talmud typically ask: "What is the distinction in principle (*be-mai qa mipalegi*)?"[29] Conversely, in a dispute evidently about what is to be thought (a difference in principle), the editors of the Talmud typically ask: "What is the actual difference in practice (*mai beineihu*)?"[30] It can be shown that when you get to the more abstract level of principles, these principles are theological ideas. And when you get to the most concrete level of acts, you are dealing with the content of *halakhah*, that is, the commandments (*mitsvot*) of the Torah. No question is so concrete that it doesn't involve some thought; no question is so abstract that it doesn't involve some act.

That messianic theology has direct political correlations has been shown quite convincingly in the work of the Israeli philosopher Aviezer Ravitsky.[31] In the case of the two types of messianic theology noted previously, interestingly enough, we see dangerous moral implications. In fact, we see the very same moral implication coming out of both of them. And it is one that causes great pain to the vast majority of the Jewish people, and greatest pain to the survivors of the Holocaust ("the saved remnant of Israel").[32]

Surely the greatest act for Jews (and their friends) to do now is to sympathetically comfort in any way those who survived the Holocaust, especially those who directly witnessed the murders and overall destruction of much of European Jewry (and their descendants too, who also suffer with them and because of their memories). One of the main ways one comforts any mourner is to let him or her initiate the conversation, to tell his or her story,

---

[29] For example, B. Berakhot 30a.
[30] Ibid., 18a.
[31] See his *Messianism, Zionism, and Jewish Religious Radicalism*.
[32] This term (*she'erit ha-pletah*) is based on Ezra 9:14.

and to listen to that story without offering any interpretation of one's own. Yet pietist, anti-Zionist theology says to the Jewish people (all of whom are survivors, however indirect one's personal and familial connections to the murderous process actually are) that your sisters and brothers, mothers and fathers, wives and husbands, daughters and sons, all of them died *because* of their own sins or because of the sin of being part of the Jewish people who had been so taken in by Zionism. On the other hand, the religio-nationalist theology says to the Jewish people that six million Jews *had to die* for there to be a Jewish state in the land of Israel. It is hard to tell which answer is more morally offensive to Jews according to traditional Jewish moral criteria. Surely, the minimal requirement when comforting mourners (*nihum avelim*) is not to cause them any emotional pain by one's words.[33] That, by the way, applies to one's words with any other human person, even if that person is not a mourner.[34]

In the case of the pietists, we could question whether working for a Jewish state in the land of Israel is a sin. Even the so-called prohibition of declaring Jewish political independence is at most one opinion, but, as we saw in the previous chapter, it is not one that codified by any of the accepted medieval legal codes. So, how could it be the reason for God allowing mass murder as a punishment for it, even if one thinks this opinion is true? Isn't punishment supposed to be commensurate with the sin?[35] Here we see the enormous theological difference between asking God – even angrily asking God – to justify Himself in the end, and our providing a conclusive human answer in the name of

---

[33] MT: Mourning, 14.1, where Maimonides sees comforting mourners to be a specific application of the general commandment to "love your neighbor as yourself" (Lev. 19:18). This general commandment of applying "loving-kindness" (*gemilut hasadim*) surely applies to those who are not literally mourners (*avelim*), as mourning is prescribed mourning for a limited period of time, but to those who still mourn in their hearts nonetheless (see Prov. 14:10); also, B. Sanhedrin 46b.
[34] For the prohibition of verbal abuse (*ona'at devarim*), M. Baba Metsia 4.10; B. Baba Metsia 58b re Lev. 25:17 and Job 4:6–7; Maimonides, *Book of Commandments*, neg. no. 251; MT: Sales, 14.13.
[35] B. Nedarim 32a re Num. 23:23.

God here and now. One would think that proponents of this kind of messianism would leave the revelation of the consequences of sin to the final messianic-redemptive revelation at the end of history, not explicate it themselves here and now. Instead, they cruelly use the Holocaust as a stick to beat down their theological opponents. If we assume with Scripture and the rabbis that God is "the judge of all the earth who practices justice [*mishpat*]" (Genesis 18:25), then isn't this theology a nearly blasphemous indictment of God Himself?

In the case of the religio-nationalists, did the Jewish victims of the Holocaust (both those who died and those who survived) choose to be sacrificed for the sake of a Jewish state? And even if they chose what could only be designated as a "suicide mission," could that be justified in the face of the norms, "one life is not set aside for another," and "your life takes precedence over the life of someone else"?[36] If the lives of six million Jews, and the continuing pain suffered by all the survivors, is the price that had to be paid for a Jewish state in the cosmic economy, isn't the price too high (as a survivor friend of mine once protested)? The end result, however good, is not worth it, at least if you follow this logic. Is it not a case of cosmic overcharge?

The moral fault of both these theologies is that their proponents are guilty of verbal abuse, in this case *theo-logical* abuse. As long as even one direct survivor of the Holocaust is still alive among us, any suggestion that his or her family and friends *had to die* because of something they did, or because of what somebody else did, or because they were means to an end they themselves could not be a part of is abusive to the extreme. The survivors are especially vulnerable to such abuse, as witnessed, for example, by how deeply pained they are by Holocaust denial. A good case can be made that as long as even one direct survivor is still among us, that person, and all of us who survived the Holocaust less directly, have the status of mourners, or perhaps orphans. Accordingly, we may not present any explanation of the

---

[36] M. Ohalot 7.6; B. Baba Metsia 62a re Lev. 25:36.

Holocaust that they could not possibly accept. As my late revered teacher Abraham Joshua Heschel (d. 1972) insisted: "The State of Israel is not an atonement. It would be blasphemy to regard it as a compensation."[37]

We can learn the immorality of such theological explanations of the Holocaust from the rebuke of God to the three "friends" of Job (Eliphaz, Bildad, and Zophar), who when they came to comfort him in his mourning condemned him instead. Thus God says to them, "You have not spoken to Me correctly" (Job 42:7). The medieval commentator Rashi interprets this admonition to be saying: "you should have comforted him as Elihu did, but it was not enough that Job was in sorrow and suffering, you added rebellion [*pesha*] to your own sins by vexing him [*le-haqnito*]." It is important to note that the text reads, "You have not spoken to Me [*elei*] correctly," whereas Rashi seems to interpret it to mean the way the friends spoke to Job *about* God's ways.[38] Furthermore, Rashi's interpretation is consistent with the mention of this verse in the Talmud, when "Rava says that a person is not to be appeased at the time of his pain (*nitpas be-sha'at tsa'aro*)."[39] Finally, when Maimonides says that the line (*shurah*) of those who come to comfort the mourners are to say to them, "May you be comforted by God," David ibn Abi Zimra (d. 1589) notes: "their sole obligation [*dvar shel hiyyuv*] is to comfort the mourner."[40] Totalizing explanations, which the victims themselves would have hardly given, cannot possibly be comforting inasmuch as they are inevitably hurtful.

Another Messianism

Many of the proponents of anti-Zionist messianism seem to be guilty of hatred of most of the Jewish people, and many of the

---

[37] *Israel: An Echo of Eternity* (New York: Farrar, Straus and Giroux, 1969), 113.
[38] Rashi seems to understand *elei* ("to Me") as it were written *alei* ("about Me"). In fact, this reading does appear in some manuscripts. See note of G. Beer on Job 42:7–8, Biblia Hebraica, 7th ed, edited by R. Kittel (Stuttgart: Privilegium Württemberg Bibelanstalt, 1951), p. 1154.
[39] B. Baba Batra 16b.
[40] MT: Mourning, 13.1-2 and note of David ibn Abi Zimra (Radbaz) thereon.

proponents of religio-nationalist messianism seem to be oblivious to the emotional scars in the hearts of Holocaust survivors. By avoiding these extremes, transcendent messianism can play an important role in Jewish political activity, such as the activity involved in the reestablishment of the State of Israel and its continued life and strength. Indeed, it can provide an important context for Jewish political activity, one that keeps it realistic and bound by Jewish moral criteria precisely because it deflects from any pseudo-messianic futurism. One might even say it is the best sublimation of political fanaticism. Transcendent messianism keeps our attention in the present and to its needs. In my mind, this kind of transcendent messianism, having eschewed pseudo-messianic historical judgments, lends itself to an adequate theological connection between the Holocaust and the reestablishment of the State of Israel much better than the extensive messianism of the religio-nationalists or that of the pietists. On this point, I have learned much from the thought of the Israeli philosopher Yeshayahu Leibowitz (d. 1994).[41]

The question is: How does our primary moral duty to comfort the mourners of Auschwitz (and the other killing fields) enable us to constitute a coherent theology that intends the same God both in the Holocaust and in the reestablishment of the State of Israel? Here again, we need to look to the *halakhah* to get a practical handle on a theoretical issue. I would suggest that we look at the obligations of any survivor. "Rav Yehudah said in the name of Rav there are four people who must give thanks: those who went down to the sea, those who have gone into the wilderness, one who was sick and then was healed, and one who was imprisoned and released."[42] But what if some of these people do not want to thank God for their being saved? Why not? Well, this reluctance, even refusal, could come from a feeling of unworthiness. Perhaps, they were saved but others with them were lost. Perhaps these survivors feel as if the wrong people were saved, that the

---

[41] For his critique of the attempt to turn redemption into a political program, see his *Judaism, the Jewish People, and the State of Israel* [Heb.] (Jerusalem: Schocken, 1976), 401–4, 415–18.
[42] B. Berakhot 54b.

truly righteous were lost, and the ones who really deserved to live in fact died. I have heard these feelings from some Holocaust survivors who are my friends. Today we call it "survivor's guilt." This is the person who would rather share his flask of water with his companion in the desert and die with him rather than drink it all himself and live as a survivor. The reason given there is "let not one of them have to see the death of his fellow."[43]

Why God let one person live and another person, even many persons, die is a mystery. Why did God rescue only a few, but did not rescue so many? This question should not be answered by any human being. It is on the eschatological agenda of questions we may ask God in the end-time. Theodicy is not only not called for; I think it is forbidden. God will justify Himself in the world-yet-to-come, but in ways we cannot even imagine.

Those whom the survivors wanted to survive with them did not survive. They were murdered horribly. Yet, the commandment to live, not die is not dependent on one's sense of his or her own worthiness or unworthiness to live. As the Talmud puts it, "The Torah was not given to the subservient angels."[44] Indeed, the more authoritative opinion of Rabbi Akivah insists in the above Talmudic case that at the moment of survival one's own life takes precedence.[45] One's obligation to live is greater than one's obligation to identify with the dead. One finds the opinion in the Talmud that no one can claim to be worthy to live.[46] But that excuses no one from the duty to live, especially to live for the sake of the covenant. As a well-known hymn in the Yom Kippur liturgy puts it: "God, look to the covenant, not to our corrupt inclinations (*v'al tefen la-yetser*)."[47]

Transposing this to the theological level, we need to separate our anger with God over the amount of death and suffering in

---

[43] B. Baba Metsia 62a.
[44] B. Kiddushin 54a and parallels.
[45] B. Baba Metsia 62a re Lev. 25:36. For the rule that Rabbi Akivah's opinion is to be followed in the event of a dissenting opinion of one of his colleagues, see B. Eruvin 46b.
[46] B. Shabbat 55a-b re Ezek. 18:20.
[47] See, for example, *The High Holyday Prayer Book*, ed. and trans. Ben Zion Bokser (New York: Hebrew Publishing Co., 1959), 285.

Another Messianism 247

the Holocaust from the judgment made by a number of contemporary Jewish thinkers that the Holocaust falsifies the fundamental covenantal promise made by God to Israel. That promise, however, would be falsified only if either all the Jews had been destroyed, or the surviving Jews were so demoralized that they could not go on as Jews and were thus to commit religious and cultural suicide. But that judgment is not true; in fact, its converse has been verified in this world. Two thirds of the Jewish people did survive, and in many ways, most especially in the reestablishment of the State of Israel, the Jewish people have done much more than merely survive. That is true, and in the light of the obligation to comfort the mourners of the Holocaust, what greater comfort could we possibly give them than to demonstrate that truth to them by pointing to all the Jews living flourishing Jewish lives today? "I shall not die but live, to declare the works of the Lord" (Psalms 118:17). The Holocaust must be judged ultimately to have been a very costly failure, but a failure nonetheless, certainly for its perpetrators.

The reestablishment of the State of Israel is the best indication that the Jewish people's will to live was not killed in and by Auschwitz. In the case of the reestablishment of the State of Israel, there can be a "holy day" (*yom tov*) and Jews can even say *Hallel* (the psalms of praise said on most holy days).[48] Why? Didn't many die at this time too? The answer, I think, is because the Jewish people only narrowly escaped the Holocaust, and the defeat of the murderers came only through the hands of others. But in the case of Israel Independence Day (*yom ha'atsma`ut*), which was discussed in Chapter 1, Jews not only celebrate their escape from death at the hands of their enemies, but they also celebrate their at least temporary victory over them. God gave the victory to the Jewish people. But there is a difference in the way Jews thank God for having some of them survive and the way Jews thank God for letting Israel triumph. Nevertheless, the God who saved some Jews from Hitler and the God who enabled the

---

[48] See David Novak, *The Election of Israel* (Cambridge: Cambridge University Press, 1995), 174.

Jewish people to reestablish the State of Israel is neither a God whose covenant has been falsified nor a God whose final and unique messianic victory has yet come. Those Jews we who are alive today still have more to thank God for than contend with God about. As Abraham Joshua Heschel put it in his own inimitable way: "And yet, there is no answer to Auschwitz … to try to answer is to commit blasphemy. Israel enables us to bear the agony of Auschwitz without radical despair, to sense a ray of God's radiance in the jungle of history."[49]

So, what is the theological connection between the Holocaust and the reestablishment of State of Israel? If by "connection" one means some sort of causal relation, then there is none and there should be none, at least not by any theological criteria. If there were any such causal relation, then it would seem Jews would have to accept the Holocaust in one way or another for the blessing of the State of Israel. But the State of Israel does not have to claim the Holocaust as its necessary precondition in any theologically cogent way.

Making a causal connection between any two events would have to be linear, one event coming after the other. But that is not the only type of relation. There are also analogical relations. Here the events are not viewed in any linear sequence; instead, they are viewed as having certain similarities. These similarities lie side by side, as it were; one is neither prior nor subsequent to the other. (There is no case here of *post hoc ergo propter hoc*.) The connection between the events is not linear, not causal. The similarities are located in the very similar responses that are prescribed for those who have experienced this event. God is to be thanked now for survival then. That salvation does not admit of any theodicy because the ways of God are mysterious. The ultimate secrets are yet to be revealed. "The secrets [*ha-nistarot*] are God's; for us and our children there is [only] doing all the words of this Torah, which are revealed [*ha-niglot*]" (Deuteronomy 29:28). Any attempt to reveal now what is now to be hidden can only be destructive to oneself and painfully abusive to others.

---

[49] *Israel: An Echo of Eternity*, 115.

The Holocaust and the reestablishment of the State of Israel both pose great challenges to the Jewish people to remain faithful to the covenant. Each also poses a temptation: the Holocaust tempts Jews to believe they are so weak that the covenant and its responsibilities are beyond them. The reestablishment of the State of Israel tempts Jews to believe they are so strong that the covenant and its responsibilities are behind them. So there is a dialectical relation between the two events: each tempers the excesses of the other. By tempering the fear of the Holocaust with the joy of the State of Israel, and by tempering the joy of the State of Israel with the fear of the Holocaust, Jews (and their friends) are able to speak to God and of God in the world, without presuming to speak for God or in place of God. That is the true task of Jewish theology at this juncture of history – nothing more and nothing less.

Index

Abravanel, Isaac, 195, 195n84
Ahad Ha'Am, 66–67, 67n35, 68, 68n38, 69–73, 73n49, 75–77, 77n57, 78–81, 84, 96, 170, 235n13
Akiva (Rabbi), 185n66, 203n21, 211n42, 246, 246n45
Alakalai, Judah, 234, 234n13,n15
Anselm of Canterbury, 174n38
Arendt, Hannah, 13, 13n15
Aristotle, 8n5, 18, 24, 41n51, 94, 94n17, 102, 102n39, 112n63, 120n4, 121, 229
Aschheim, S. E., 13n16
Auden, W.H., 207
Avineri, Shlomo, 234n10

Balfour Declaration, 3, 49, 168
Barak, Aharon, 153, 153n2, 154–155, 199
Barak, Ehud, 227–228
Batnitzky, Leora, 15n20
Beer, G., 244n38
Begin, Menachem, 65
Ben-Gurion, David, 23–24, 24n2, 25, 25n5, 26, 35–37
di Boten, Abraham (*Lehem Mishne*), 213n52
brit, *see* covenant

Britain, 3, 32, 65, 141, 166
Buber, Martin, 103n44, 135n34, 138, 185n66, 234n10

Canada, 162, 165, 174
Catholic Church, 45, 61, 162
Charter of Rights and Freedoms (Canadian), 165
Christianity, 20, 29, 33, 37, 59, 61–62, 131, 143, 210, 218, 223
de Clermont-Tonnere, Stanislas, 60–61
Cohen, Hermann, 34, 34n32, 76, 95n20, 104n45, 214n56
Common Law, English, 166
community, 59
converts, *see* ger
covenant, 15, 20, 27, 27n8, 28, 30, 59, 67–68, 80, 91, 98, 104, 107, 126–129, 132, 133–134, 136–138, 140, 143, 148–149, 163–164, 164n22, 178–179, 189–191, 219, 229, 232, 246, 248–249

David ibn Abi Zimra (*Radbaz*), 244, 244n40
Declaration of Independence (Israel), 4n1, 141, 141n51, 144, 154n2, 167, 167n25, 171, 176, 199, 199n6

251

Declaration of Independence
   (United States), 163
Dreyfus, Alfred, 51, 62
Drukman, Haim, 236n16

Edels, Samuel (*Maharsha*), 184–5
Eger, Akiva, 203n21
Elon, Amos, 53n11
Elon, Menachem, 83n65
Emon, Anver, 218n67
ends, *see* teleology
Epstein, Yehiel Michal (*Arokh ha-Shulhan*), 198n1
Ereignis, *see* root experience
Eshkoli-Wagman, Hannah, 237n19
excommunication, 23, 46

Fackenheim, Emil, 8, 64
Federbush, Simon, 89n5, 203n20

ger, 27n8, 139, 144, 148, 174, 178–179, 200–202, 202n15, 203, 203n21, 204, 204n22, 205, 206–208, 212–218, 223–224
Ginzberg, Asher, *see* Ahad Ha'Am
Ginzberg, Louis, 126n18, 151n75, 188
Goethe, Johann Wolfgang, 77, 77n57
Goldman, Shalom, 20n16
Gordon, Aaron David, 68n38, 72n45, 77n56,n57
Gordon, Judah Leib, 5, 5n1, 33
Gumbiner, Abraham (*Magen Avraham*), 189n76

Habermas, Jürgen, 161n19
Halakhah, 9, 27, 49, 54–55, 83, 87–88, 92, 154, 156–158, 176, 203n22, 204n22, 208, 214, 240–241, 245
Halevi, Judah, 145n60
Halivni, David Weiss, 14n22
Hanukkah, 9–11
Hatam, Sofer, 72
Hatikvah, 55, 142
Hayyim ibn Attar (*Or Hayyim*), 108, 181n52
Hazony, Yoram, 56n15

Hebrew University of Jerusalem, 46
Hegel, G.W.F., 24
Hertzberg, Arthur, 68
Herzl, Theodor, 51–53, 53n11, 54, 55–58, 62–64, 68, 78, 82, 84, 90, 96, 141, 154–155, 167, 169, 177, 236n17
Herzog, Isaac Halevi, 88n3, 185n68
Heschel, Abraham Joshua, 12, 90n10, 92, 244, 248
Hillel the Elder, 206
Hillel, School of, 100n33
Hirschensohn, Chaim, 49
historicism, 10
Hobbes, Thomas, 40
Holocaust, 4, 17, 19, 133, 176, 224–233, 236–237, 239–241, 243–249
Husserl, Edmund, 95n19, 100, 100n31

Islam, *see* Muslims
Ishmael (Rabbi), 211n42
Israel Independence Day, 9, 247

Jacob ben Asher (*Baal ha-Turim*), 42n54, 122n9, 189n76, 203n21, 215n58
Jefferson, Thomas, 33, 163
Jerusalem Temple, 11, 31, 39, 44–45, 56–57, 101, 148, 151, 182n54, 186, 187n71, 194, 201, 204–205, 207, 238
Jewish Law, *see Halakhah*
Josephus, 39, 88–90

Kabbalah, 42, 97, 133n32, 234, 234n9
Kalischer, Zvi Hirsch, 234, 234n11, 235, 235n13
Kant, Immanuel, 8, 15n18, 24, 73n48
Kaplan, Mordecai, 80
Karo, Joseph, 182n57, 189n76, 203n21, 204n22, 205, 205n26, 207n33, 212n48, 215n58
Kaufmann, Yehezkel, 49n3, 69n39, 79, 79n59, 136
kenesset, *see* community

Index

Kimhi, David (*Radaq*), 102n40, 103n43, 202n16
Klatzkin, Joseph, 48–49, 49n3, 50
Klausner, Joseph, 46
Kook, Abraham Isaac, 236, 236n17
Kook, Tzvi Yehudah, 187n72, 235, 236n16, 237, 239n26, 240n27
Korn, Bertram W., 198n3
Kornberg, Jacques, 51n9, 63n28, 66n33

League of Nations, 3, 168
Leibowitz, Yeshayahu, 57, 158n11, 245
Lichtenstein, Aharon, 177n44
Lieberman, Saul, 208n34

Maccabees, 10
Maimon, Judah Leib, 157, 157n10
Maimonides (*Rambam*), 12n12, 32n27, 36n34, 79–80, 94, 96n24, 100n33, 102, 102n37, 107n49, 110, 113n65, 115, 121n6, 137n43, 143n56, 159n12,n13, 170, 172–173, 180, 180n47,n48, 181, 181n52, 182–183, 185n66, 187n71, 189, 189n76, 200, 204–205, 209–210, 212–213, 217–222, 238, 242n33,n34, 244
Maritain, Jaques, 17n21
Mason, Richard, 34n31
McManners, J., 61n26
Meiri, Menachem, 210, 213n51
Mendelssohn, Moses, 34
Messiah, 35–36, 46, 185n66, 230, 233–234, 236n17, 238–240
millenarianism, 21
mitsvah, 12, 140, 179–180, 182, 182n54, 183, 187n71,n72, 191
Muslims, 21, 28n12, 131, 143, 158, 210, 218

Nadler, Steven, 24n3, 45n66
Nahmanides (*Ramban*), 32n24, 109n58, 131n29, 179–180, 180n47, 181, 181n51,n52, 182–183, 183n58, 187n72, 189n76, 200, 222–223

nationalism, 16, 21, 49–51, 58, 66, 69, 70n40, 75, 141, 234n10, 235
Nature, 32–33, 41, 68, 73n49, 77–78, 80, 89n5, 97, 102, 103n42, 105, 108–111, 163–164, 168–169
Netanyahu, Benjamin, 65
Nietzsche, Friedrich, 160, 160n17
Noah, Mordecai Manuel, 235n13
Noahide Law, 130–131, 172, 175–176, 203, 203n21, 204, 204n22, 205–206, 213, 217–220, 222–223
Novak, David, 18n24, 24n2, 27n7, 28n9,n13, 32n24,n25, 46n67, 59n24, 76n53, 92n16, 99n30, 101n35, 103n44, 107n50, 109n58, 113n65, 115n67, 130n27, 132n21, 135n36, 136n38, 139n48, 143n55,n56, 159n14, 160n16, 163n21, 166n24, 175n41, 176n42, 183n58, 186n70, 192n80, 195n85, 198n2, 201n10,n12, 208n34, 209n37, 210n40, 211n43, 222n75, 240n28, 247n48

O'Donovan, Oliver, 222n75
Orthodox Judaism, 12, 46, 72, 87, 230, 234

Palestine, 3–4, 4n1, 49, 141, 206, 209, 234n10, 236
Passover, 9, 109, 239n25
Pereira, Salamon Rodrigues, 23–25
Philo, 94
Plato, 8n5, 24, 94, 102n41, 123, 220n69, 229
propaganda, 14, 98
Protestantism, 15, 61, 198

Raphall, Morris, 198n3
Rashi, 31n20,n21, 89n6, 114, 115n67, 120, 126n20, 137n43, 144n57,n59, 157n8, 170n27, 181n52, 182n54, 184n63, 185n66, 202n16, 244, 244n38
Ravitzky, Aviezer, 236, 236n15,n16, 241
Rawls, John, 17n23

realpolitik, 5, 15, 58, 151, 156, 168, 171, 195, 223
Reform Judaism, 33–34, 72, 157
Reines, Isaac Jacob, 70n40, 235
revelation, 30, 33, 42, 60, 62, 81, 83–84, 87, 94–95, 97, 100n33, 135, 139, 142n54, 143, 155, 159, 165–166, 171, 180, 205, 236, 243
rights, 2, 4–5, 21, 51, 156, 163–165, 168–169, 173–175, 175n41, 176–177, 196, 198–200, 203, 205–209, 211–213, 217
rhetoric, 3–6, 14, 54, 56, 68, 169, 228, 235
Rohrlich, Ruby, 226n1
Rome, 39, 44, 209
root experience, 8
rootless cosmopolitan, 6, 6n1, 144
Rosenzweig, Franz, 103–104, 104n45, 112
Rousseau, Jean-Jaques, 38, 38n39, 40
Rubenstein, Richard, 231–232, 232n6, 233

Saadiah Gaon, 15, 94
San Remo Resolution, 3
Sartre, Jean-Paul, 51
Schiller, Friedrich, 63
Scholem, Gershom, 13, 13n15, 101n36, 239n24
Schwartz, Daniel B., 25n5, 26n6, 33n28, 46n67
Schwartz, Dov, 235n11, 237n19
science, 41, 43, 54–55, 57, 62, 69, 97, 109–110, 145n60
secularism, 33–34, 44, 46, 48, 153–156, 159–162, 165, 171
Sen, Amartya, 161n19
Shabbtai Zevi, 37
Shammai, School of, 100, 100n33
Shimoni, Gideon, 52n10, 67n35, 142n54, 235n14
Simon, Ernst, 81n63
social contract, 27, 27n8, 40, 139, 164
social justice, 14, 192
sojourner, *see* ger

Solomon ibn Adret (*Rashba*), 150n71, 176n43, 203n21
Soloveitchik, Joseph B., 152n77
Soviet Union, 4, 17, 168, 186, 228
Spiegel, Shalom, 124n15
Spinoza, Baruch, 22–24, 24n2,n3, 25, 25n5, 26–27, 28n9, 29–35, 35n34, 36–47, 77, 77n57, 78, 90, 103n42, 134, 136, 229
Strauss, Leo, 85n68

Teitelbaum, Joel (Satmar Rebbe), 185n67, 230, 239
teleology, 5, 8, 15, 73n49, 102, 132, 193
theocracy, 39, 44–45, 54–55, 86–90, 93–95, 99
Theology, 26–28, 36, 38, 40, 42–43, 67, 70, 88, 92, 94–97, 97n27, 98, 101n35, 182–183, 229–230, 232–233, 238, 240–243, 245, 249
Tradition, 9, 11–14, 16, 18–19, 21, 21n16, 24, 26–27, 30, 33–35, 42, 48, 55, 62, 73, 77–79, 81–84, 89, 94–95, 99, 107, 122–123, 131, 133n32, 141, 143, 145, 153–160, 166, 170–173, 177, 182, 188, 199, 201, 204, 222, 231, 239n25, 242

United States of America, 4, 16, 33, 162–164, 168, 186, 198, 228

Vidal of Tolosa, 133n32, 201n13
Vovelle, Michel, 162n20

Walzer, Michael, 87n1
deWitt, Johan, 45
Wissenschaft, *see* science
Wittgenstein, Ludwig, 95n21, 104n46, 127n21

Yad Vashem, 228
Yom ha`Atsma'ut, *see* Israel Independence Day
Yovel, Yirmiyahu, 34n31, 37, 37n37

Zisberg, Yaakov, 181n49, 183n60, 185n68, 187n72
Zohar, David, 49n4

Printed in Great Britain
by Amazon